S.S. ASTRO

Asashio Sogo Teachers' ROom

NEGI BANNO 1

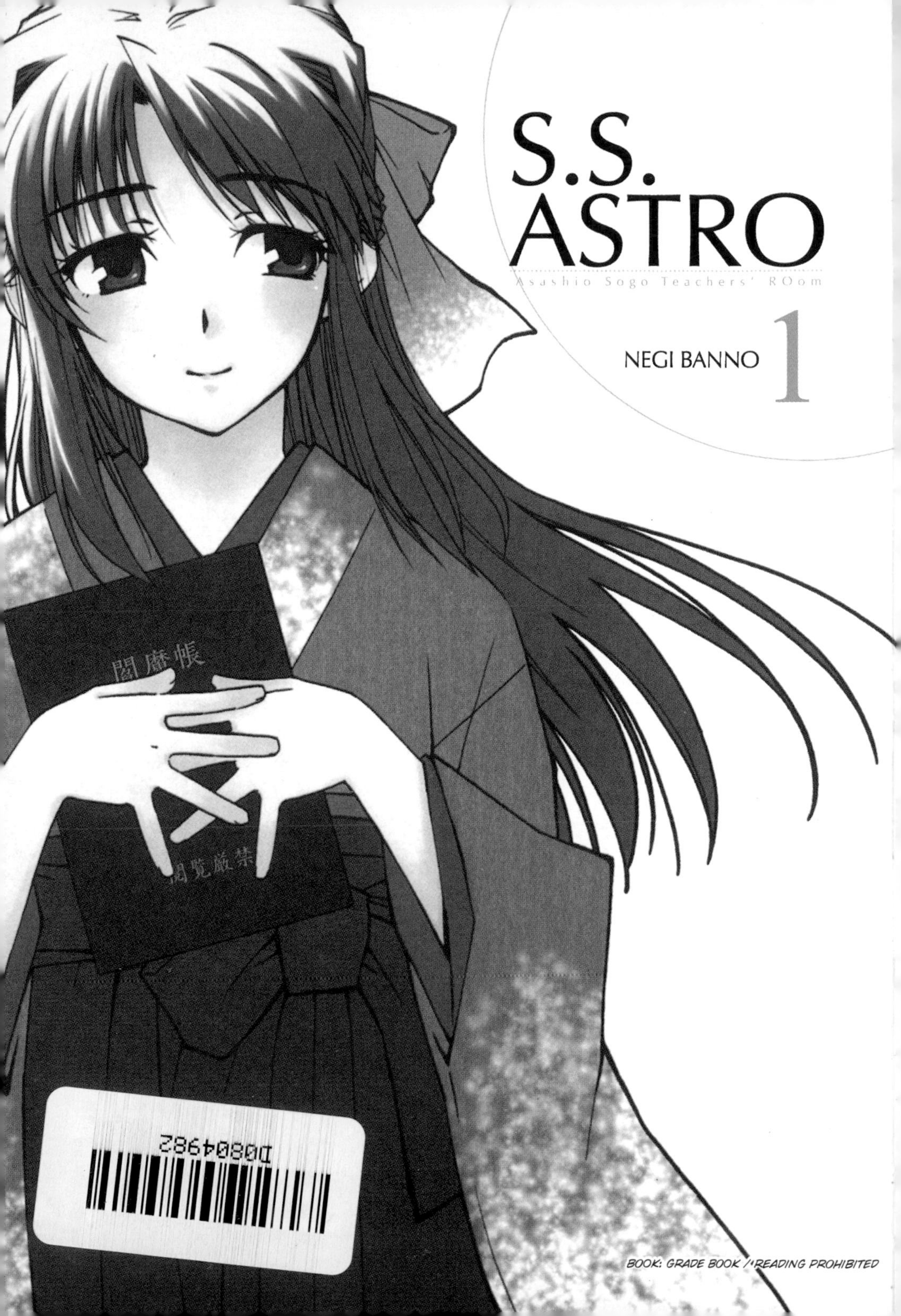
閻魔帳
閲覧厳禁
BOOK: GRADE BOOK / READING PROHIBITED

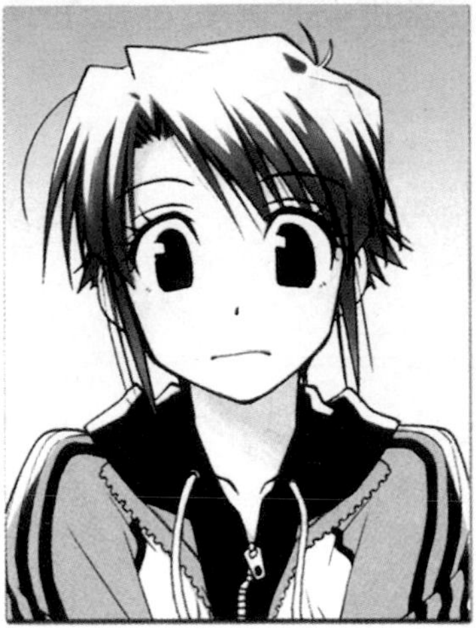

NAME	MAKI, IZUMI	牧
KANJI	牧 和泉	
JOB	PHYSICAL EDUCATION TEACHER	
NOTE	LET'S BE ADULTS.	

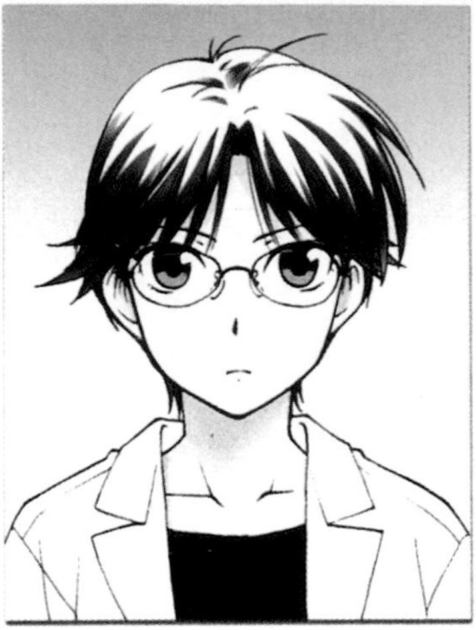

NAME	ARAI, SETSUNA	荒井
KANJI	荒井 準名	
JOB	NURSING TEACHER	
NOTE	EVERYTHING IN MODERATION.	

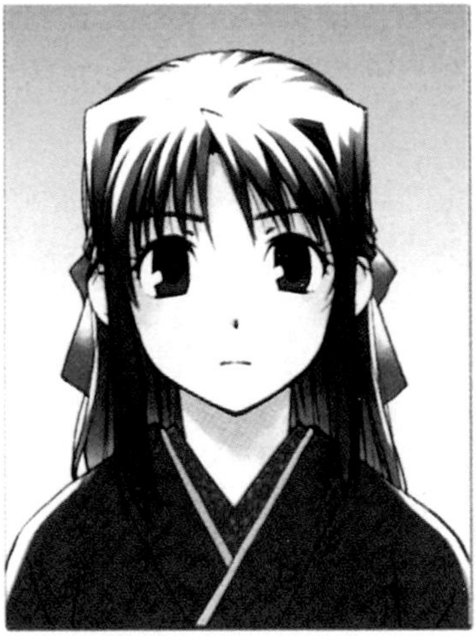

NAME	NAGUMO, YUKO	南雲
KANJI	南雲 有子	
JOB	JAPANESE TEACHER	
NOTE	THE TEACHERS' LOUNGE SMELLS LIKE SOY SAUCE.	

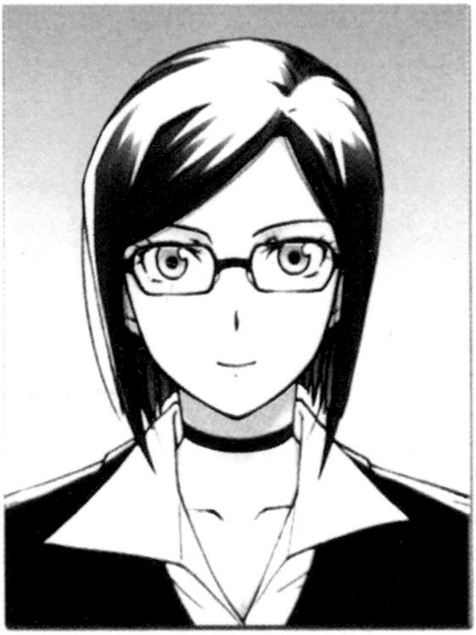

NAME	KARASUMA, KANAME	烏丸
KANJI	烏丸 かなめ	
JOB	FOREIGN LANGUAGE TEACHER	
NOTE	SETTLE DOWN, PEOPLE.	

ASASHIO INTEGRATED PUBLIC HIGH SCHOOL OF TOKYO

Color Illustration Collection

From *Carat*, Nov. 2005

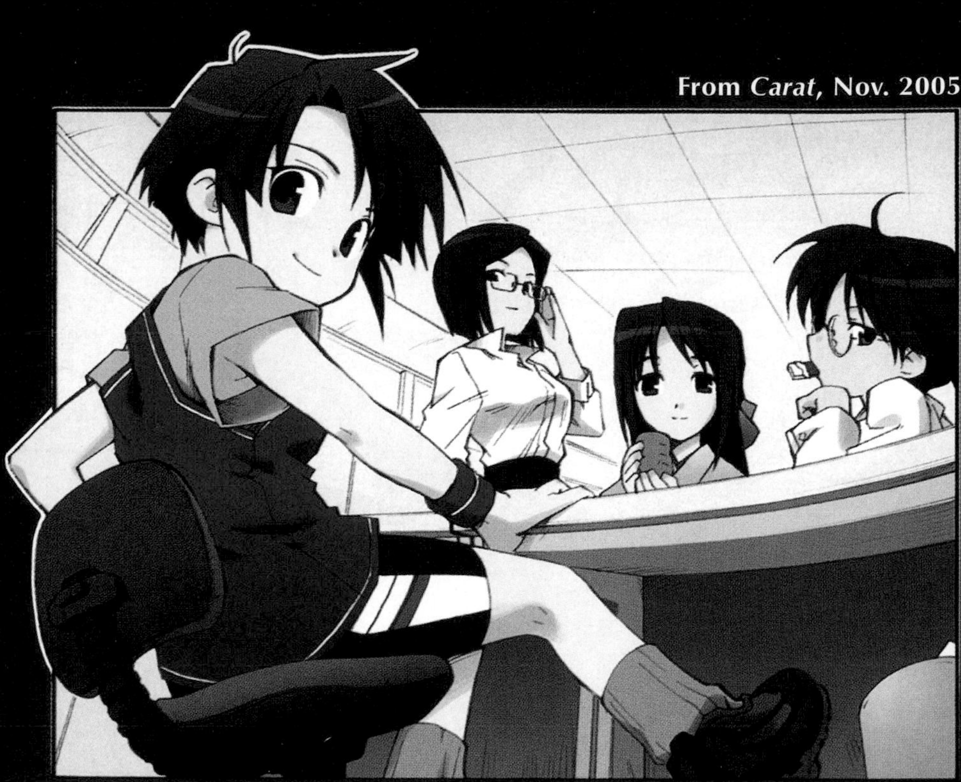

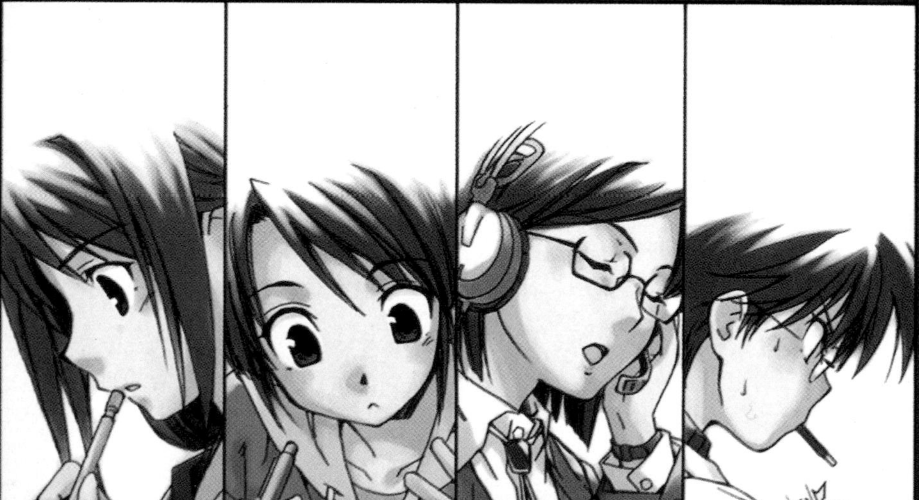

From *Carat*, Jan. 2006

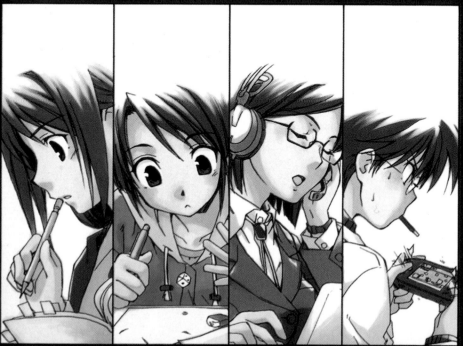

S.S. ASTRO

Asashio Sogo Teachers' ROom

From *Carat*, Mar. 2006

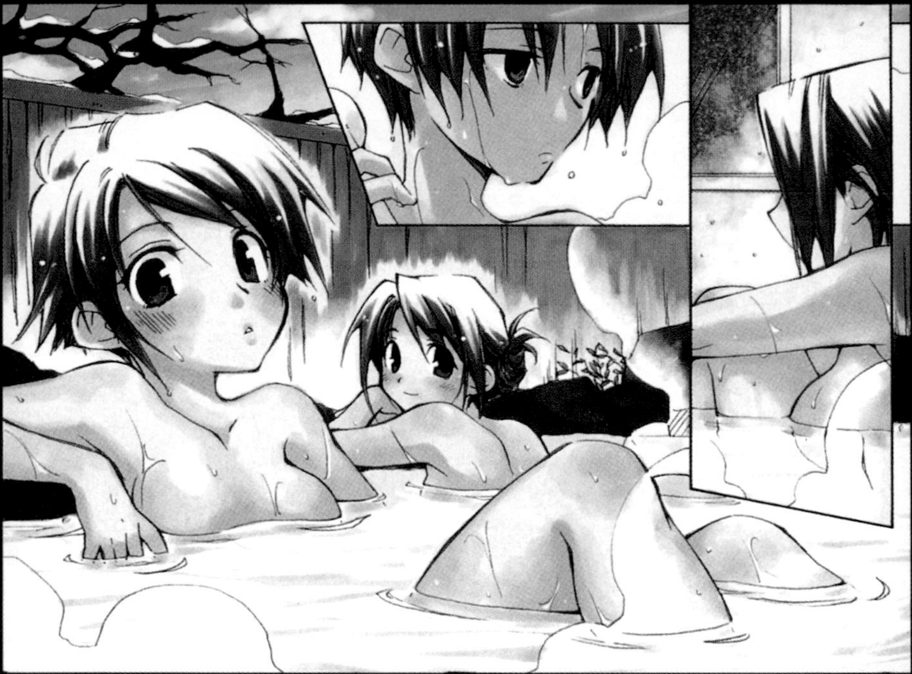

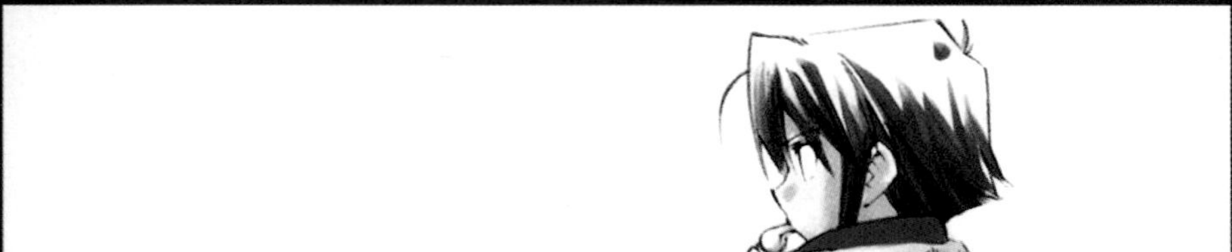

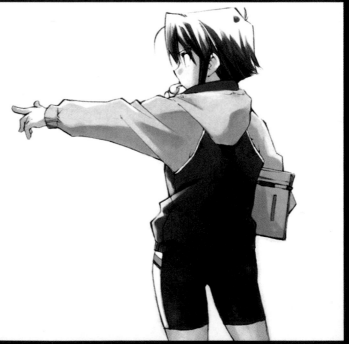

From *Carat*, May 2006

S.S. ASTRO

Asashio Sogo Teachers' ROom

From *Carat*, Jul. 2006

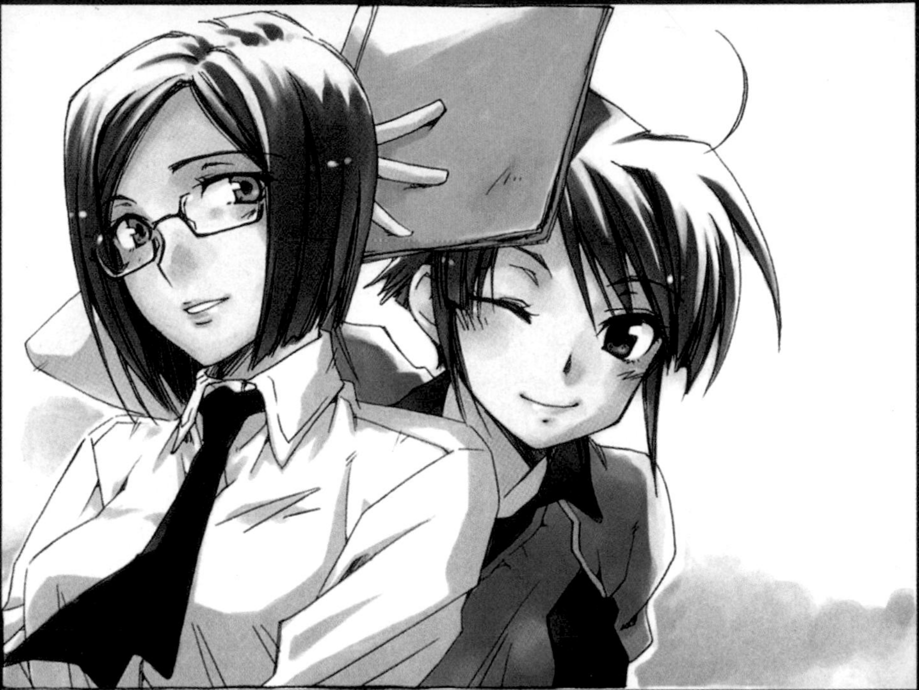

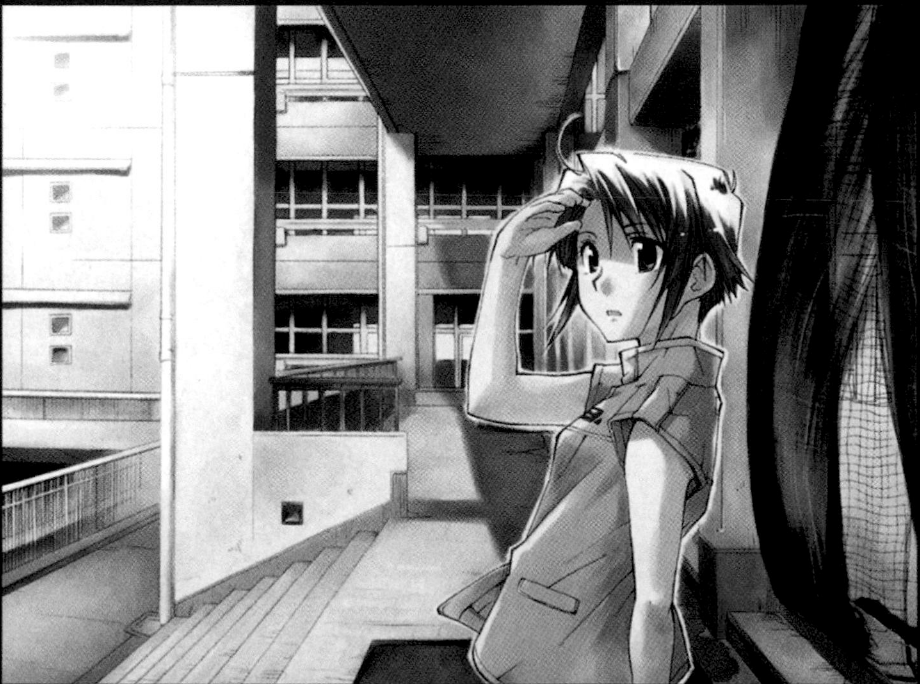

From *Carat*, Sep. 2006

S.S. ASTRO

Asashio Sogo Teachers' ROom

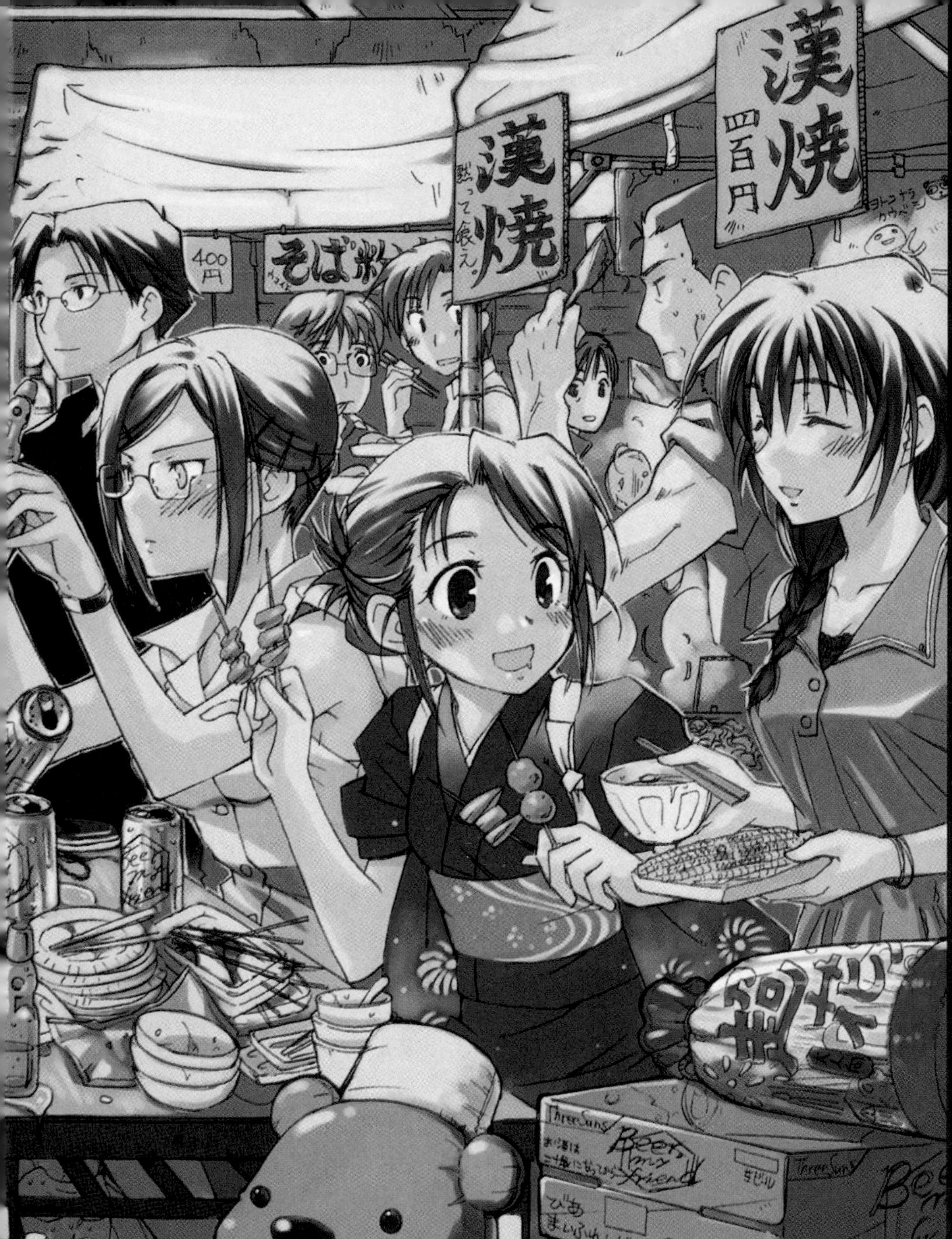
漢焼
四百円
漢焼
黙って喰え。
400円
Beer my friend
350ml×24

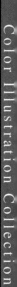

SIGNS: MANLY ROAST: ¥400 / MANLY ROAST: SHUT UP AND EAT IT.
SOBA NOODLES: YUMMY! / ¥400
BAG: SUPER FIREWORKS: ADULTS ONLY
BOXES: ALCOHOL IS ILLEGAL FOR MINORS TO CONSUME. / "BEER MY FRIEND"

S.S. ASTRO

Asashio Sogo Teachers' ROom

Color Illustration Collection

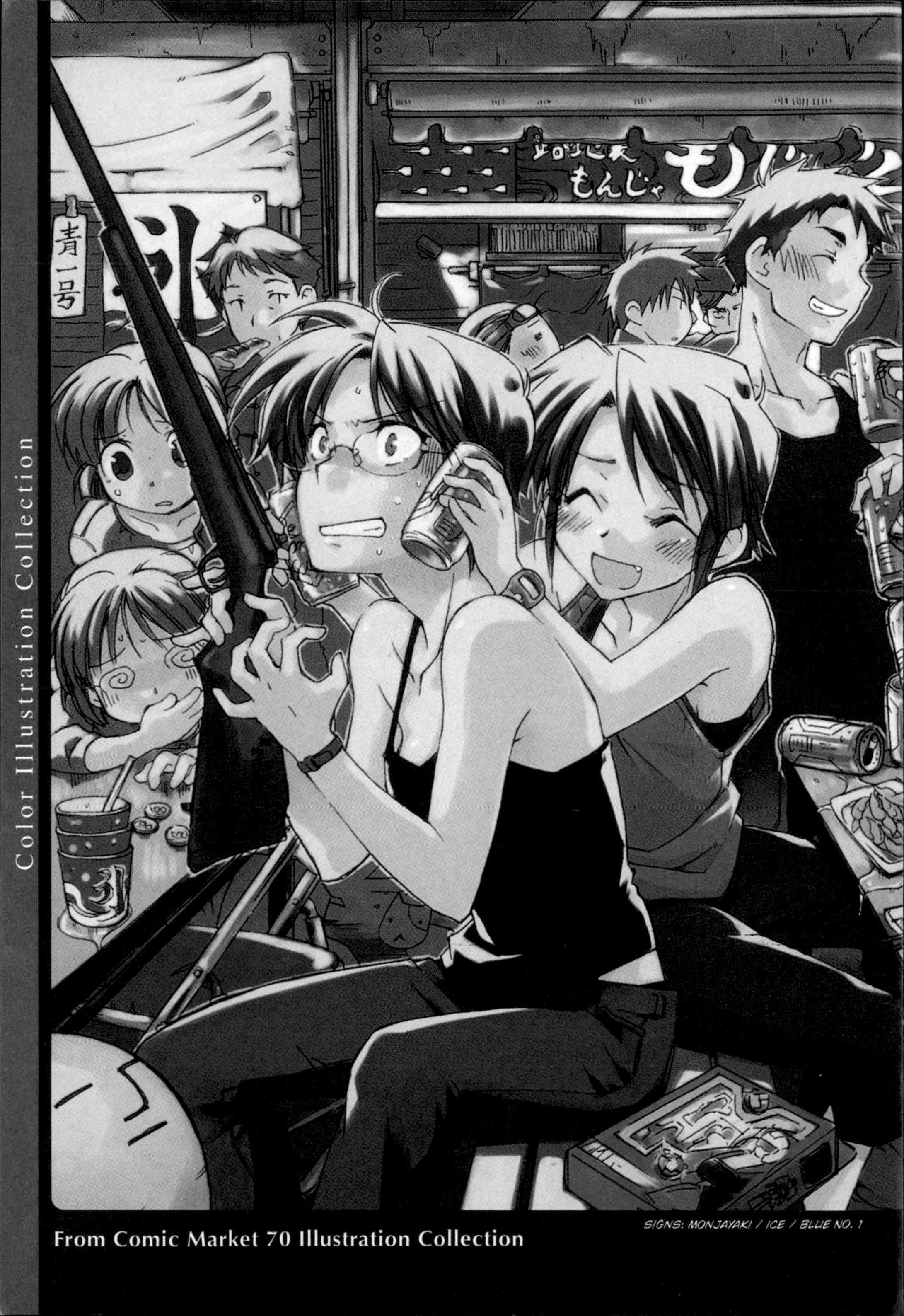
青一号
もんじゃ

SIGNS: MONJAYAKI / ICE / BLUE NO. 1

From Comic Market 70 Illustration Collection

Comic Market 70
Limited Edition Bath Towel

From *Carat*, Nov. 2006

S.S. ASTRO
Asashio Sogo Teachers' ROom

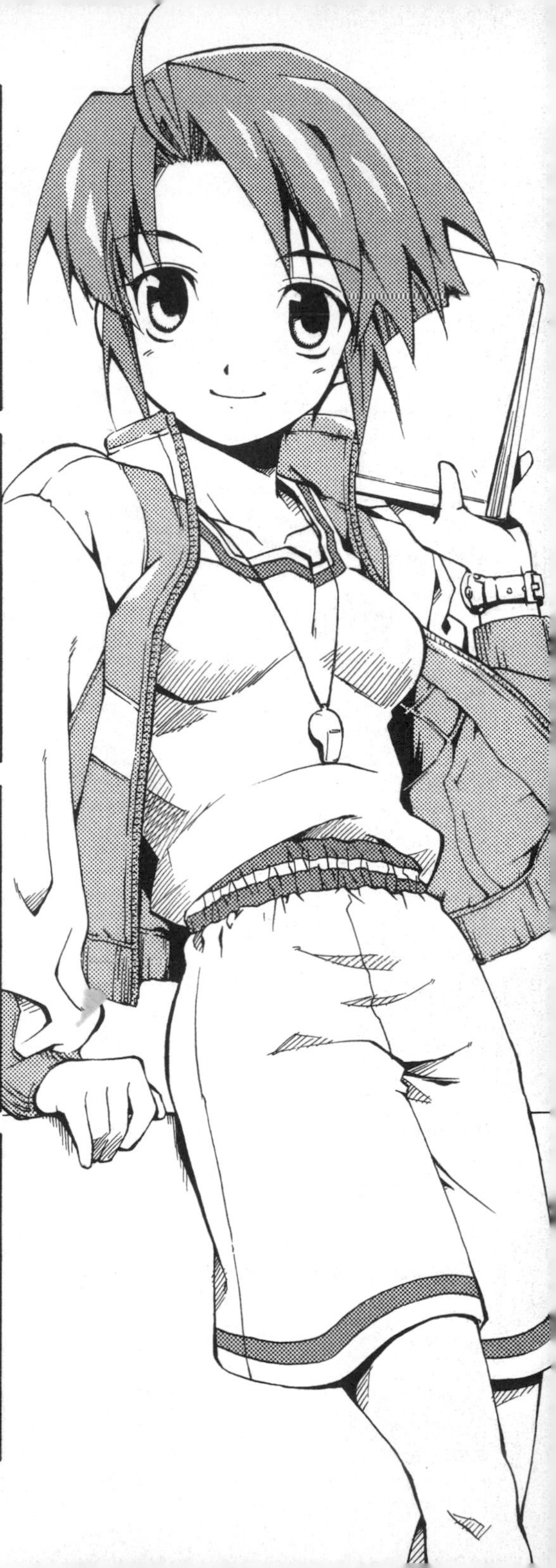

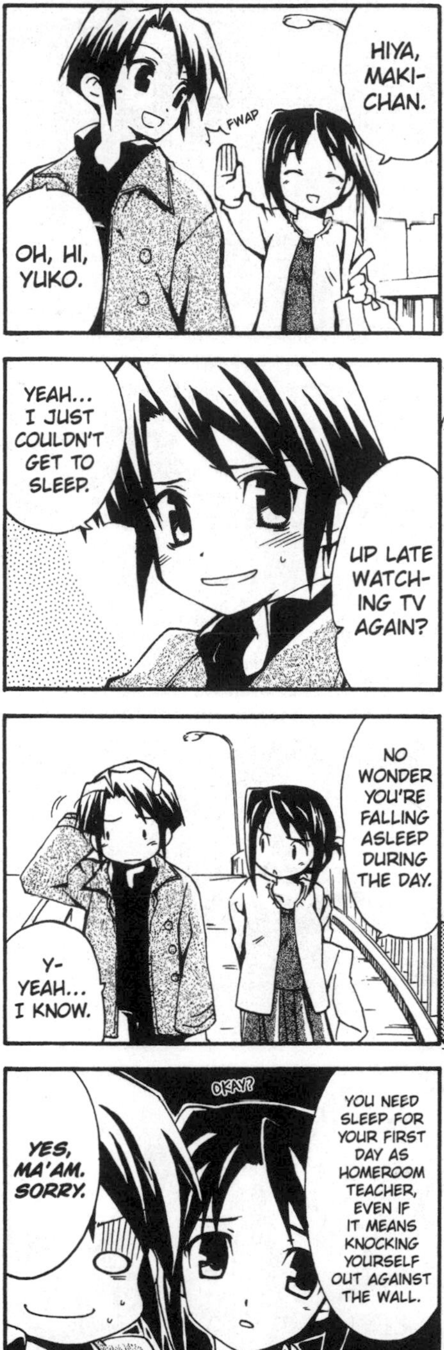
HIYA, MAKI-CHAN.
FWAP
OH, HI, YUKO.
UP LATE WATCHING TV AGAIN?
YEAH... I JUST COULDN'T GET TO SLEEP.
NO WONDER YOU'RE FALLING ASLEEP DURING THE DAY.
Y-YEAH... I KNOW.
YOU NEED SLEEP FOR YOUR FIRST DAY AS HOMEROOM TEACHER, EVEN IF IT MEANS KNOCKING YOURSELF OUT AGAINST THE WALL.
OKAY?
YES, MA'AM. SORRY.

SIGN: ASASHIO INTEGRATED PUBLIC HIGH SCHOOL OF TOKYO

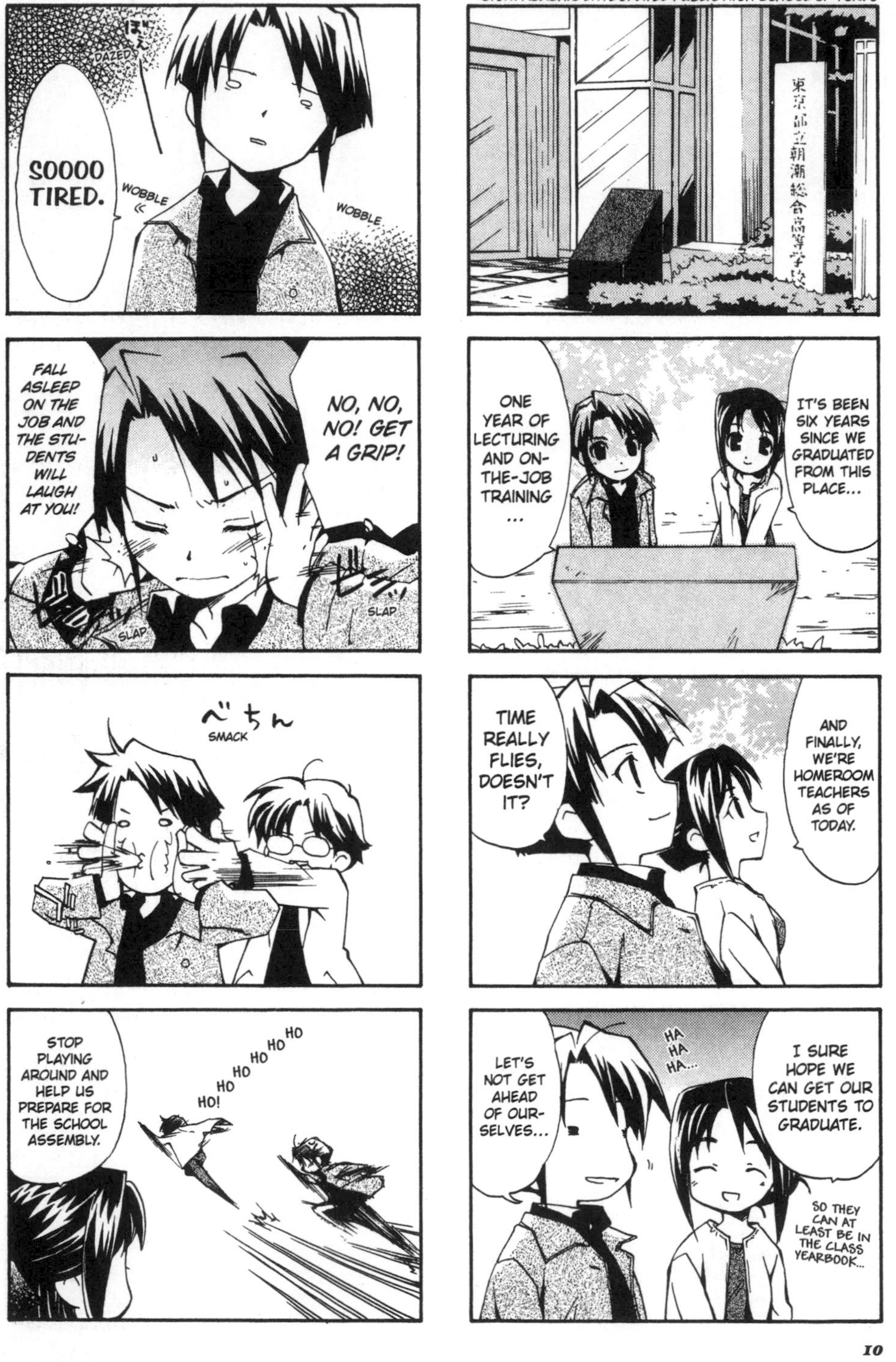
東京都立朝潮総合高等学校
IT'S BEEN SIX YEARS SINCE WE GRADUATED FROM THIS PLACE...
ONE YEAR OF LECTURING AND ON-THE-JOB TRAINING ...
AND FINALLY, WE'RE HOMEROOM TEACHERS AS OF TODAY.
TIME REALLY FLIES, DOESN'T IT?
I SURE HOPE WE CAN GET OUR STUDENTS TO GRADUATE.
HA HA HA...
LET'S NOT GET AHEAD OF OURSELVES...
SO THEY CAN AT LEAST BE IN THE CLASS YEARBOOK...
DAZED
SOOOO TIRED.
WOBBLE
WOBBLE
NO, NO, NO! GET A GRIP!
FALL ASLEEP ON THE JOB AND THE STUDENTS WILL LAUGH AT YOU!
SLAP
SLAP
べちん
SMACK
HO HO HO HO HO HO!
STOP PLAYING AROUND AND HELP US PREPARE FOR THE SCHOOL ASSEMBLY.

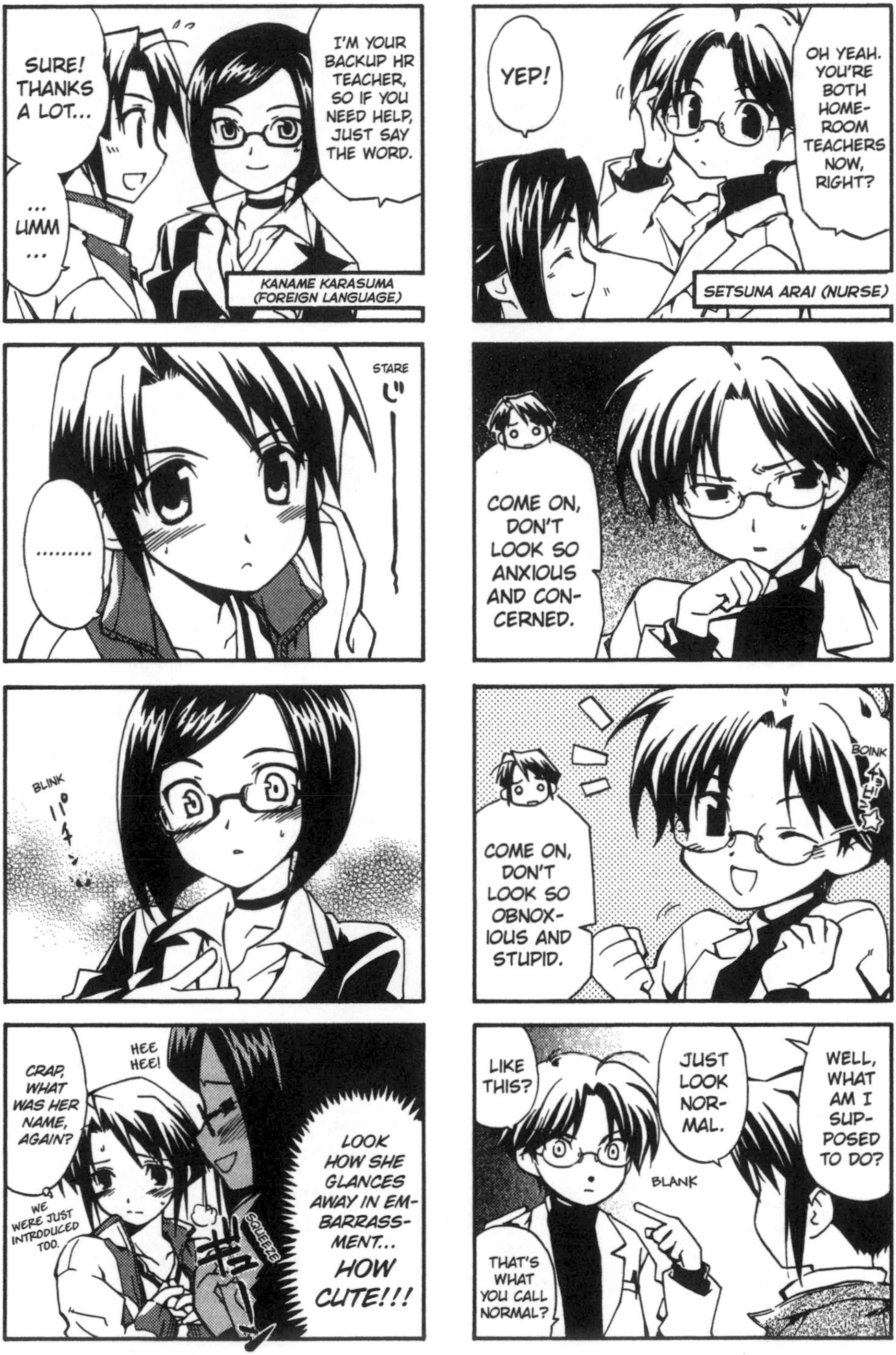
OH YEAH. YOU'RE BOTH HOME-ROOM TEACHERS NOW, RIGHT?
YEP!
SETSUNA ARAI (NURSE)
I'M YOUR BACKUP HR TEACHER, SO IF YOU NEED HELP, JUST SAY THE WORD.
SURE! THANKS A LOT...
... UMM ...
KANAME KARASUMA (FOREIGN LANGUAGE)
COME ON, DON'T LOOK SO ANXIOUS AND CONCERNED.
STARE
....
BOINK
COME ON, DON'T LOOK SO OBNOXIOUS AND STUPID.
BLINK
WELL, WHAT AM I SUPPOSED TO DO?
JUST LOOK NORMAL.
LIKE THIS?
BLANK
THAT'S WHAT YOU CALL NORMAL?
HEE HEE!
CRAP, WHAT WAS HER NAME, AGAIN?
WE WERE JUST INTRODUCED TOO.
LOOK HOW SHE GLANCES AWAY IN EMBARRASSMENT... HOW CUTE!!!
SQUEEZE

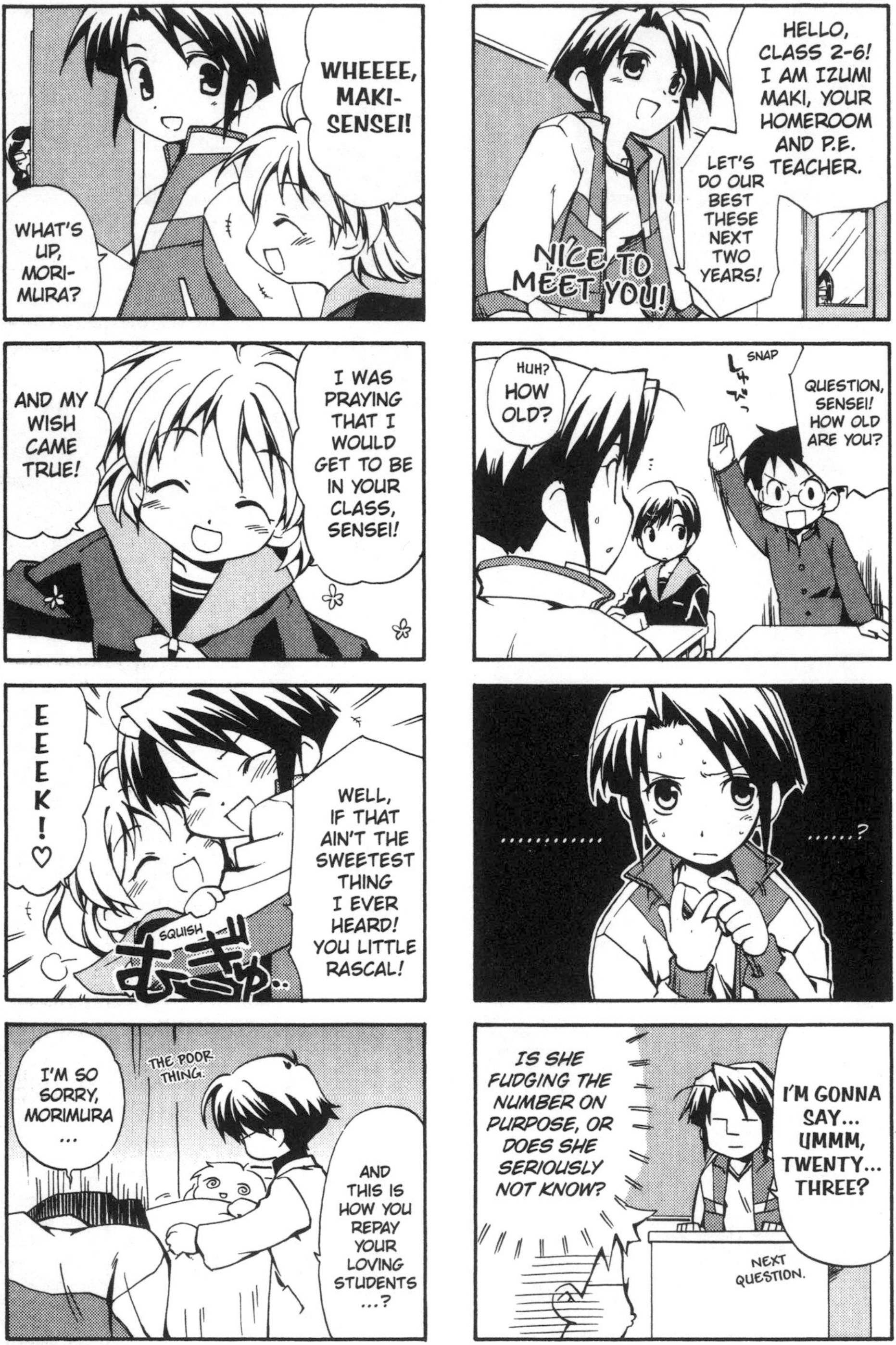
HELLO, CLASS 2-6! I AM IZUMI MAKI, YOUR HOMEROOM AND P.E. TEACHER.
LET'S DO OUR BEST THESE NEXT TWO YEARS!
NICE TO MEET YOU!
SNAP
QUESTION, SENSEI! HOW OLD ARE YOU?
HUH? HOW OLD?
......?
....
I'M GONNA SAY... UMMM, TWENTY... THREE?
IS SHE FUDGING THE NUMBER ON PURPOSE, OR DOES SHE SERIOUSLY NOT KNOW?
NEXT QUESTION.
WHEEEE, MAKI-SENSEI!
WHAT'S UP, MORI-MURA?
I WAS PRAYING THAT I WOULD GET TO BE IN YOUR CLASS, SENSEI!
AND MY WISH CAME TRUE!
WELL, IF THAT AIN'T THE SWEETEST THING I EVER HEARD! YOU LITTLE RASCAL!
EEEEK!♡
SQUISH
むぎゅ..
AND THIS IS HOW YOU REPAY YOUR LOVING STUDENTS ...?
THE POOR THING.
I'M SO SORRY, MORIMURA ...

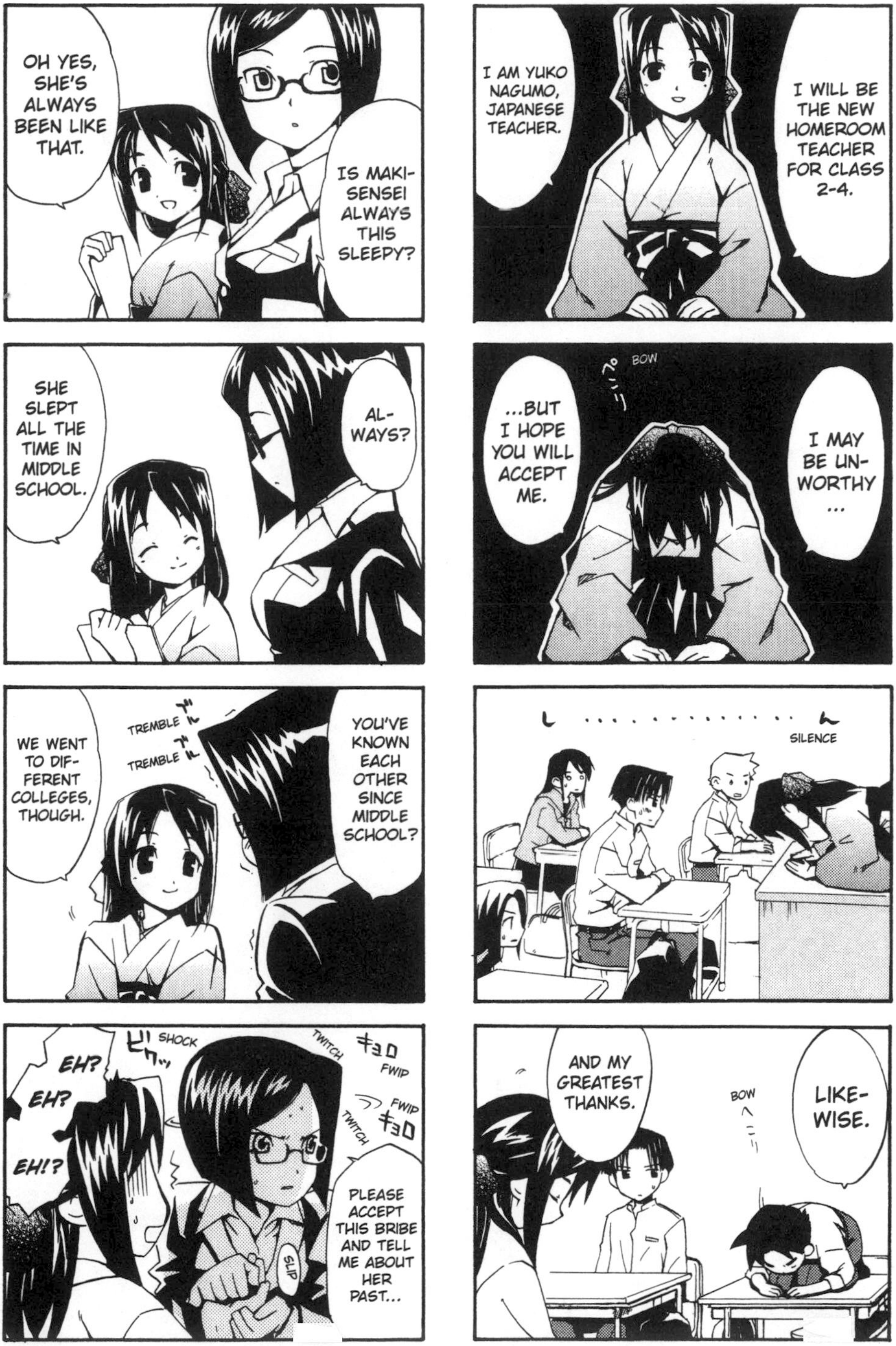
I WILL BE THE NEW HOMEROOM TEACHER FOR CLASS 2-4.
I AM YUKO NAGUMO, JAPANESE TEACHER.
BOW
I MAY BE UN-WORTHY ...
...BUT I HOPE YOU WILL ACCEPT ME.
SILENCE
LIKE-WISE.
BOW
AND MY GREATEST THANKS.
IS MAKI-SENSEI ALWAYS THIS SLEEPY?
OH YES, SHE'S ALWAYS BEEN LIKE THAT.
AL-WAYS?
SHE SLEPT ALL THE TIME IN MIDDLE SCHOOL.
YOU'VE KNOWN EACH OTHER SINCE MIDDLE SCHOOL?
TREMBLE
TREMBLE
WE WENT TO DIF-FERENT COLLEGES, THOUGH.
TWITCH
FWIP
FWIP
TWITCH
SHOCK
EH?
EH?
EH!?
PLEASE ACCEPT THIS BRIBE AND TELL ME ABOUT HER PAST...
SLIP

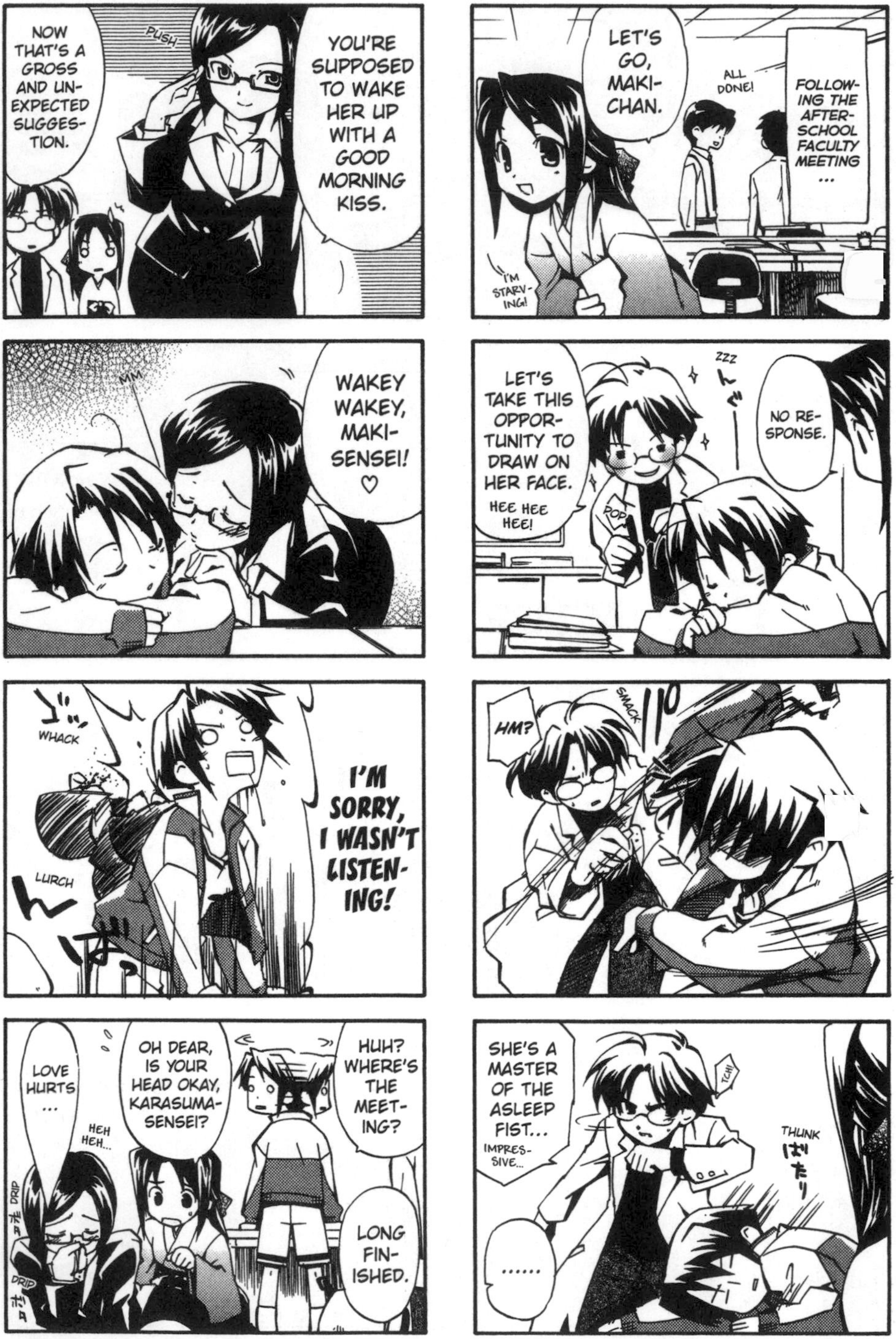
FOLLOWING THE AFTER-SCHOOL FACULTY MEETING...
ALL DONE!
LET'S GO, MAKI-CHAN.
I'M STARVING!
ZZZ
NO RESPONSE.
LET'S TAKE THIS OPPORTUNITY TO DRAW ON HER FACE.
HEE HEE HEE!
POP
SMACK
HM?
TCH!
THUNK
ぱたり
SHE'S A MASTER OF THE ASLEEP FIST...
IMPRESSIVE...
......
YOU'RE SUPPOSED TO WAKE HER UP WITH A GOOD MORNING KISS.
PUSH
NOW THAT'S A GROSS AND UNEXPECTED SUGGESTION.
WAKEY WAKEY, MAKI-SENSEI! ♡
MM
I'M SORRY, I WASN'T LISTENING!
WHACK
LURCH
HUH? WHERE'S THE MEETING?
LONG FINISHED.
OH DEAR, IS YOUR HEAD OKAY, KARASUMA-SENSEI?
LOVE HURTS...
HEH HEH...
DRIP
DRIP

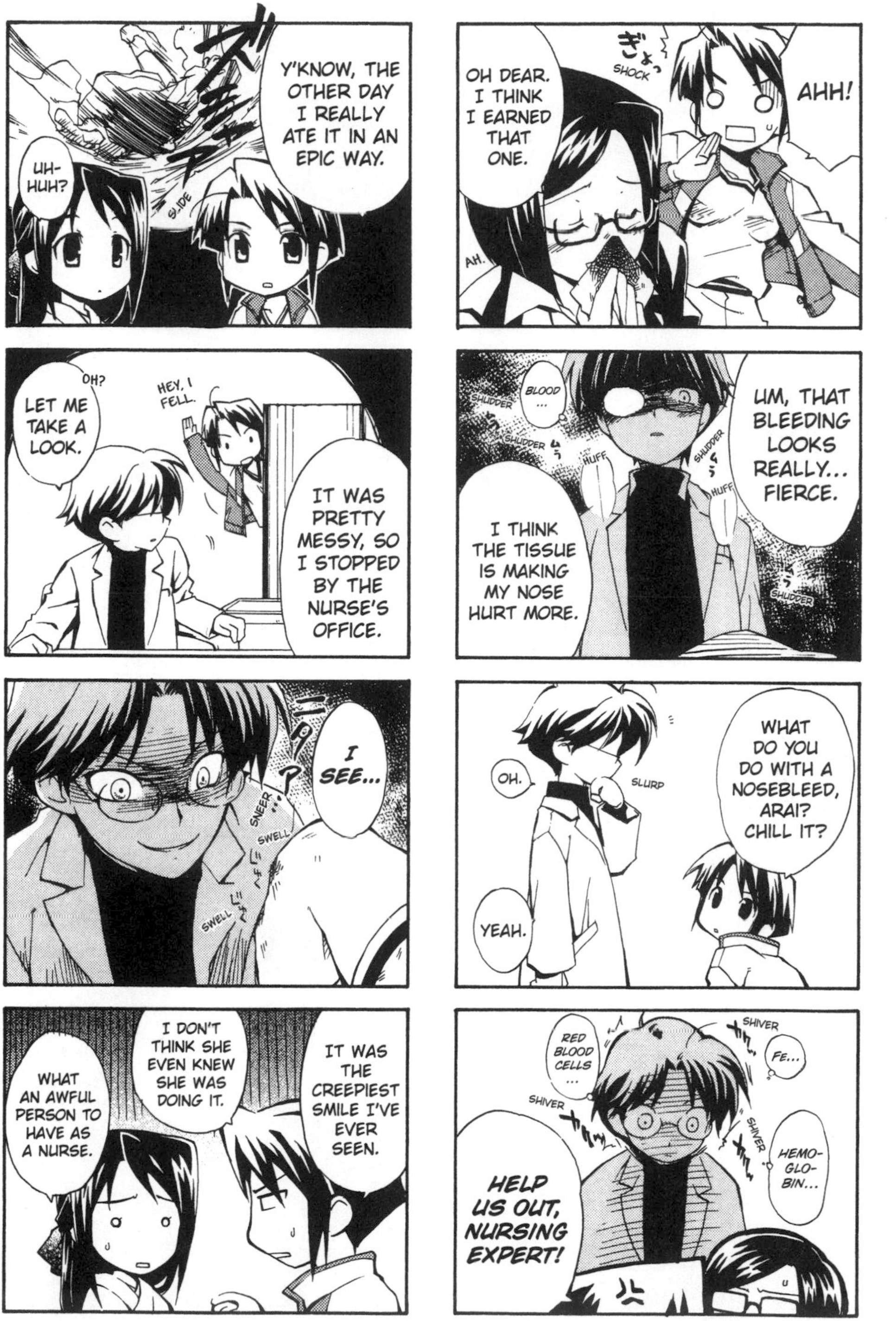
ぎょっ
SHOCK
AHH!
OH DEAR. I THINK I EARNED THAT ONE.
AH.
UM, THAT BLEEDING LOOKS REALLY... FIERCE.
SHUDDER
HUFF
I THINK THE TISSUE IS MAKING MY NOSE HURT MORE.
BLOOD ...
SHUDDER
SHUDDER
HUFF
SHUDDER
WHAT DO YOU DO WITH A NOSEBLEED, ARAI? CHILL IT?
SLURP
OH.
YEAH.
SHIVER
FE...
SHIVER
HEMO-GLOBIN...
RED BLOOD CELLS ...
SHIVER
HELP US OUT, NURSING EXPERT!
Y'KNOW, THE OTHER DAY I REALLY ATE IT IN AN EPIC WAY.
SLIDE
UH-HUH?
IT WAS PRETTY MESSY, SO I STOPPED BY THE NURSE'S OFFICE.
HEY, I FELL.
OH?
LET ME TAKE A LOOK.
I SEE...
SNEER
SWELL
SWELL
IT WAS THE CREEPIEST SMILE I'VE EVER SEEN.
I DON'T THINK SHE EVEN KNEW SHE WAS DOING IT.
WHAT AN AWFUL PERSON TO HAVE AS A NURSE.

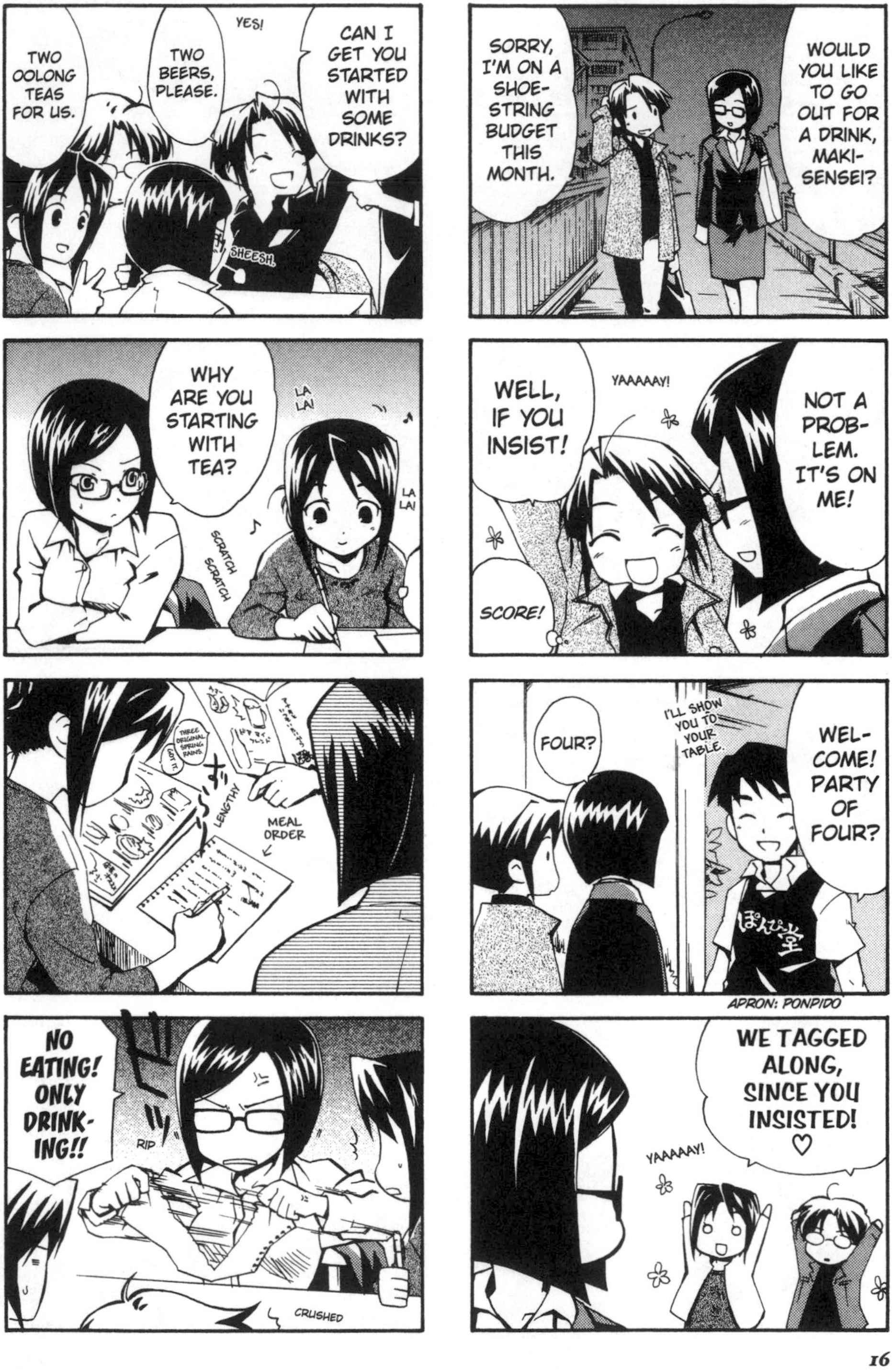
WOULD YOU LIKE TO GO OUT FOR A DRINK, MAKI-SENSEI?
SORRY, I'M ON A SHOE-STRING BUDGET THIS MONTH.
NOT A PROB-LEM. IT'S ON ME!
YAAAAAY!
WELL, IF YOU INSIST!
SCORE!
WEL-COME! PARTY OF FOUR?
I'LL SHOW YOU TO YOUR TABLE.
FOUR?
APRON: PONPIDO
WE TAGGED ALONG, SINCE YOU INSISTED! ♡
YAAAAAY!
CAN I GET YOU STARTED WITH SOME DRINKS?
YES!
TWO BEERS, PLEASE.
TWO OOLONG TEAS FOR US.
SHEESH.
WHY ARE YOU STARTING WITH TEA?
LA LA!
LA LA!
SCRATCH SCRATCH
THREE ORIGINAL SPRING RAINS.
GOT IT.
LENGTHY
MEAL ORDER
NO EATING! ONLY DRINK-ING!!
RIP
CRUSHED

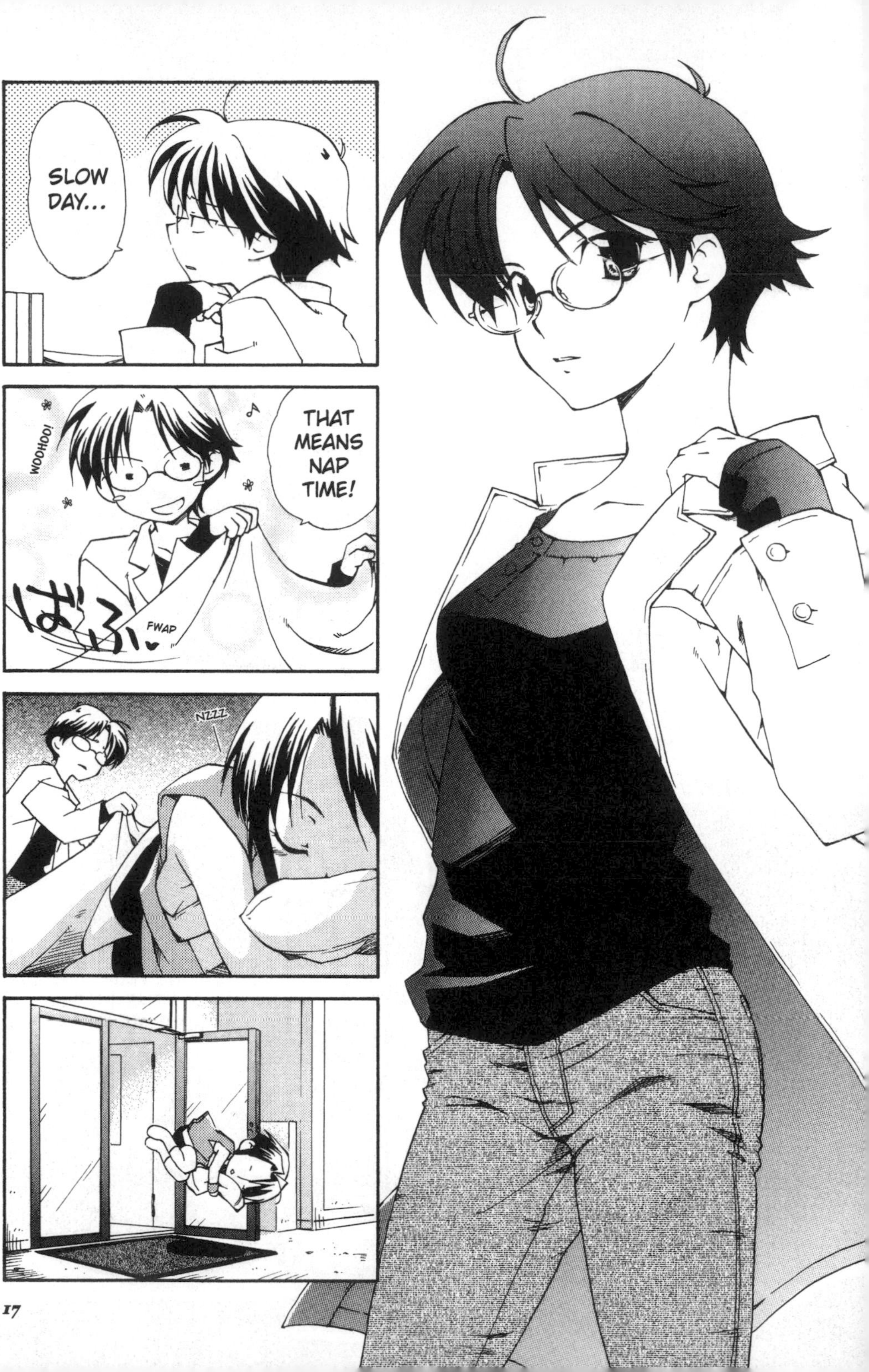
SLOW DAY...
THAT MEANS NAP TIME!
WOOHOO!
ぱふ
FWAP
NZZZ

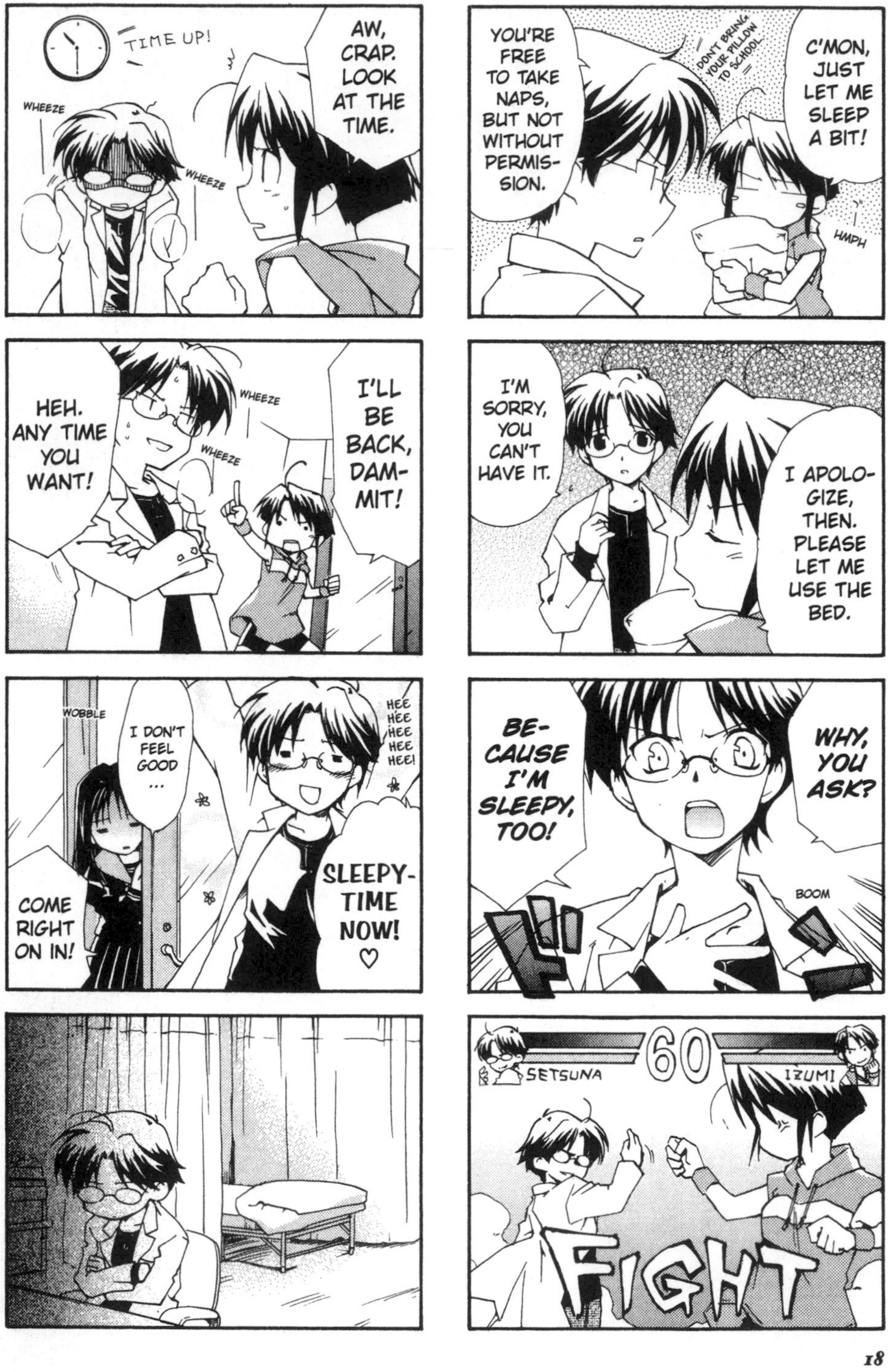
C'MON, JUST LET ME SLEEP A BIT!
DON'T BRING YOUR PILLOW TO SCHOOL
YOU'RE FREE TO TAKE NAPS, BUT NOT WITHOUT PERMISSION.
HMPH
TIME UP!
AW, CRAP. LOOK AT THE TIME.
WHEEZE
WHEEZE
I'M SORRY, YOU CAN'T HAVE IT.
I APOLOGIZE, THEN. PLEASE LET ME USE THE BED.
I'LL BE BACK, DAMMIT!
WHEEZE
WHEEZE
HEH. ANY TIME YOU WANT!
WHY, YOU ASK?
BECAUSE I'M SLEEPY, TOO!
BOOM
HEE HEE HEE HEE HEE!
I DON'T FEEL GOOD ...
WOBBLE
SLEEPY-TIME NOW! ♡
COME RIGHT ON IN!
60
IZUMI
SETSUNA
FIGHT

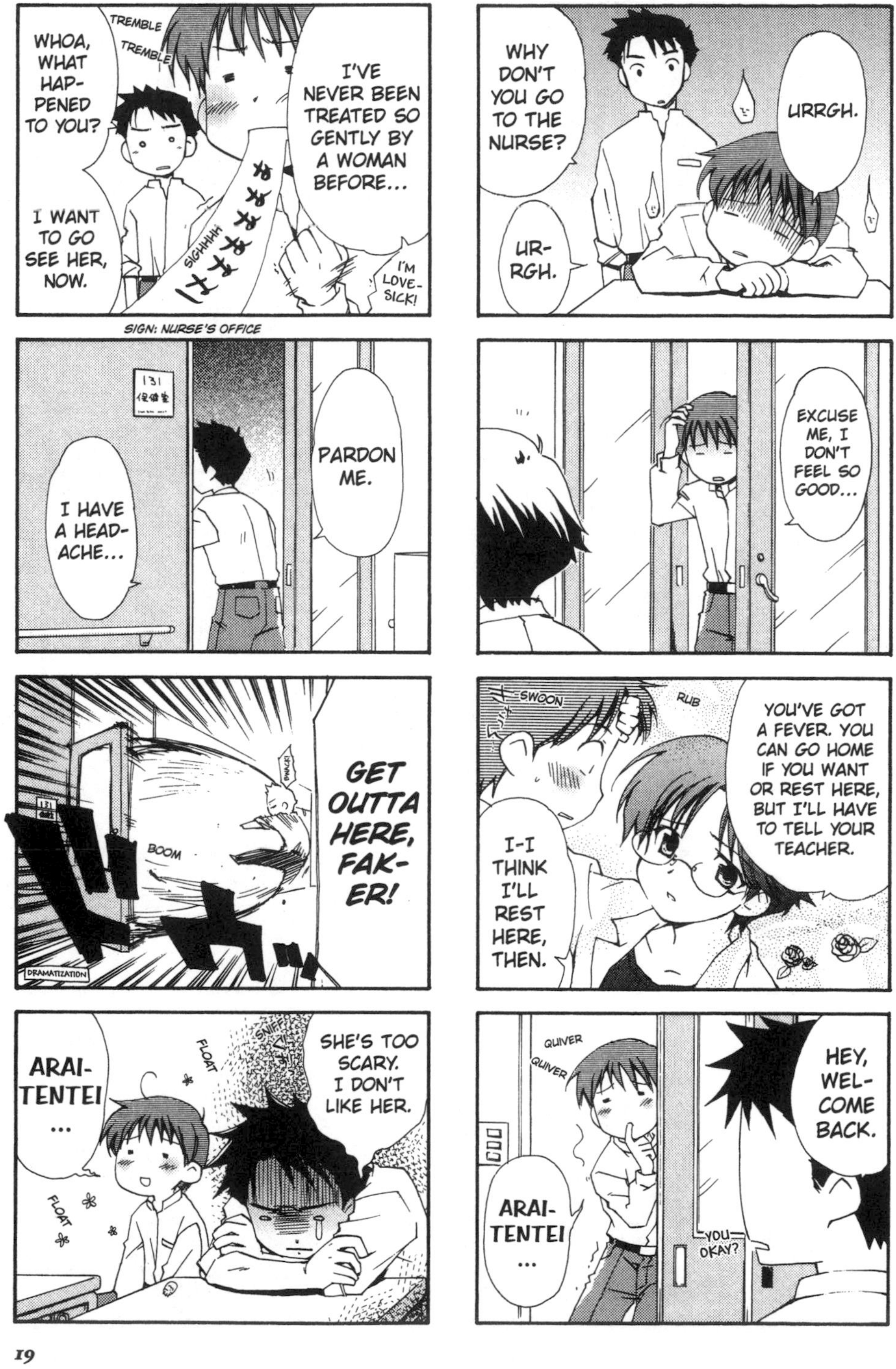
URRGH.
WHY DON'T YOU GO TO THE NURSE?
UR-RGH.
EXCUSE ME, I DON'T FEEL SO GOOD...
RUB
SWOON
YOU'VE GOT A FEVER. YOU CAN GO HOME IF YOU WANT OR REST HERE, BUT I'LL HAVE TO TELL YOUR TEACHER.
I-I THINK I'LL REST HERE, THEN.
HEY, WELCOME BACK.
QUIVER
QUIVER
YOU OKAY?
ARAI-TENTEI ...
I'VE NEVER BEEN TREATED SO GENTLY BY A WOMAN BEFORE...
TREMBLE
TREMBLE
WHOA, WHAT HAPPENED TO YOU?
I'M LOVE-SICK!
SIGHHHH
I WANT TO GO SEE HER, NOW.
SIGN: NURSE'S OFFICE
PARDON ME.
I HAVE A HEADACHE...
GET OUTTA HERE, FAKER!
SWACK!
BOOM
DRAMATIZATION
SHE'S TOO SCARY. I DON'T LIKE HER.
SNIFF
FLOAT
ARAI-TENTEI ...
FLOAT

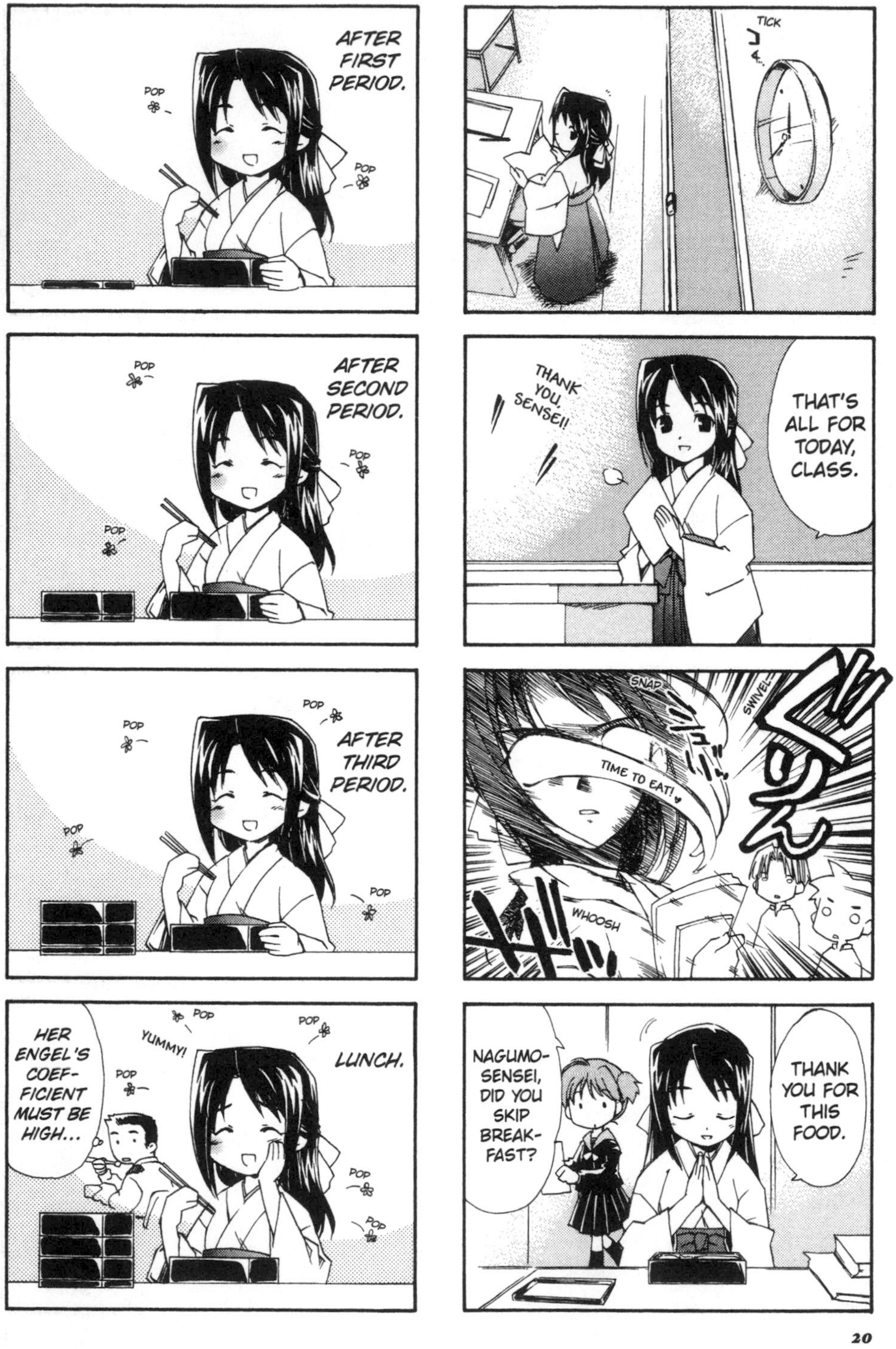
TICK
THAT'S ALL FOR TODAY, CLASS.
THANK YOU, SENSEI!!
SWIVEL
SNAP
TIME TO EAT!♥
WHOOSH
THANK YOU FOR THIS FOOD.
NAGUMO-SENSEI, DID YOU SKIP BREAK-FAST?
AFTER FIRST PERIOD.
POP
POP
AFTER SECOND PERIOD.
POP
POP
POP
AFTER THIRD PERIOD.
POP
POP
POP
POP
LUNCH.
POP
POP
YUMMY!
POP
HER ENGEL'S COEF-FICIENT MUST BE HIGH...
POP
POP

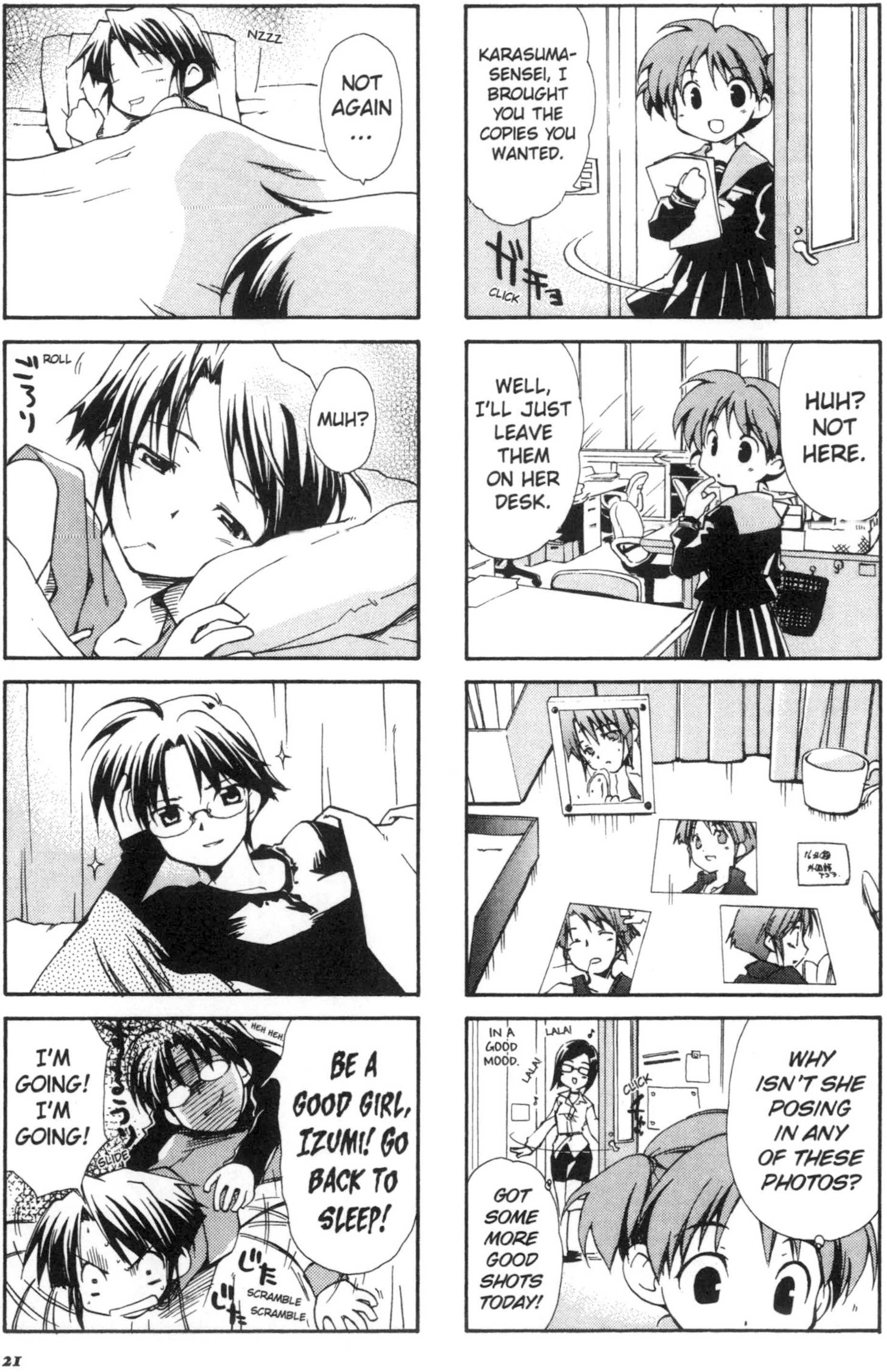
KARASUMA-SENSEI, I BROUGHT YOU THE COPIES YOU WANTED.
CLICK
HUH? NOT HERE.
WELL, I'LL JUST LEAVE THEM ON HER DESK.
WHY ISN'T SHE POSING IN ANY OF THESE PHOTOS?
IN A GOOD MOOD.
LALA!
LALA!
CLICK
GOT SOME MORE GOOD SHOTS TODAY!
NZZZ
NOT AGAIN ...
ROLL
MUH?
BE A GOOD GIRL, IZUMI! GO BACK TO SLEEP!
HEH HEH
I'M GOING! I'M GOING!
SLIDE
SCRAMBLE
SCRAMBLE

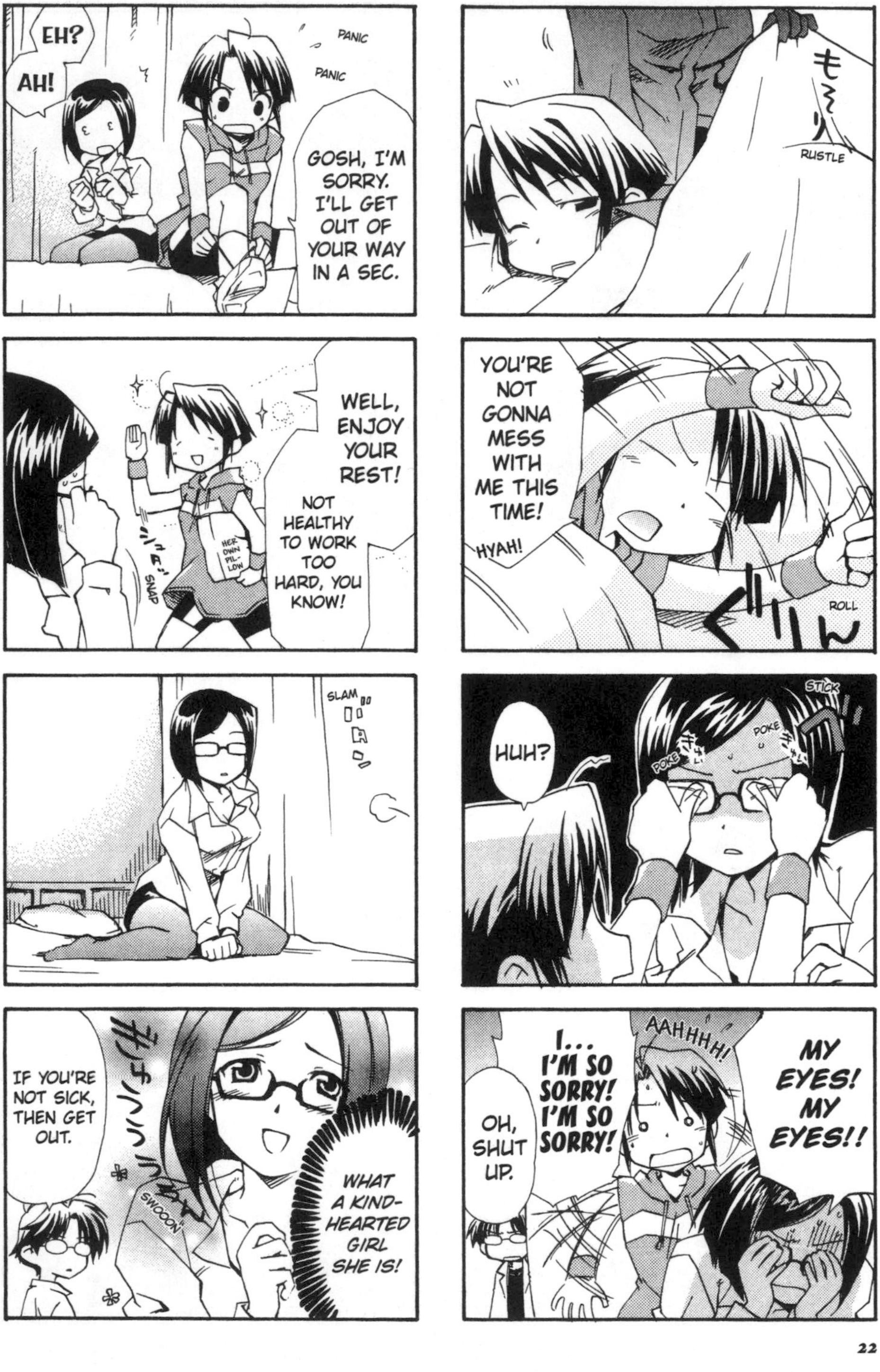
もぞり
RUSTLE
YOU'RE NOT GONNA MESS WITH ME THIS TIME!
HYAH!
ぐりん
ROLL
STICK
POKE
POKE
HUH?
AAHHHH!
MY EYES! MY EYES!!
I... I'M SO SORRY! I'M SO SORRY!
OH, SHUT UP.
PANIC
PANIC
EH?
AH!
GOSH, I'M SORRY. I'LL GET OUT OF YOUR WAY IN A SEC.
WELL, ENJOY YOUR REST!
NOT HEALTHY TO WORK TOO HARD, YOU KNOW!
HER DOWN PILLOW
SNAP
SLAM
IF YOU'RE NOT SICK, THEN GET OUT.
WHAT A KIND-HEARTED GIRL SHE IS!
SWOOON

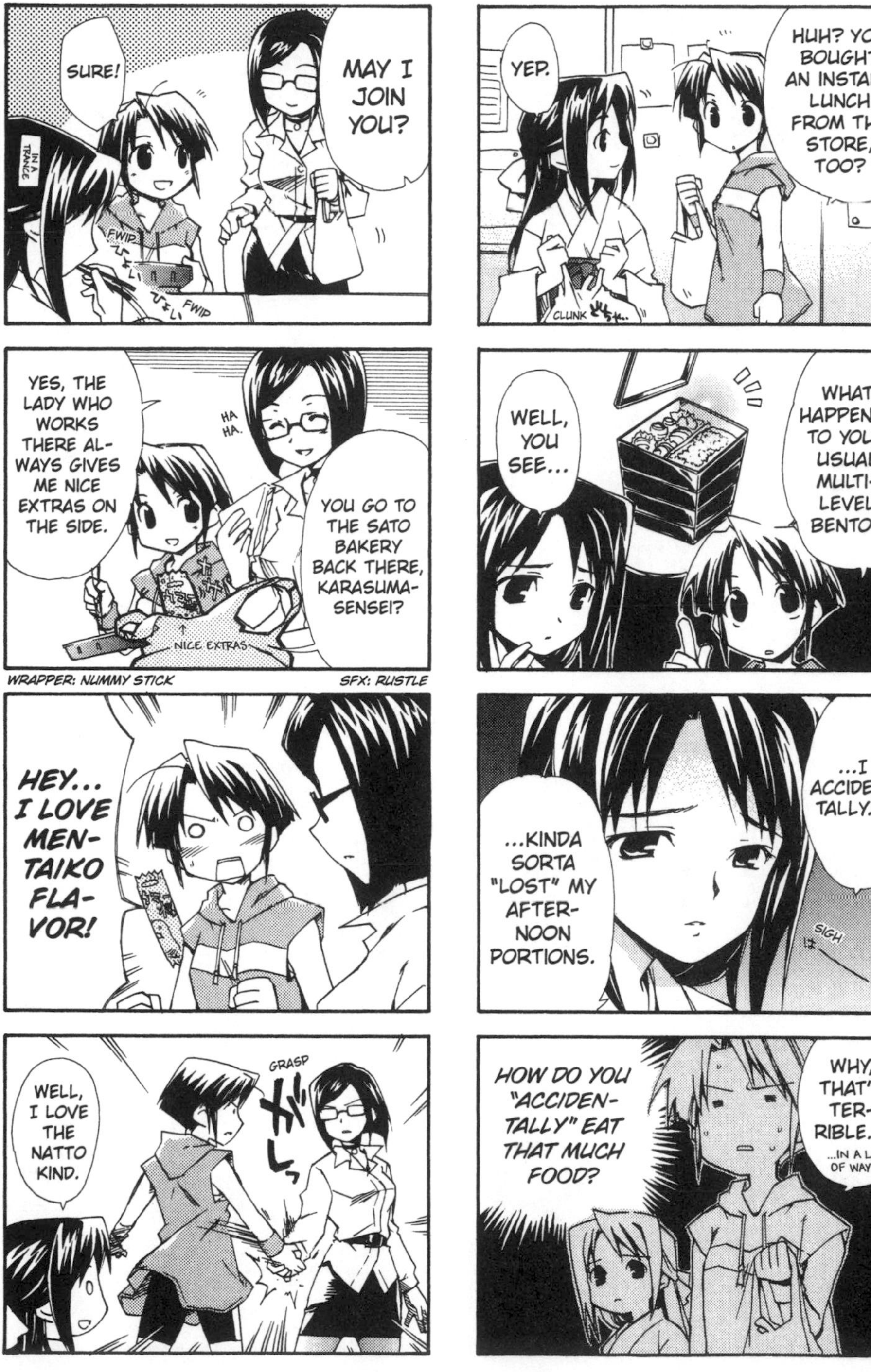
HUH? YOU BOUGHT AN INSTANT LUNCH FROM THE STORE, TOO?
YEP.
CLUNK
WHAT HAPPENED TO YOUR USUAL MULTI-LEVEL BENTO?
WELL, YOU SEE...
...I ACCIDENTALLY...
...KINDA SORTA "LOST" MY AFTERNOON PORTIONS.
SIGH
WHY, THAT'S TERRIBLE...
...IN A LOT OF WAYS.
HOW DO YOU "ACCIDENTALLY" EAT THAT MUCH FOOD?
MAY I JOIN YOU?
SURE!
IN A TRANCE
FWIP
FWIP
YOU GO TO THE SATO BAKERY BACK THERE, KARASUMA-SENSEI?
HA HA.
YES, THE LADY WHO WORKS THERE ALWAYS GIVES ME NICE EXTRAS ON THE SIDE.
NICE EXTRAS
WRAPPER: NUMMY STICK
SFX: RUSTLE
HEY... I LOVE MENTAIKO FLAVOR!
GRASP
WELL, I LOVE THE NATTO KIND.

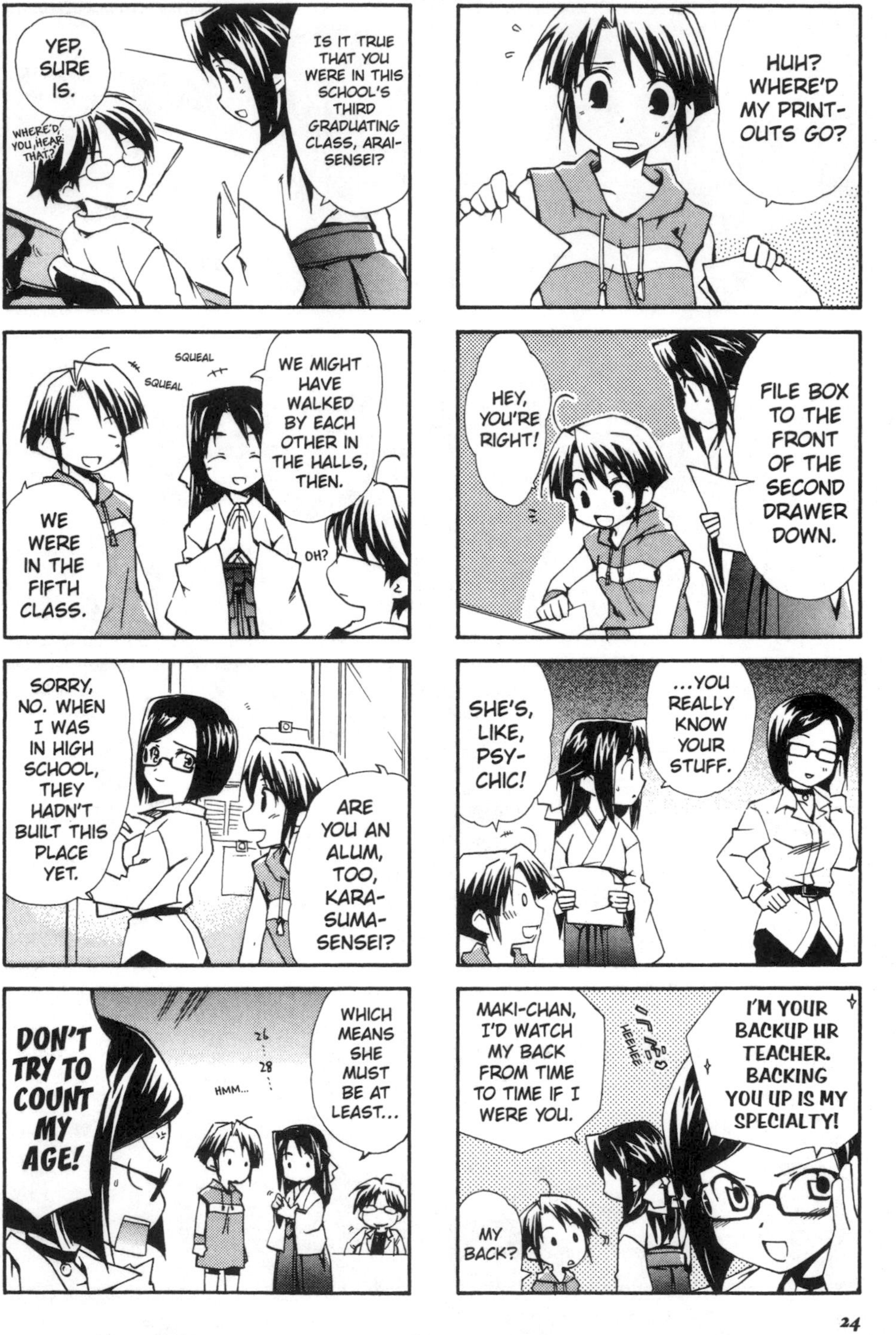
HUH? WHERE'D MY PRINT-OUTS GO?
FILE BOX TO THE FRONT OF THE SECOND DRAWER DOWN.
HEY, YOU'RE RIGHT!
...YOU REALLY KNOW YOUR STUFF.
SHE'S, LIKE, PSY-CHIC!
I'M YOUR BACKUP HR TEACHER. BACKING YOU UP IS MY SPECIALTY!
HEEHEE
MAKI-CHAN, I'D WATCH MY BACK FROM TIME TO TIME IF I WERE YOU.
MY BACK?
IS IT TRUE THAT YOU WERE IN THIS SCHOOL'S THIRD GRADUATING CLASS, ARAI-SENSEI?
YEP, SURE IS.
WHERE'D YOU HEAR THAT?
WE MIGHT HAVE WALKED BY EACH OTHER IN THE HALLS, THEN.
SQUEAL
SQUEAL
OH?
WE WERE IN THE FIFTH CLASS.
ARE YOU AN ALUM, TOO, KARASUMA-SENSEI?
SORRY, NO. WHEN I WAS IN HIGH SCHOOL, THEY HADN'T BUILT THIS PLACE YET.
WHICH MEANS SHE MUST BE AT LEAST...
26... 28...
HMM...
DON'T TRY TO COUNT MY AGE!

IZUMI MAKI

CLASS: HEALTH AND PHYSICAL EDUCATION TEACHER
GENDER: FEMALE
PERSONALITY: CLOSET PERVERT
LEVEL: 3

E: JERSEY
E: WHISTLE
E: LOW-PRESSURE PILLOW
E: UMAA BO

(SKIN) HEALTH POINTS: SQUISHY
MENTAL POINTS: RELATIVELY NORMAL PERSON
STRENGTH: CAN'T KILL A BEAR
SPEED: THERE'S ALWAYS TOMORROW
STAMINA: PLENTY
INTELLIGENCE: GAVE UP
LUCK: ENOUGH TO BE THE MAIN CHARACTER
GUTS: HATES TO LOSE

¥: ON A SHOESTRING BUDGET THIS MONTH...

S.S. ASTRO

Asashio Sogo Teachers' ROom

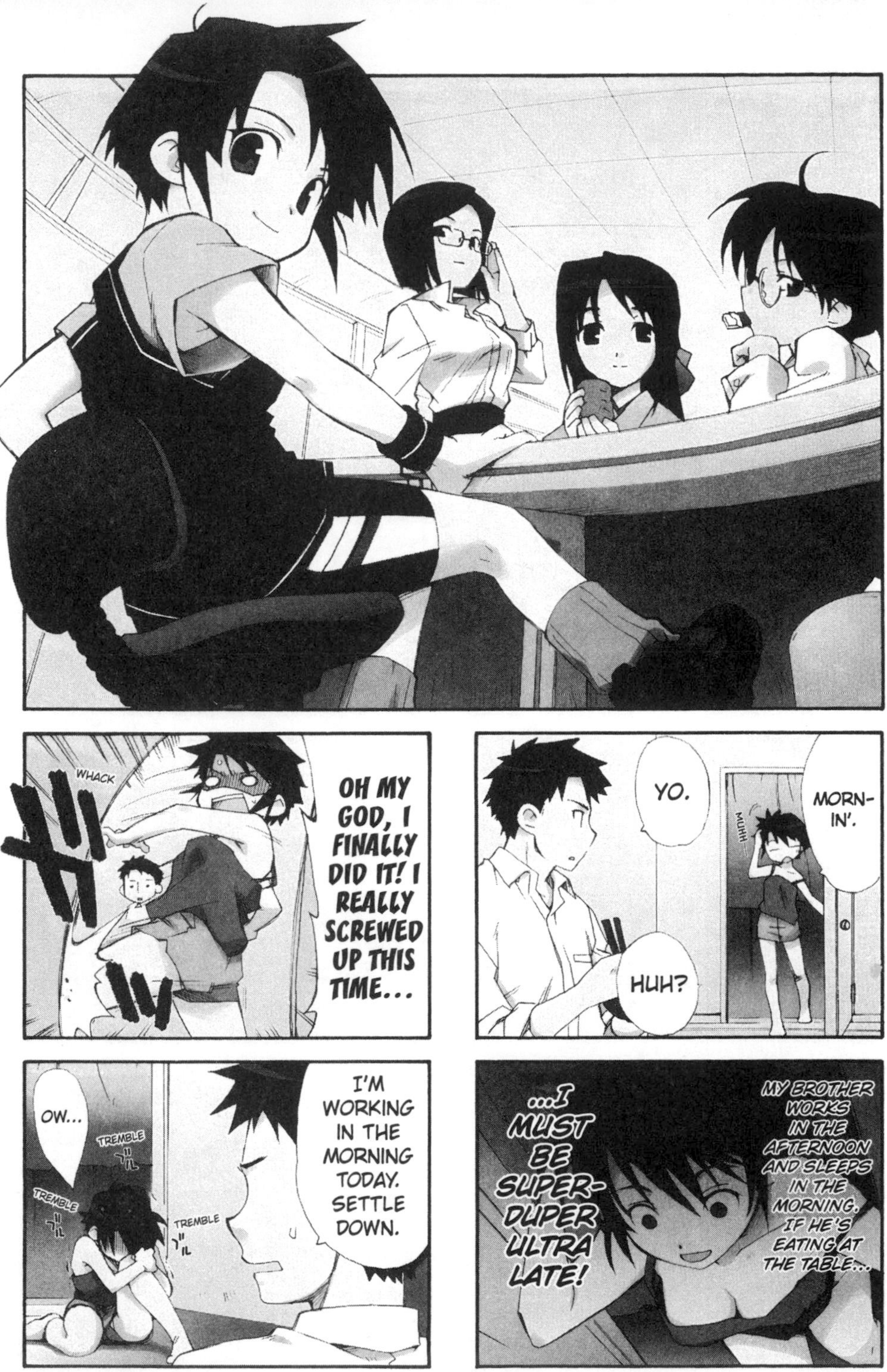
MORN- IN'.
YO.
MUHH—
HUH?
OH MY GOD, I FINALLY DID IT! I REALLY SCREWED UP THIS TIME...
WHACK
MY BROTHER WORKS IN THE AFTERNOON AND SLEEPS IN THE MORNING. IF HE'S EATING AT THE TABLE...
...I MUST BE SUPER-DUPER ULTRA LATE!
I'M WORKING IN THE MORNING TODAY. SETTLE DOWN.
OW...
TREMBLE
TREMBLE
TREMBLE

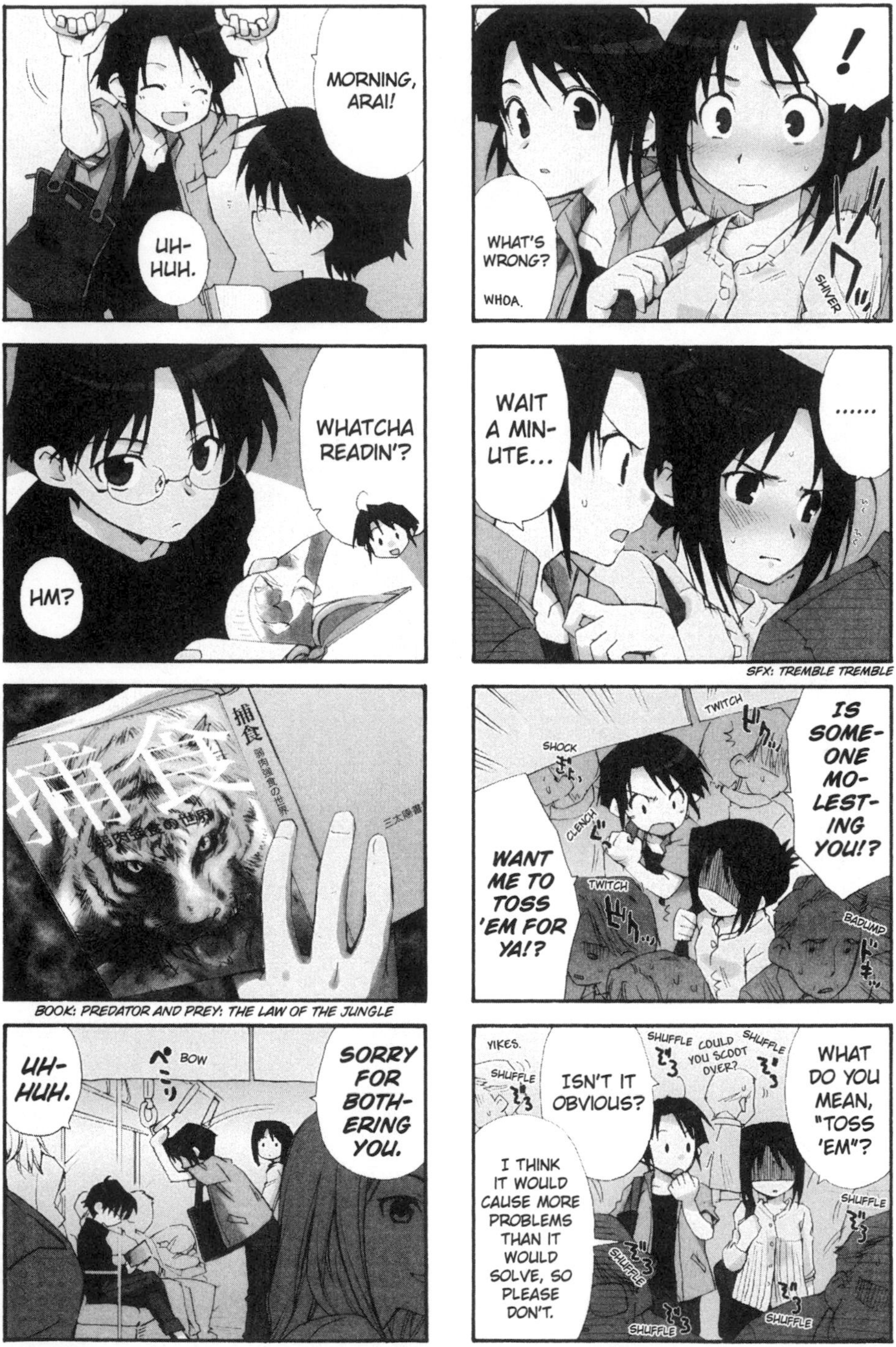
!
WHAT'S WRONG?
WHOA.
SHIVER
......
WAIT A MIN-UTE...
SFX: TREMBLE TREMBLE
IS SOME-ONE MO-LEST-ING YOU!?
TWITCH
SHOCK
CLENCH
WANT ME TO TOSS 'EM FOR YA!?
TWITCH
BADUMP
WHAT DO YOU MEAN, "TOSS 'EM"?
SHUFFLE
COULD YOU SCOOT OVER?
SHUFFLE
ISN'T IT OBVIOUS?
YIKES.
SHUFFLE
I THINK IT WOULD CAUSE MORE PROBLEMS THAN IT WOULD SOLVE, SO PLEASE DON'T.
SHUFFLE
SHUFFLE
SHUFFLE
SHUFFLE
MORNING, ARAI!
UH-HUH.
WHATCHA READIN'?
HM?
BOOK: PREDATOR AND PREY: THE LAW OF THE JUNGLE
SORRY FOR BOTH-ERING YOU.
BOW
UH-HUH.

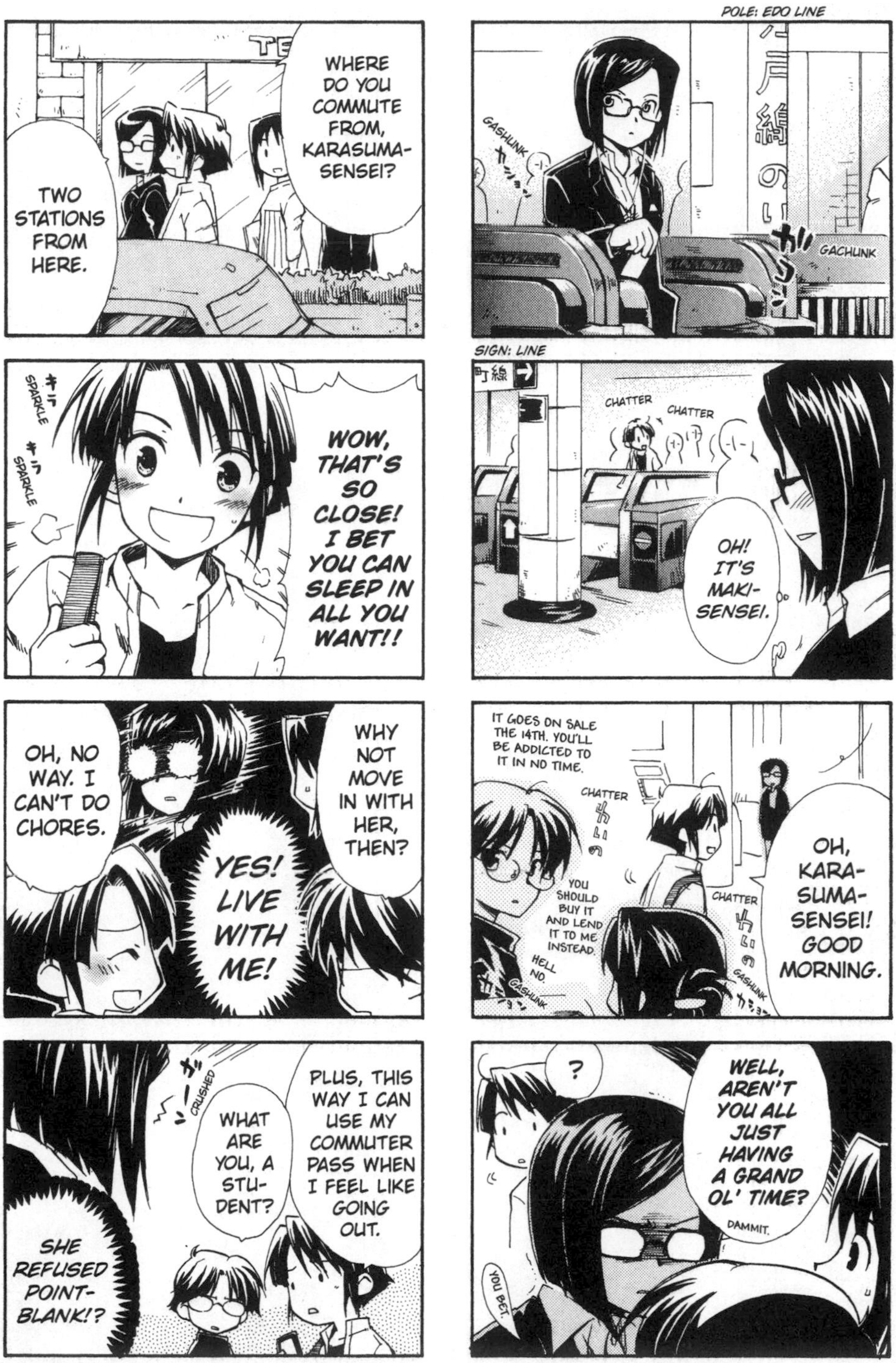
POLE: EDO LINE
GACHUNK
GASHLUNK
SIGN: LINE
CHATTER
CHATTER
OH! IT'S MAKI-SENSEI.
OH, KARA-SUMA-SENSEI! GOOD MORNING.
CHATTER
IT GOES ON SALE THE 14TH. YOU'LL BE ADDICTED TO IT IN NO TIME.
CHATTER
YOU SHOULD BUY IT AND LEND IT TO ME INSTEAD.
HELL NO.
GASHLUNK
GASHLUNK
WELL, AREN'T YOU ALL JUST HAVING A GRAND OL' TIME?
DAMMIT.
?
YOU BET.
WHERE DO YOU COMMUTE FROM, KARASUMA-SENSEI?
TWO STATIONS FROM HERE.
WOW, THAT'S SO CLOSE! I BET YOU CAN SLEEP IN ALL YOU WANT!!
SPARKLE
SPARKLE
WHY NOT MOVE IN WITH HER, THEN?
YES! LIVE WITH ME!
OH, NO WAY. I CAN'T DO CHORES.
PLUS, THIS WAY I CAN USE MY COMMUTER PASS WHEN I FEEL LIKE GOING OUT.
CRUSHED
WHAT ARE YOU, A STUDENT?
SHE REFUSED POINT-BLANK!?

SIGN: ASASHIO

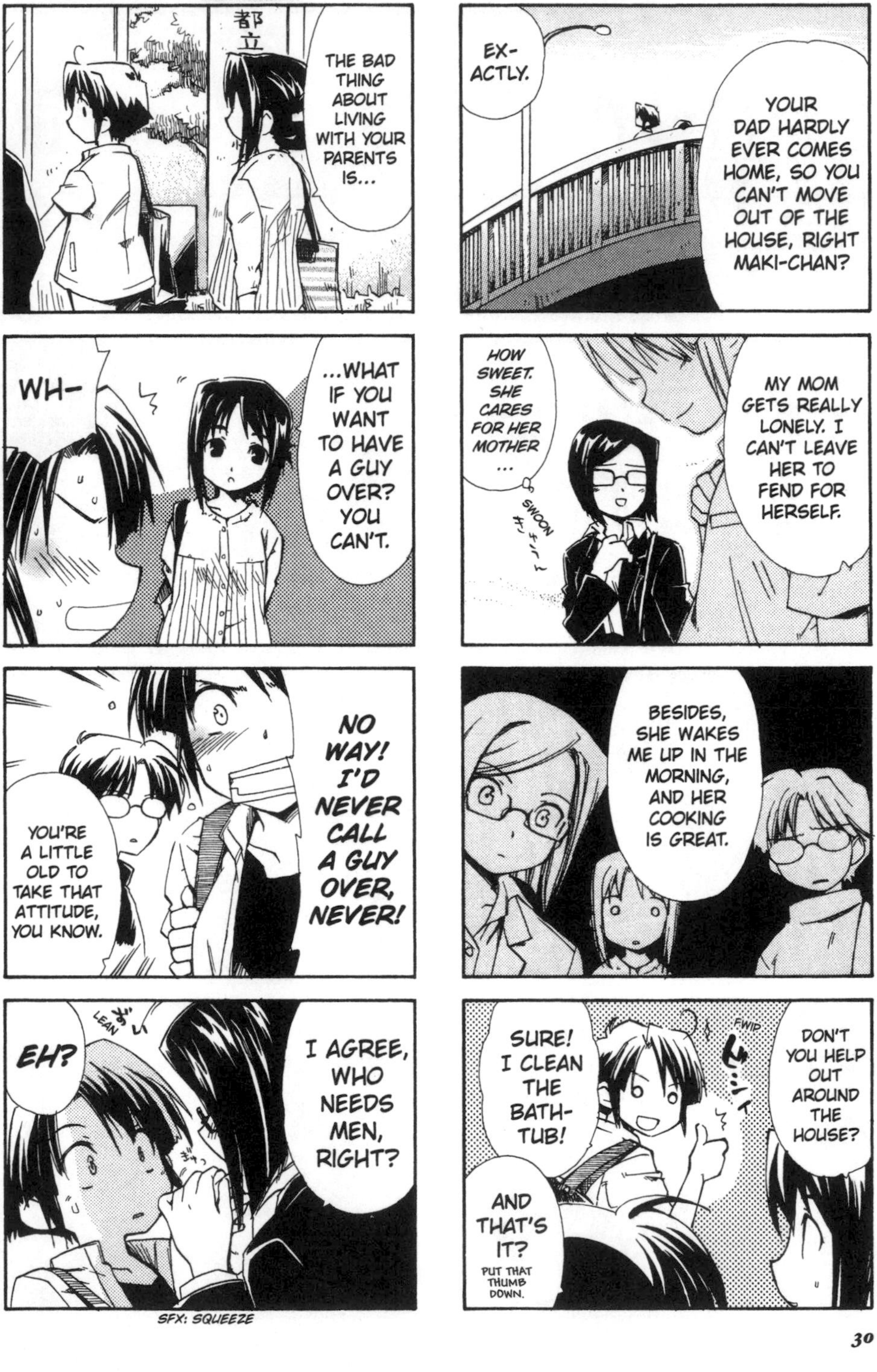
YOUR DAD HARDLY EVER COMES HOME, SO YOU CAN'T MOVE OUT OF THE HOUSE, RIGHT MAKI-CHAN?
EX-ACTLY.
MY MOM GETS REALLY LONELY. I CAN'T LEAVE HER TO FEND FOR HERSELF.
HOW SWEET. SHE CARES FOR HER MOTHER …
SWOON
BESIDES, SHE WAKES ME UP IN THE MORNING, AND HER COOKING IS GREAT.
DON'T YOU HELP OUT AROUND THE HOUSE?
FWIP
SURE! I CLEAN THE BATH-TUB!
AND THAT'S IT?
PUT THAT THUMB DOWN.
都立
THE BAD THING ABOUT LIVING WITH YOUR PARENTS IS…
…WHAT IF YOU WANT TO HAVE A GUY OVER? YOU CAN'T.
WH-
NO WAY! I'D NEVER CALL A GUY OVER, NEVER!
YOU'RE A LITTLE OLD TO TAKE THAT ATTITUDE, YOU KNOW.
I AGREE, WHO NEEDS MEN, RIGHT?
LEAN
EH?

SFX: SQUEEZE

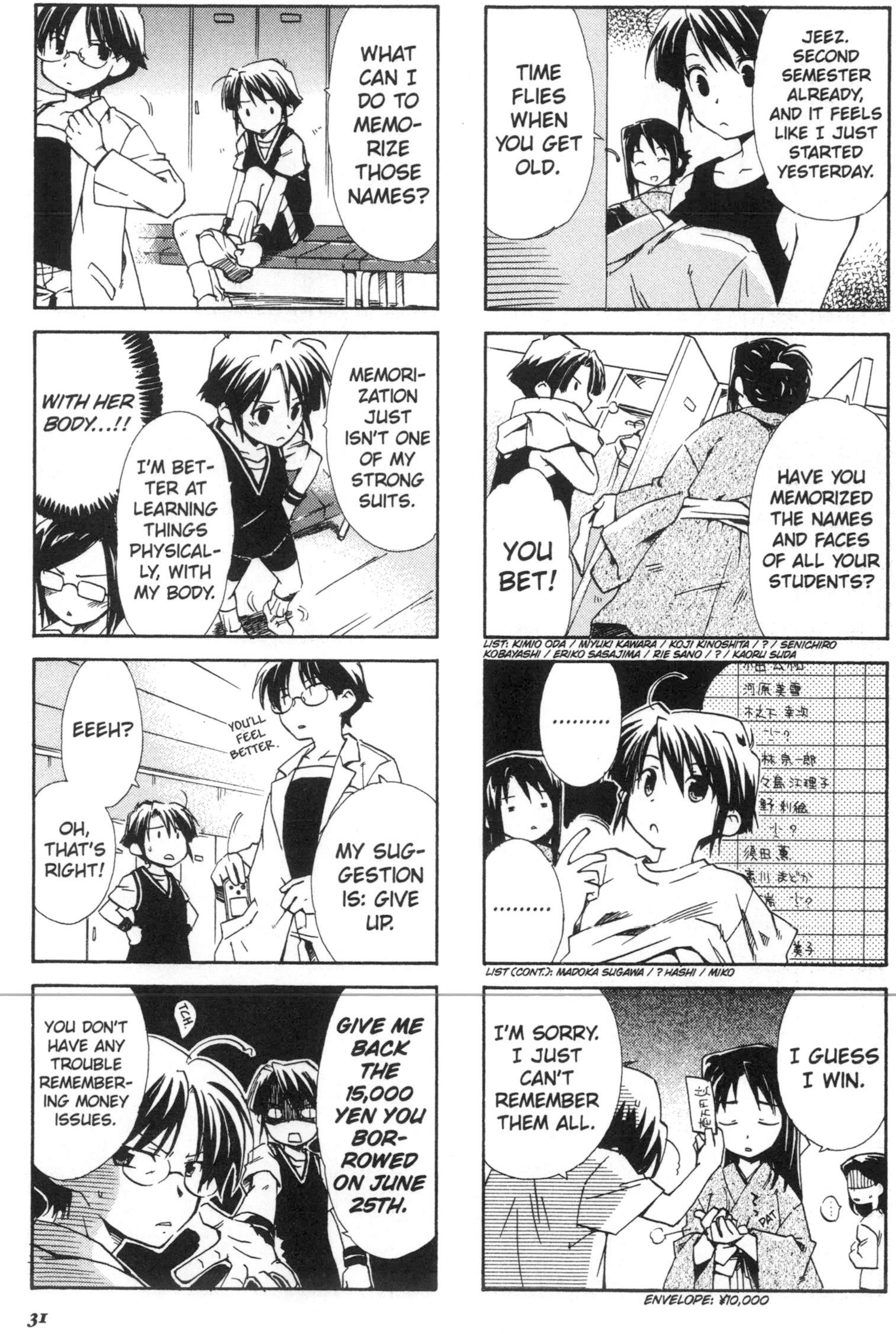
JEEZ. SECOND SEMESTER ALREADY, AND IT FEELS LIKE I JUST STARTED YESTERDAY.
TIME FLIES WHEN YOU GET OLD.
HAVE YOU MEMORIZED THE NAMES AND FACES OF ALL YOUR STUDENTS?
YOU BET!
LIST: KIMIO ODA / MIYUKI KAWARA / KOJI KINOSHITA / ? / SENICHIRO KOBAYASHI / ERIKO SASAJIMA / RIE SANO / ? / KAORU SUDA
....
....
LIST (CONT.): MADOKA SUGAWA / ? HASHI / MIKO
I GUESS I WIN.
I'M SORRY. I JUST CAN'T REMEMBER THEM ALL.
...
PAT
ENVELOPE: ¥10,000
WHAT CAN I DO TO MEMO-RIZE THOSE NAMES?
MEMORI-ZATION JUST ISN'T ONE OF MY STRONG SUITS.
I'M BET-TER AT LEARNING THINGS PHYSICAL-LY, WITH MY BODY.
WITH HER BODY...!!
MY SUG-GESTION IS: GIVE UP.
YOU'LL FEEL BETTER.
EEEH?
OH, THAT'S RIGHT!
GIVE ME BACK THE 15,000 YEN YOU BOR-ROWED ON JUNE 25TH.
TCH.
YOU DON'T HAVE ANY TROUBLE REMEMBER-ING MONEY ISSUES.

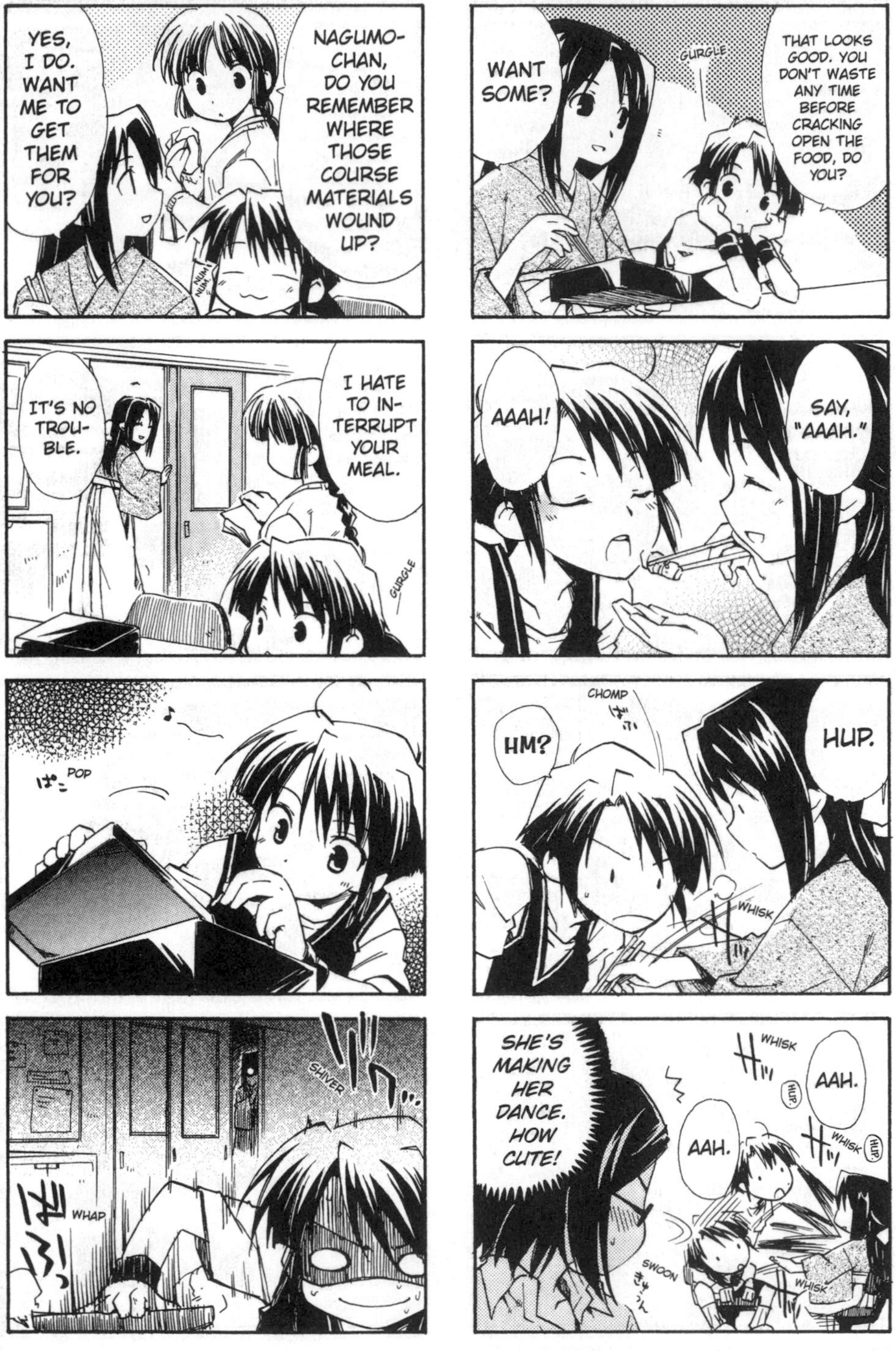
THAT LOOKS GOOD. YOU DON'T WASTE ANY TIME BEFORE CRACKING OPEN THE FOOD, DO YOU?
GURGLE
WANT SOME?
SAY, "AAAH."
AAAH!
HUP.
CHOMP
HM?
WHISK
WHISK
AAH.
HUP.
WHISK
HUP.
AAH.
SHE'S MAKING HER DANCE. HOW CUTE!
WHISK
SWOON
NAGUMO-CHAN, DO YOU REMEMBER WHERE THOSE COURSE MATERIALS WOUND UP?
YES, I DO. WANT ME TO GET THEM FOR YOU?
NUM NUM.
I HATE TO INTERRUPT YOUR MEAL.
IT'S NO TROUBLE.
GURGLE
POP
SHIVER
WHAP

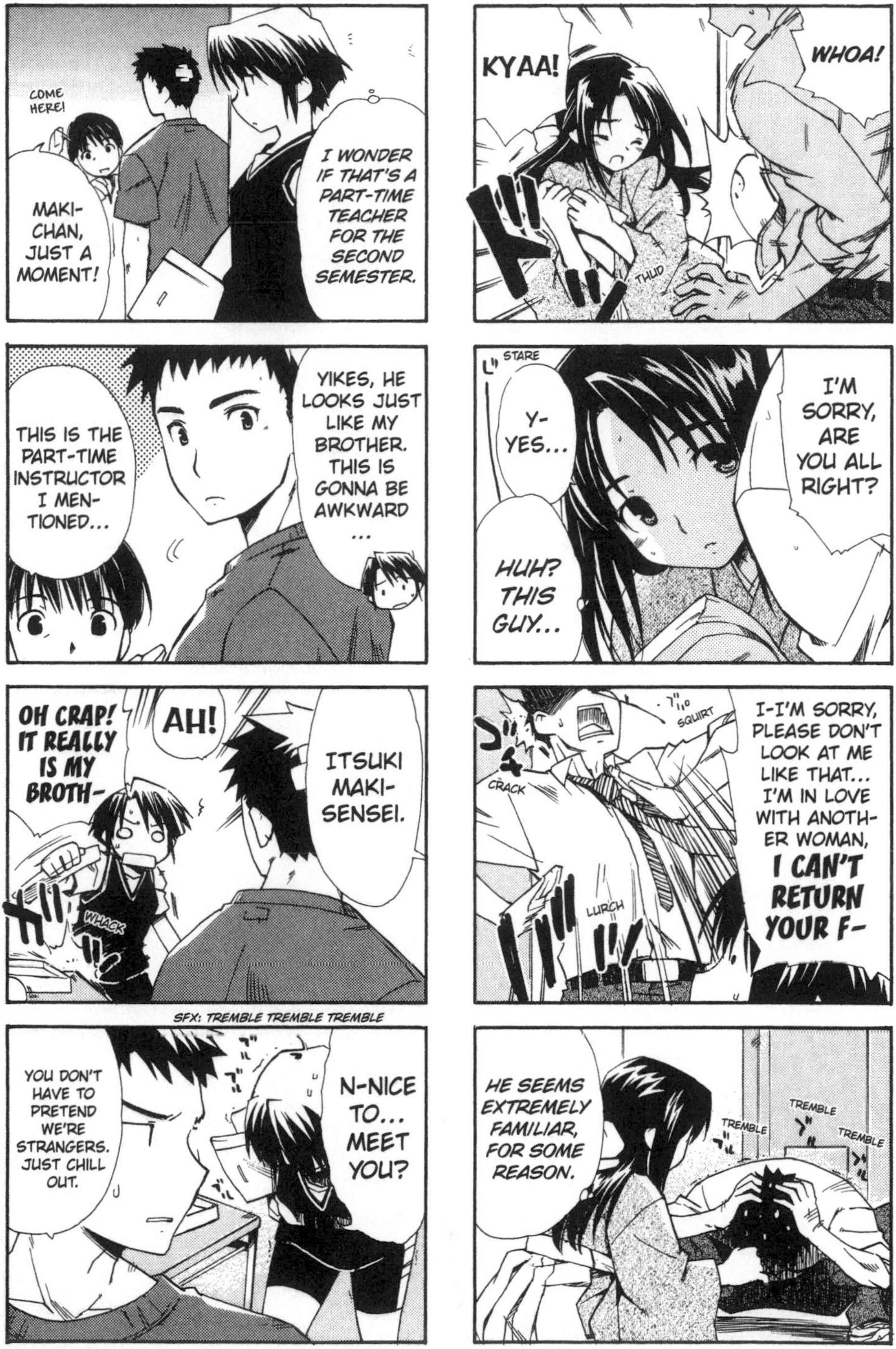
WHOA!
KYAA!
THUD
I'M SORRY, ARE YOU ALL RIGHT?
STARE
Y-YES...
HUH? THIS GUY...
SQUIRT
I-I'M SORRY, PLEASE DON'T LOOK AT ME LIKE THAT... I'M IN LOVE WITH ANOTHER WOMAN, I CAN'T RETURN YOUR F-
CRACK
LURCH
TREMBLE
TREMBLE
TREMBLE
HE SEEMS EXTREMELY FAMILIAR, FOR SOME REASON.
I WONDER IF THAT'S A PART-TIME TEACHER FOR THE SECOND SEMESTER.
COME HERE!
MAKI-CHAN, JUST A MOMENT!
YIKES, HE LOOKS JUST LIKE MY BROTHER. THIS IS GONNA BE AWKWARD...
THIS IS THE PART-TIME INSTRUCTOR I MENTIONED...
ITSUKI MAKI-SENSEI.
AH!
OH CRAP! IT REALLY IS MY BROTH-
WHACK
SFX: TREMBLE TREMBLE TREMBLE
N-NICE TO... MEET YOU?
YOU DON'T HAVE TO PRETEND WE'RE STRANGERS. JUST CHILL OUT.

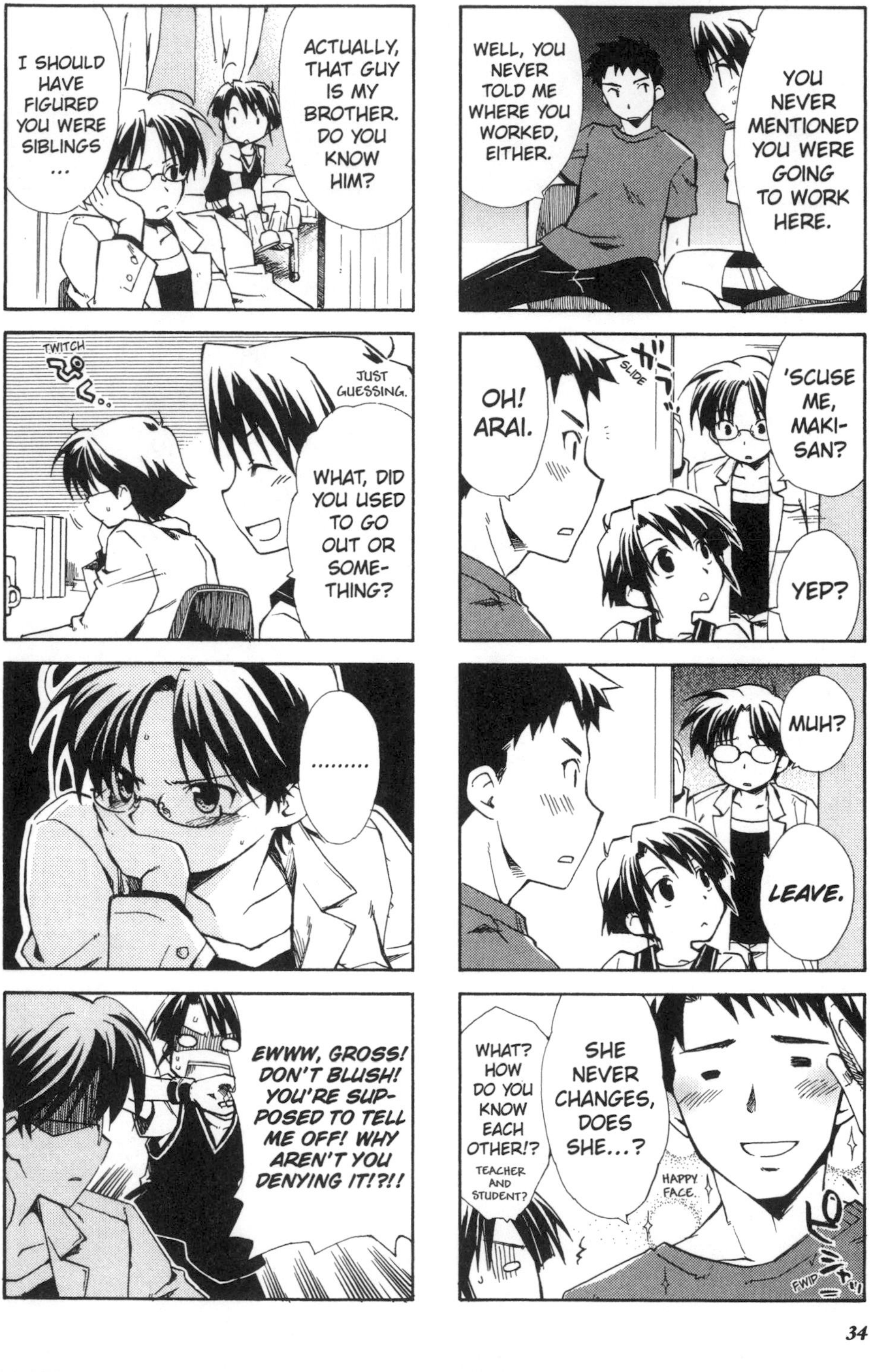
YOU NEVER MENTIONED YOU WERE GOING TO WORK HERE.
WELL, YOU NEVER TOLD ME WHERE YOU WORKED, EITHER.
'SCUSE ME, MAKI-SAN?
SLIDE
OH! ARAI.
YEP?
MUH?
LEAVE.
SHE NEVER CHANGES, DOES SHE...?
WHAT? HOW DO YOU KNOW EACH OTHER!?
TEACHER AND STUDENT?
HAPPY FACE.
FWIP
ACTUALLY, THAT GUY IS MY BROTHER. DO YOU KNOW HIM?
I SHOULD HAVE FIGURED YOU WERE SIBLINGS ...
JUST GUESSING.
WHAT, DID YOU USED TO GO OUT OR SOME-THING?
TWITCH
....
EWWW, GROSS! DON'T BLUSH! YOU'RE SUP-POSED TO TELL ME OFF! WHY AREN'T YOU DENYING IT!?!!

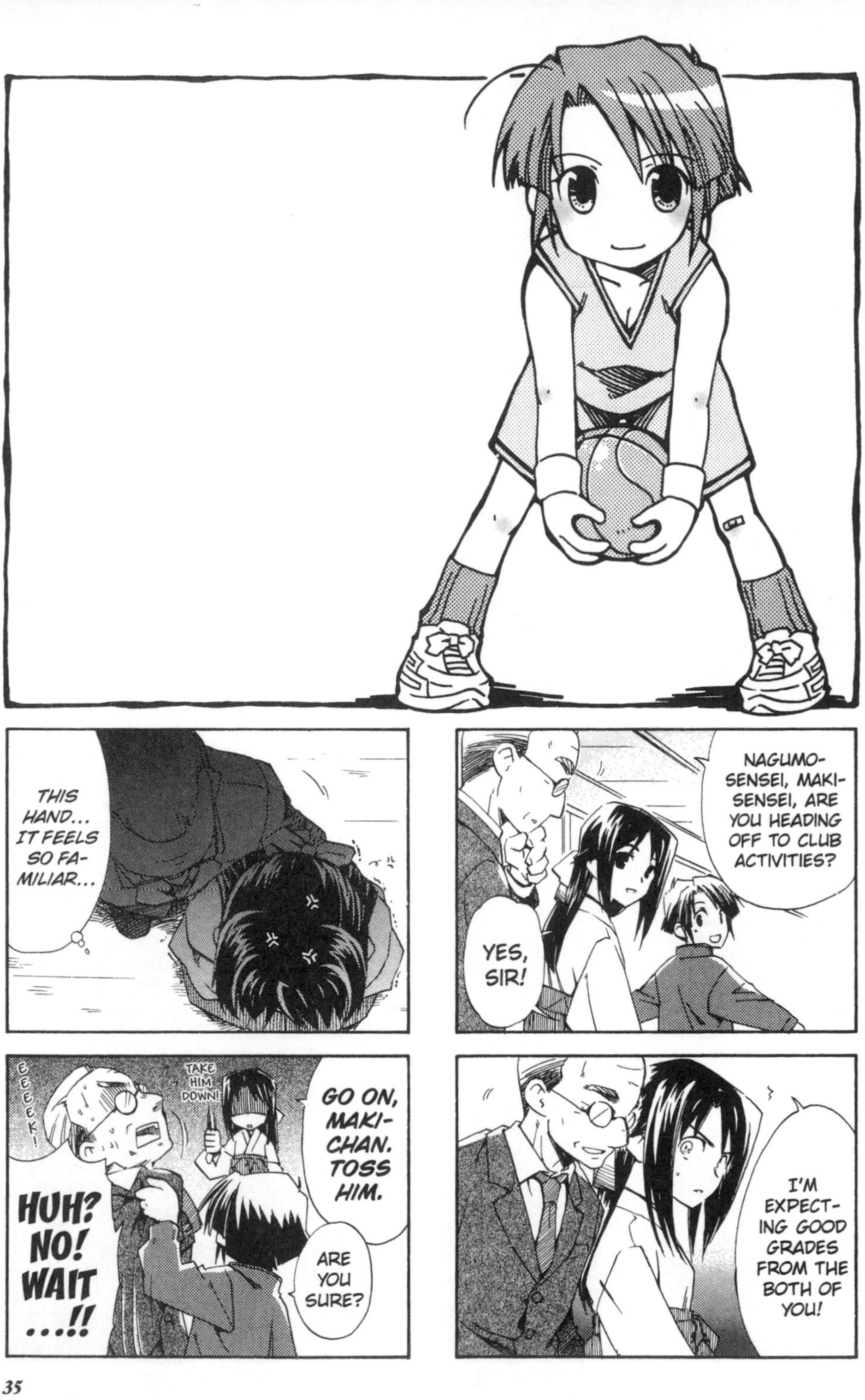
NAGUMO-SENSEI, MAKI-SENSEI, ARE YOU HEADING OFF TO CLUB ACTIVITIES?
YES, SIR!
THIS HAND... IT FEELS SO FAMILIAR...
I'M EXPECTING GOOD GRADES FROM THE BOTH OF YOU!
GO ON, MAKI-CHAN. TOSS HIM.
TAKE HIM DOWN!
EEEEK!
ARE YOU SURE?
HUH? NO! WAIT ...!!

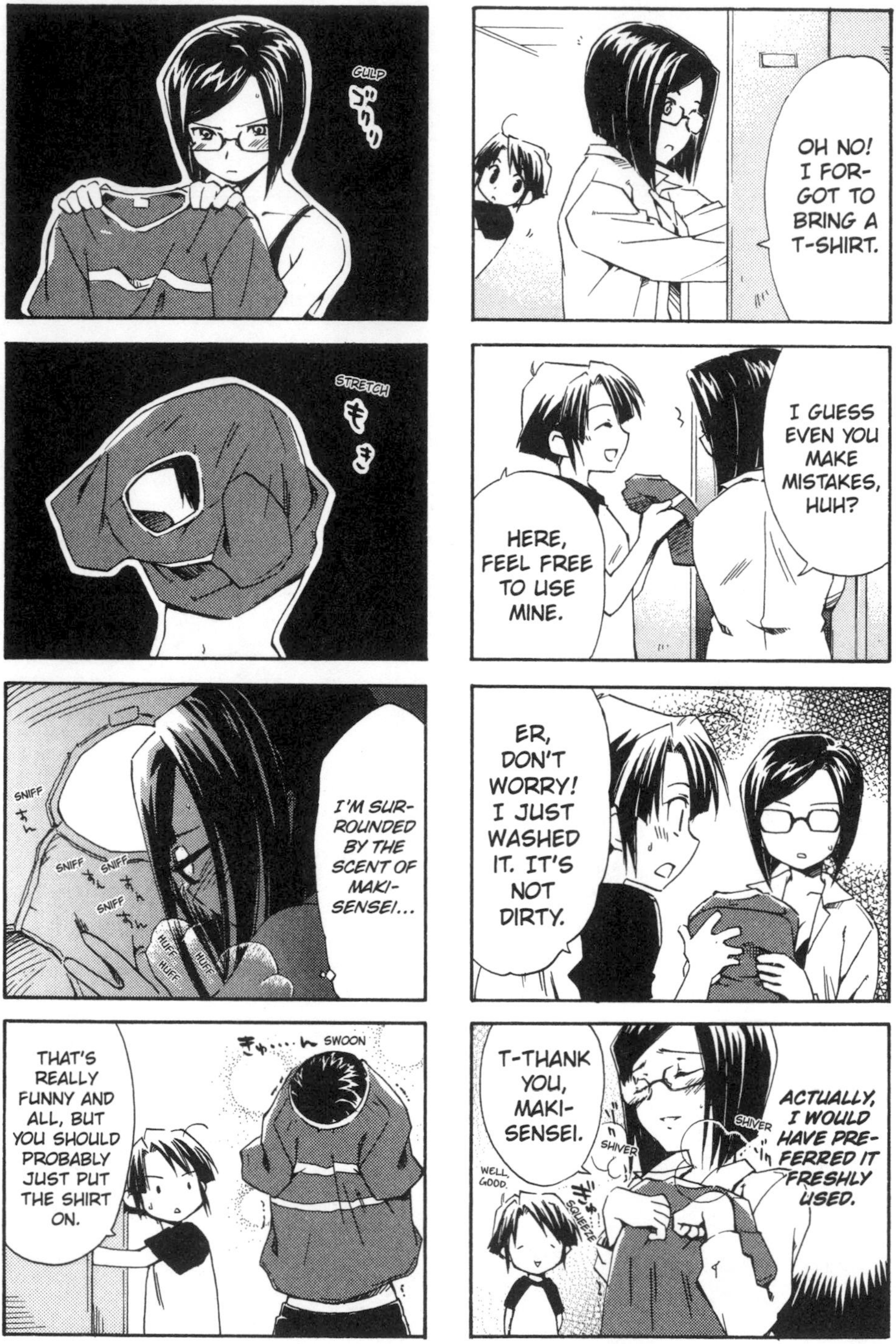
OH NO! I FORGOT TO BRING A T-SHIRT.
I GUESS EVEN YOU MAKE MISTAKES, HUH?
HERE, FEEL FREE TO USE MINE.
ER, DON'T WORRY! I JUST WASHED IT. IT'S NOT DIRTY.
T-THANK YOU, MAKI-SENSEI.
SHIVER
SHIVER
ACTUALLY, I WOULD HAVE PREFERRED IT FRESHLY USED.
WELL, GOOD.
SQUEEZE
GULP
STRETCH
SNIFF
SNIFF
SNIFF
SNIFF
HUFF
HUFF
HUFF
I'M SURROUNDED BY THE SCENT OF MAKI-SENSEI...
きゅ・・・・ん SWOON
THAT'S REALLY FUNNY AND ALL, BUT YOU SHOULD PROBABLY JUST PUT THE SHIRT ON.

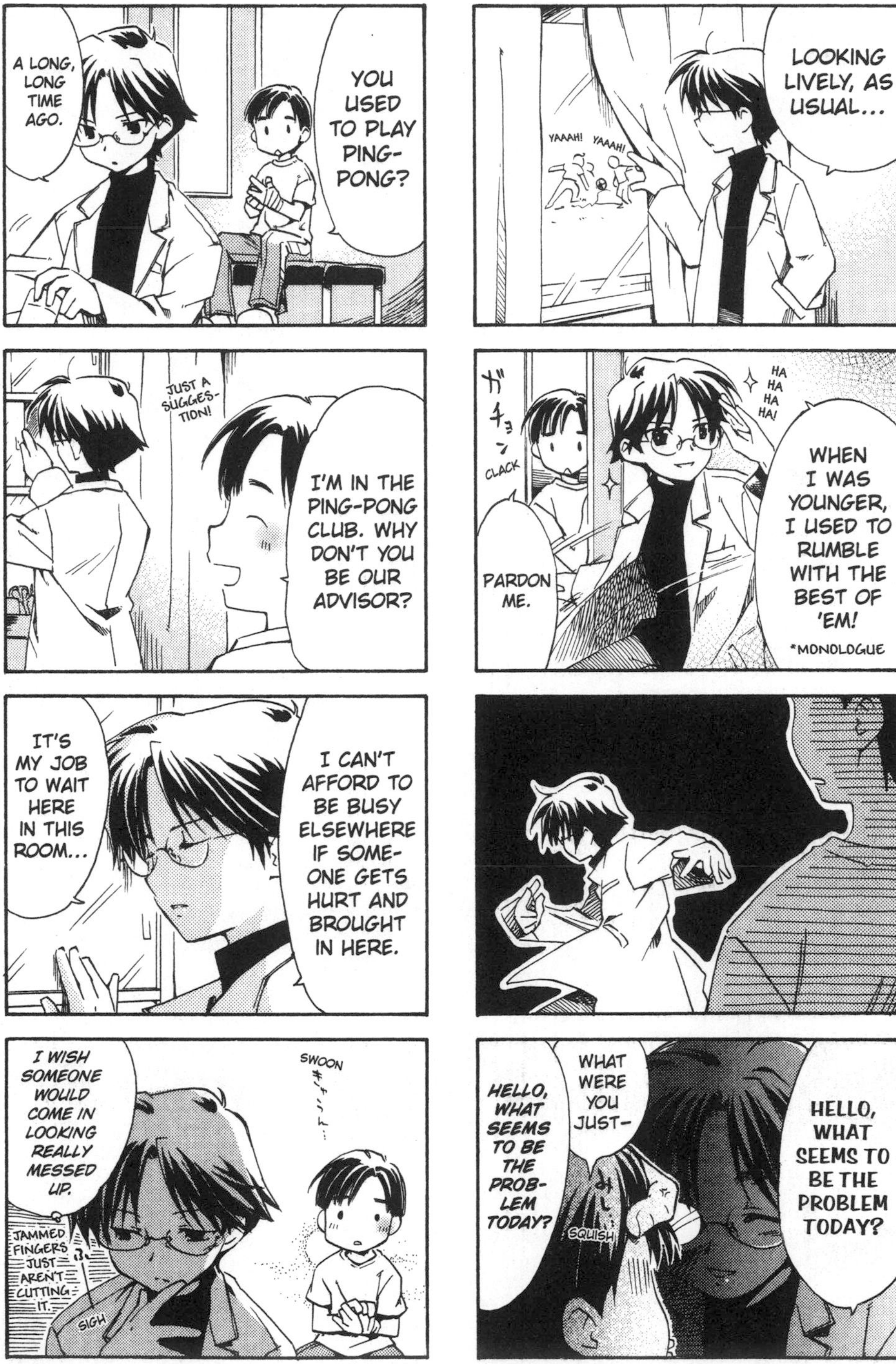
LOOKING LIVELY, AS USUAL...
YAAAH! YAAAH!
YOU USED TO PLAY PING-PONG?
A LONG, LONG TIME AGO.
WHEN I WAS YOUNGER, I USED TO RUMBLE WITH THE BEST OF 'EM!
HA HA HA HA!
*MONOLOGUE
ガチョン
CLACK
PARDON ME.
I'M IN THE PING-PONG CLUB. WHY DON'T YOU BE OUR ADVISOR?
JUST A SUGGESTION!
I CAN'T AFFORD TO BE BUSY ELSEWHERE IF SOMEONE GETS HURT AND BROUGHT IN HERE.
IT'S MY JOB TO WAIT HERE IN THIS ROOM...
HELLO, WHAT SEEMS TO BE THE PROBLEM TODAY?
WHAT WERE YOU JUST-
HELLO, WHAT SEEMS TO BE THE PROBLEM TODAY?
SQUISH
SWOON
I WISH SOMEONE WOULD COME IN LOOKING REALLY MESSED UP.
JAMMED FINGERS JUST AREN'T CUTTING IT.
SIGH

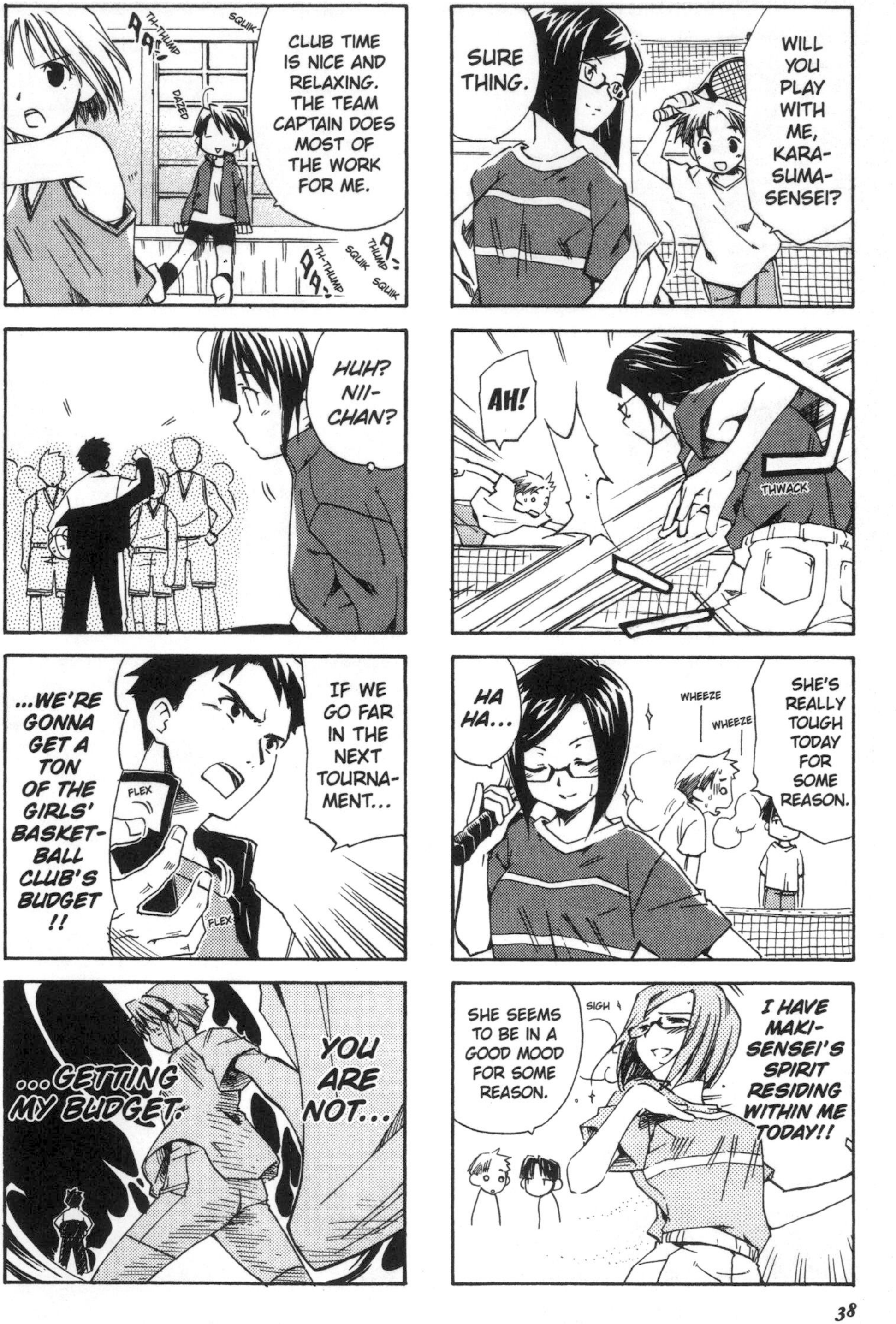
WILL YOU PLAY WITH ME, KARA-SUMA-SENSEI?
SURE THING.
AH!
THWACK
SHE'S REALLY TOUGH TODAY FOR SOME REASON.
WHEEZE
WHEEZE
HA HA...
I HAVE MAKI-SENSEI'S SPIRIT RESIDING WITHIN ME TODAY!!
SIGH
SHE SEEMS TO BE IN A GOOD MOOD FOR SOME REASON.
SQUIK
TH-THUMP
CLUB TIME IS NICE AND RELAXING. THE TEAM CAPTAIN DOES MOST OF THE WORK FOR ME.
DAZED
THUMP
SQUIK
TH-THUMP
SQUIK
HUH? NII-CHAN?
IF WE GO FAR IN THE NEXT TOURNA-MENT...
...WE'RE GONNA GET A TON OF THE GIRLS' BASKET-BALL CLUB'S BUDGET!!
FLEX
FLEX
YOU ARE NOT...
...GETTING MY BUDGET.

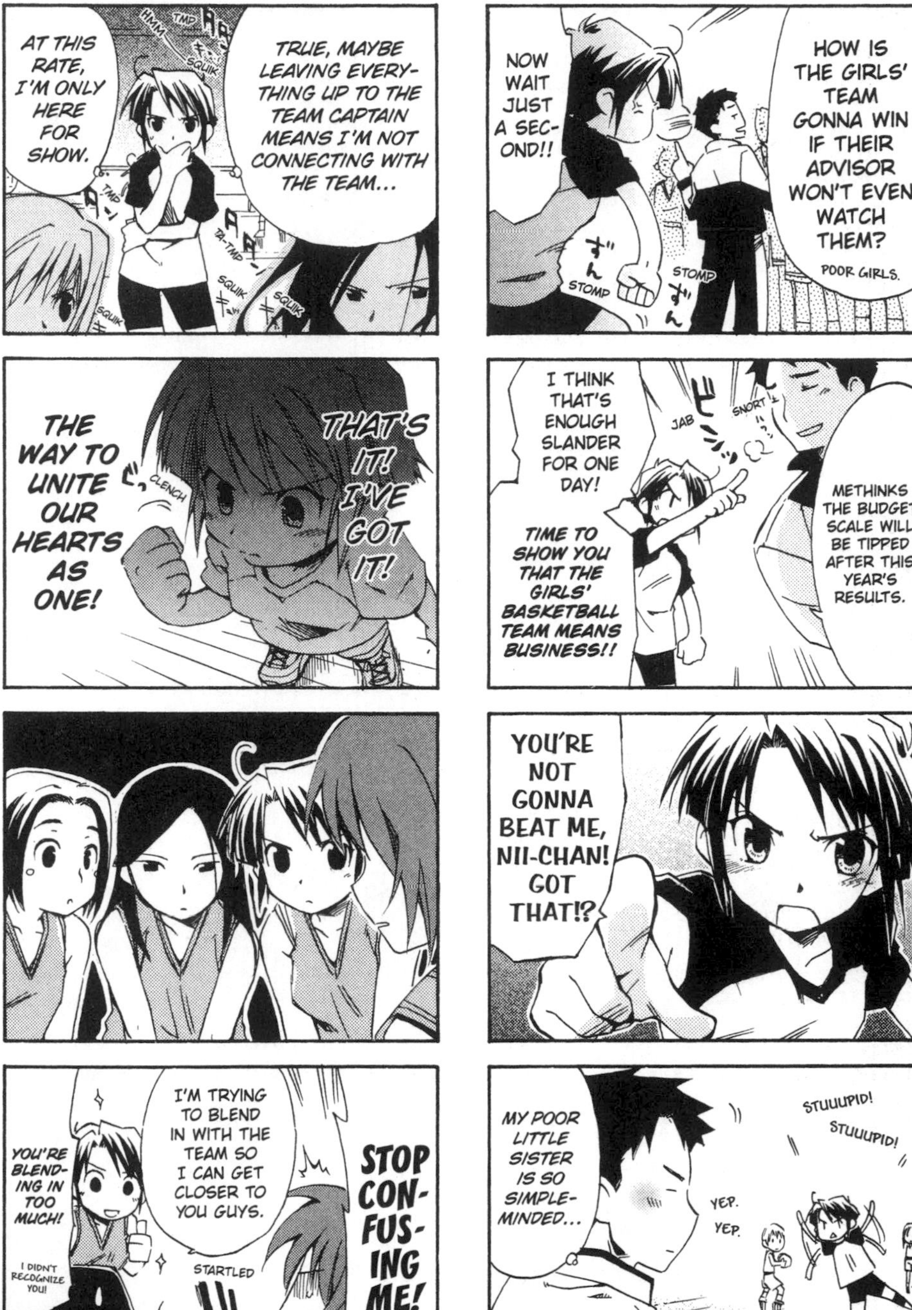
HOW IS THE GIRLS' TEAM GONNA WIN IF THEIR ADVISOR WON'T EVEN WATCH THEM?
POOR GIRLS.
NOW WAIT JUST A SEC-OND!!
STOMP
ずん
STOMP
ずん
I THINK THAT'S ENOUGH SLANDER FOR ONE DAY!
JAB
SNORT
TIME TO SHOW YOU THAT THE GIRLS' BASKETBALL TEAM MEANS BUSINESS!!
METHINKS THE BUDGET SCALE WILL BE TIPPED AFTER THIS YEAR'S RESULTS.
YOU'RE NOT GONNA BEAT ME, NII-CHAN! GOT THAT!?
MY POOR LITTLE SISTER IS SO SIMPLE-MINDED...
STUUUPID!
STUUUPID!
YEP.
YEP.
TRUE, MAYBE LEAVING EVERY-THING UP TO THE TEAM CAPTAIN MEANS I'M NOT CONNECTING WITH THE TEAM...
AT THIS RATE, I'M ONLY HERE FOR SHOW.
HMM
TMP
SQUIK
TMP
TA-TMP
SQUIK
SQUIK
SQUIK
THAT'S IT! I'VE GOT IT!
CLENCH
THE WAY TO UNITE OUR HEARTS AS ONE!
STOP CON-FUS-ING ME!
I'M TRYING TO BLEND IN WITH THE TEAM SO I CAN GET CLOSER TO YOU GUYS.
STARTLED
YOU'RE BLEND-ING IN TOO MUCH!
I DIDN'T RECOGNIZE YOU!

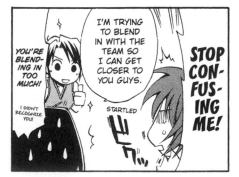

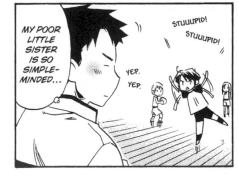

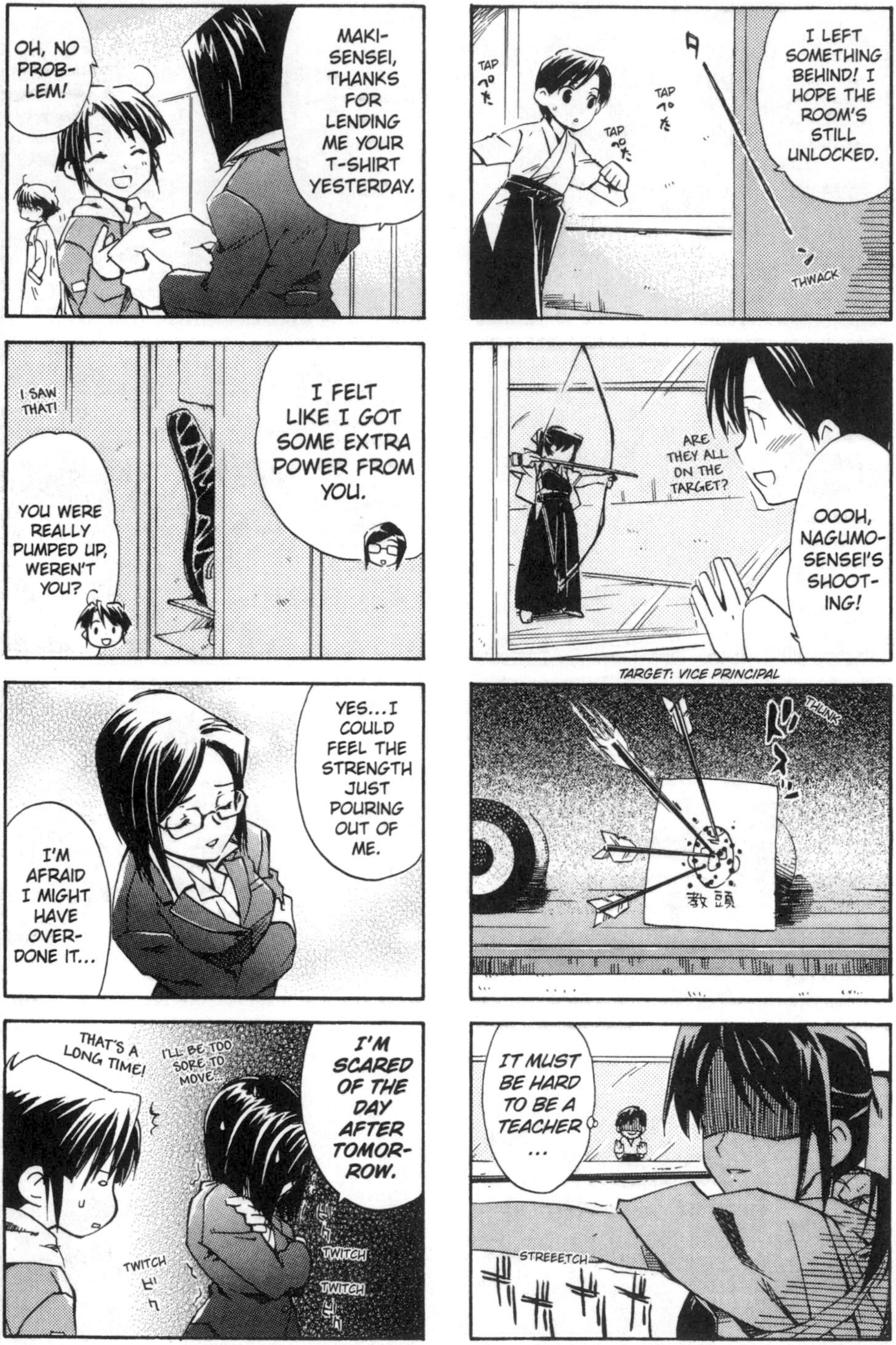
I LEFT SOMETHING BEHIND! I HOPE THE ROOM'S STILL UNLOCKED.
TAP
TAP
TAP
THWACK
OOOH, NAGUMO-SENSEI'S SHOOTING!
ARE THEY ALL ON THE TARGET?
TARGET: VICE PRINCIPAL
THUNK
教頭
IT MUST BE HARD TO BE A TEACHER...
STREEETCH
MAKI-SENSEI, THANKS FOR LENDING ME YOUR T-SHIRT YESTERDAY.
OH, NO PROBLEM!
I FELT LIKE I GOT SOME EXTRA POWER FROM YOU.
I SAW THAT!
YOU WERE REALLY PUMPED UP, WEREN'T YOU?
YES...I COULD FEEL THE STRENGTH JUST POURING OUT OF ME.
I'M AFRAID I MIGHT HAVE OVER-DONE IT...
I'M SCARED OF THE DAY AFTER TOMORROW.
I'LL BE TOO SORE TO MOVE...
THAT'S A LONG TIME!
TWITCH
TWITCH
TWITCH

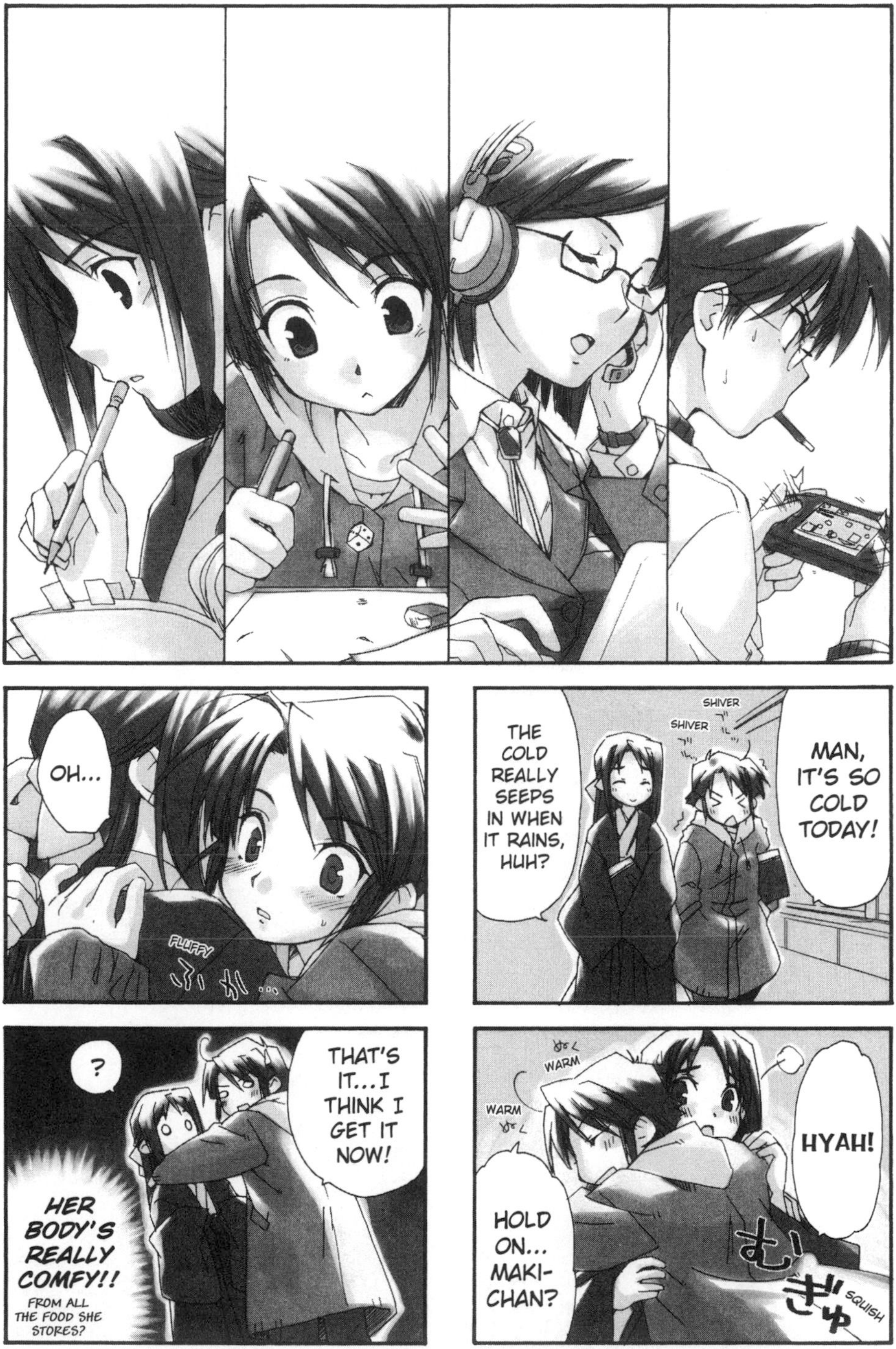
MAN, IT'S SO COLD TODAY!
SHIVER
SHIVER
THE COLD REALLY SEEPS IN WHEN IT RAINS, HUH?
OH...
FLUFFY
HYAH!
WARM
WARM
HOLD ON... MAKI-CHAN?
むぎゅ
SQUISH
THAT'S IT...I THINK I GET IT NOW!
?
HER BODY'S REALLY COMFY!!
FROM ALL THE FOOD SHE STORES?

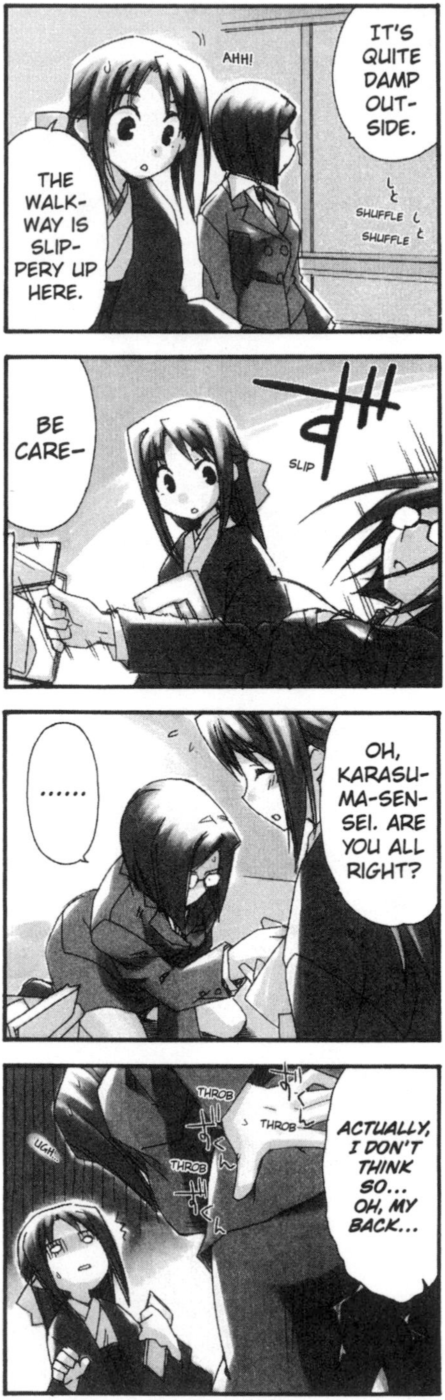
IT'S QUITE DAMP OUTSIDE.
AHH!
SHUFFLE
SHUFFLE
THE WALKWAY IS SLIPPERY UP HERE.
BE CARE-
SLIP
OH, KARASUMA-SENSEI. ARE YOU ALL RIGHT?
......
ACTUALLY, I DON'T THINK SO... OH, MY BACK...
THROB
THROB
UGH...
THROB

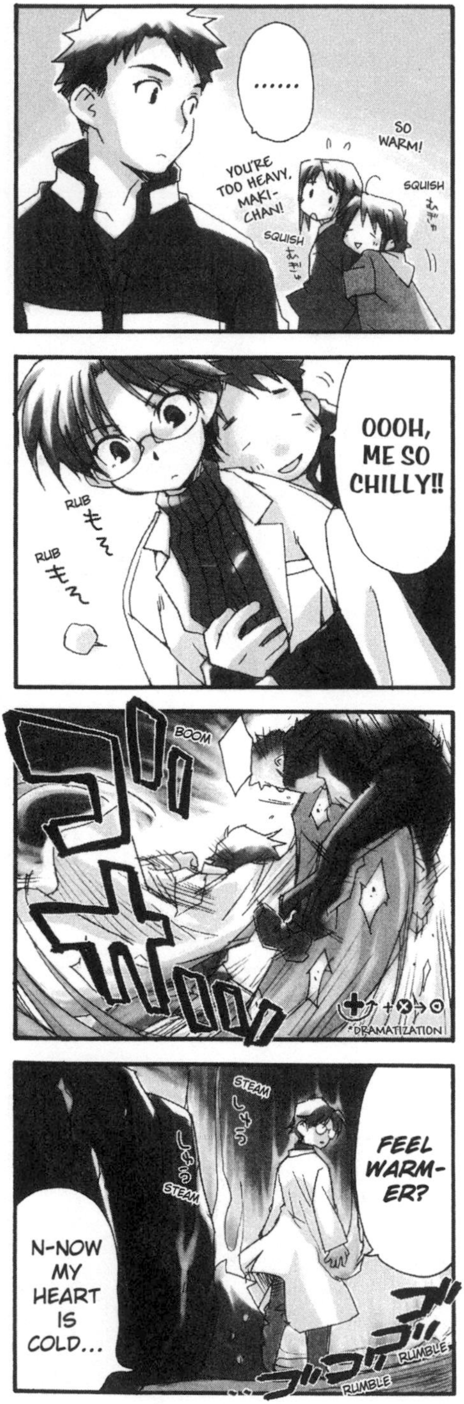
......
SO WARM!
SQUISH
YOU'RE TOO HEAVY, MAKI-CHAN!
SQUISH
OOOH, ME SO CHILLY!!
RUB
RUB
BOOM
*DRAMATIZATION
FEEL WARMER?
STEAM
STEAM
N-NOW MY HEART IS COLD...
RUMBLE
RUMBLE

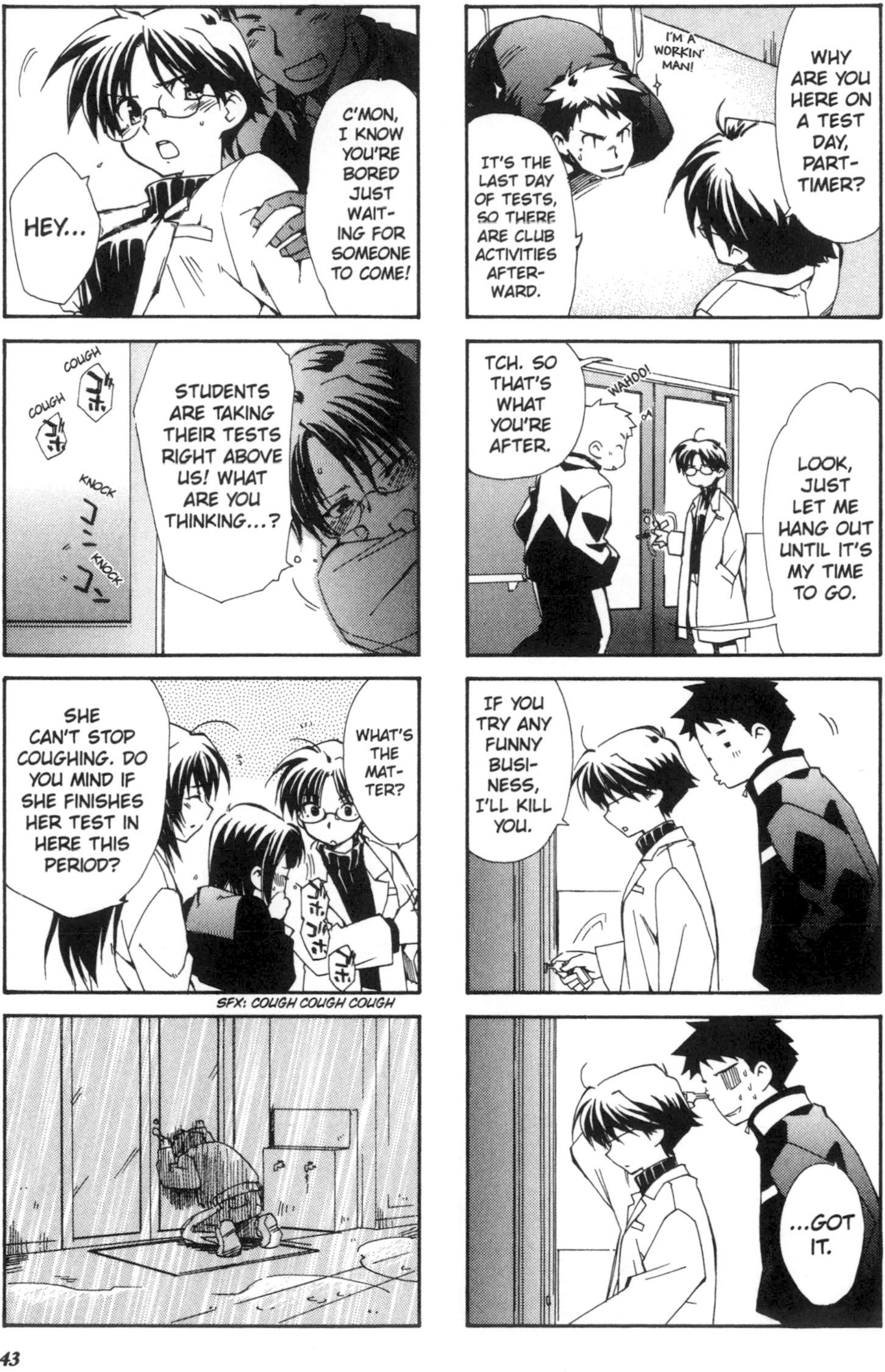

WHY ARE YOU HERE ON A TEST DAY, PART-TIMER?
I'M A WORKIN' MAN!
IT'S THE LAST DAY OF TESTS, SO THERE ARE CLUB ACTIVITIES AFTERWARD.
LOOK, JUST LET ME HANG OUT UNTIL IT'S MY TIME TO GO.
WAHOO!
TCH. SO THAT'S WHAT YOU'RE AFTER.
IF YOU TRY ANY FUNNY BUSINESS, I'LL KILL YOU.
...GOT IT.
C'MON, I KNOW YOU'RE BORED JUST WAITING FOR SOMEONE TO COME!
HEY...
STUDENTS ARE TAKING THEIR TESTS RIGHT ABOVE US! WHAT ARE YOU THINKING...?
COUGH
COUGH
KNOCK
KNOCK
WHAT'S THE MATTER?
SHE CAN'T STOP COUGHING. DO YOU MIND IF SHE FINISHES HER TEST IN HERE THIS PERIOD?

SFX: COUGH COUGH COUGH

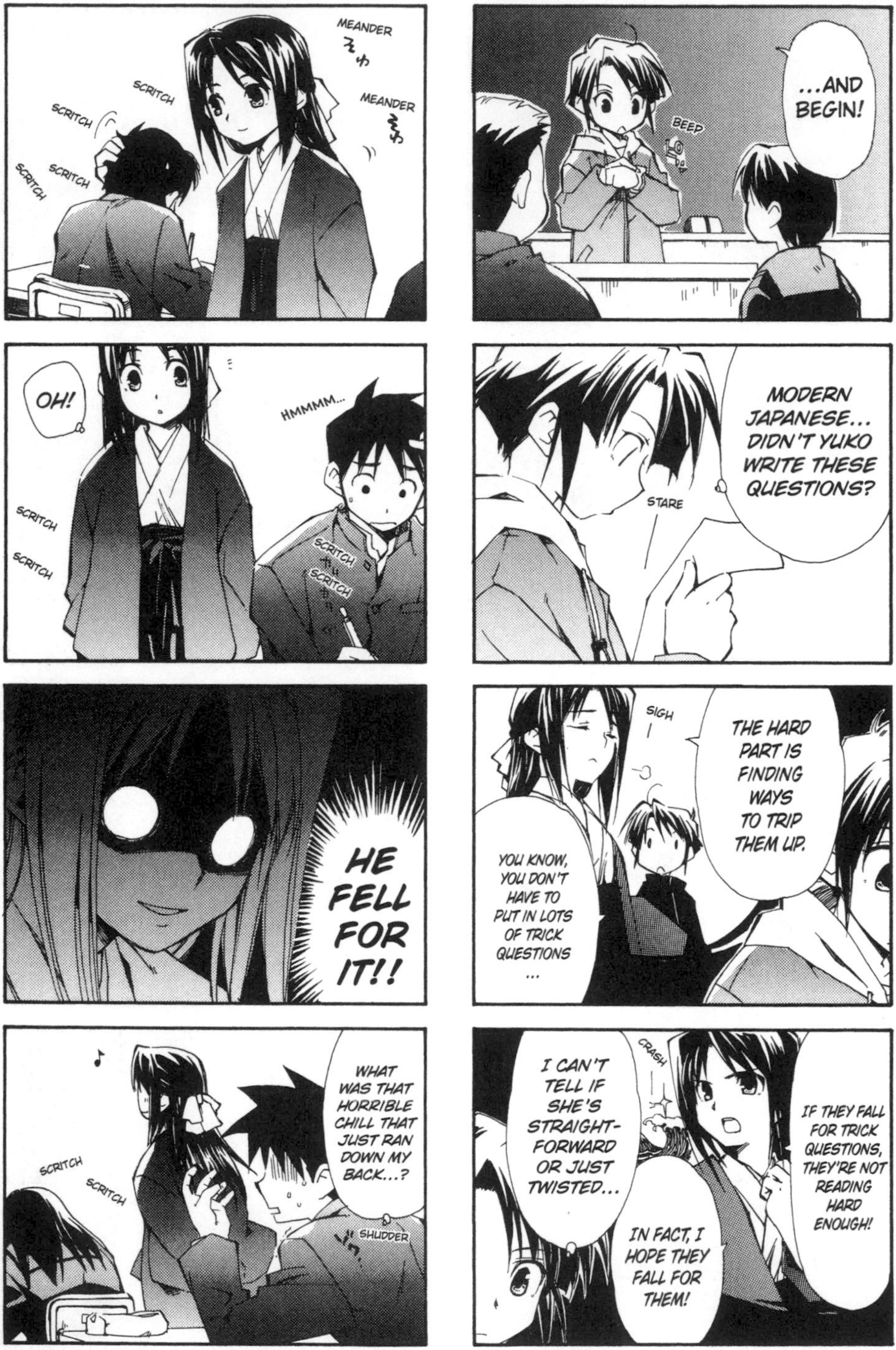
...AND BEGIN!
BEEP
MEANDER
MEANDER
SCRITCH
SCRITCH
SCRITCH
SCRITCH
MODERN JAPANESE... DIDN'T YUKO WRITE THESE QUESTIONS?
STARE
HMMMM...
OH!
SCRITCH
SCRITCH
SCRITCH
SCRITCH
SIGH
THE HARD PART IS FINDING WAYS TO TRIP THEM UP.
YOU KNOW, YOU DON'T HAVE TO PUT IN LOTS OF TRICK QUESTIONS ...
HE FELL FOR IT!!
CRASH
IF THEY FALL FOR TRICK QUESTIONS, THEY'RE NOT READING HARD ENOUGH!
I CAN'T TELL IF SHE'S STRAIGHT-FORWARD OR JUST TWISTED...
IN FACT, I HOPE THEY FALL FOR THEM!
WHAT WAS THAT HORRIBLE CHILL THAT JUST RAN DOWN MY BACK...?
SCRITCH
SCRITCH
SHUDDER

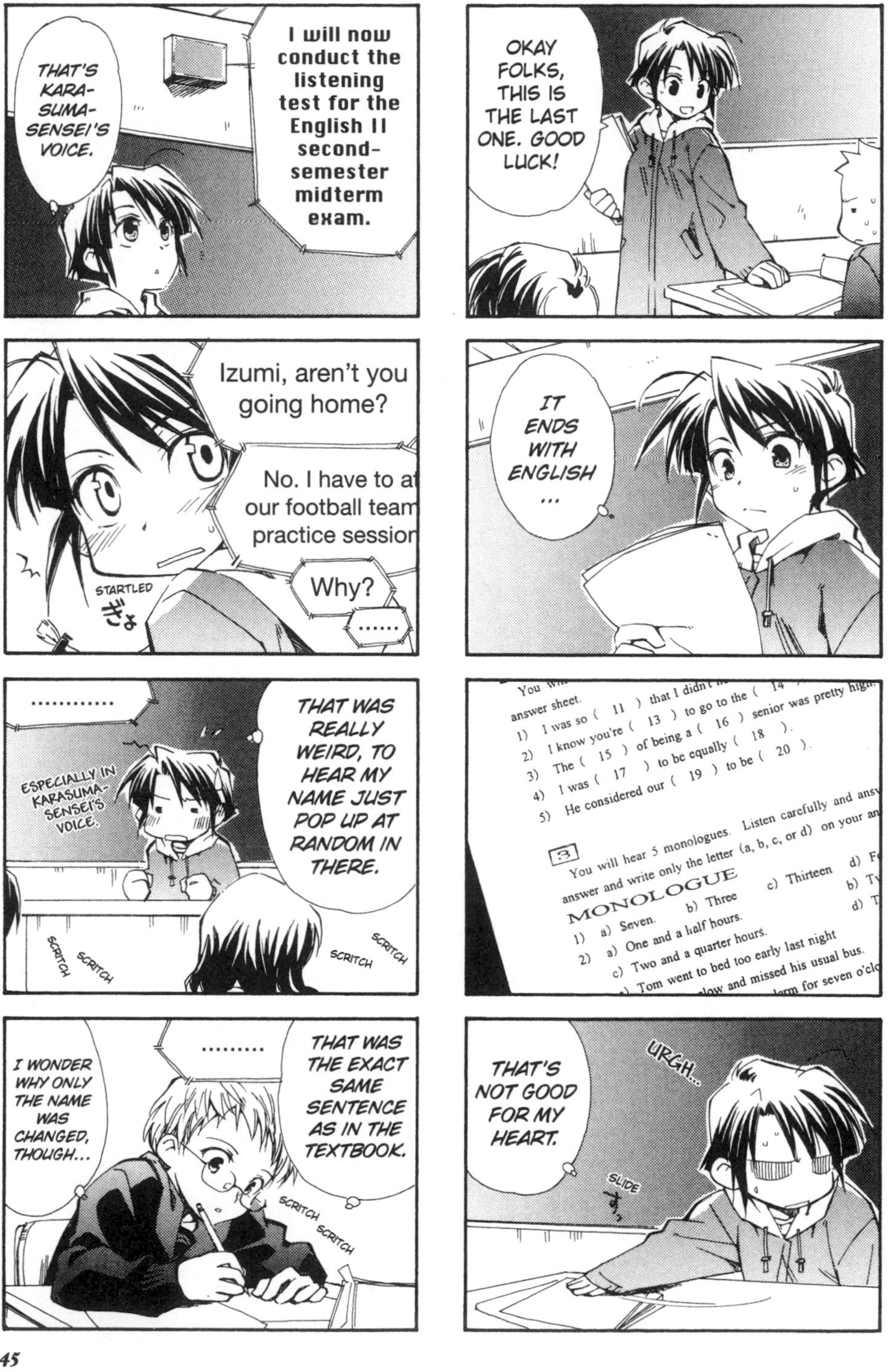
OKAY FOLKS, THIS IS THE LAST ONE. GOOD LUCK!
IT ENDS WITH ENGLISH ...
answer sheet.
1) I was so (11) that I didn't
2) I know you're (13) to go to the (14)
3) The (15) of being a (16) senior was pretty high.
4) I was (17) to be equally (18).
5) He considered our (19) to be (20).
3
You will hear 5 monologues. Listen carefully and
answer and write only the letter (a, b, c, or d) on your
MONOLOGUE
1) a) Seven. b) Three c) Thirteen
2) a) One and a half hours.
c) Two and a quarter hours.
Tom went to bed too early last night
URGH...
THAT'S NOT GOOD FOR MY HEART.
SLIDE
I will now conduct the listening test for the English II second-semester midterm exam.
THAT'S KARASUMA-SENSEI'S VOICE.
Izumi, aren't you going home?
No. I have to at our football team practice session
Why?
......
STARTLED
ぎょ
THAT WAS REALLY WEIRD, TO HEAR MY NAME JUST POP UP AT RANDOM IN THERE.
....
ESPECIALLY IN KARASUMA-SENSEI'S VOICE.
THAT WAS THE EXACT SAME SENTENCE AS IN THE TEXTBOOK.
....
I WONDER WHY ONLY THE NAME WAS CHANGED, THOUGH...

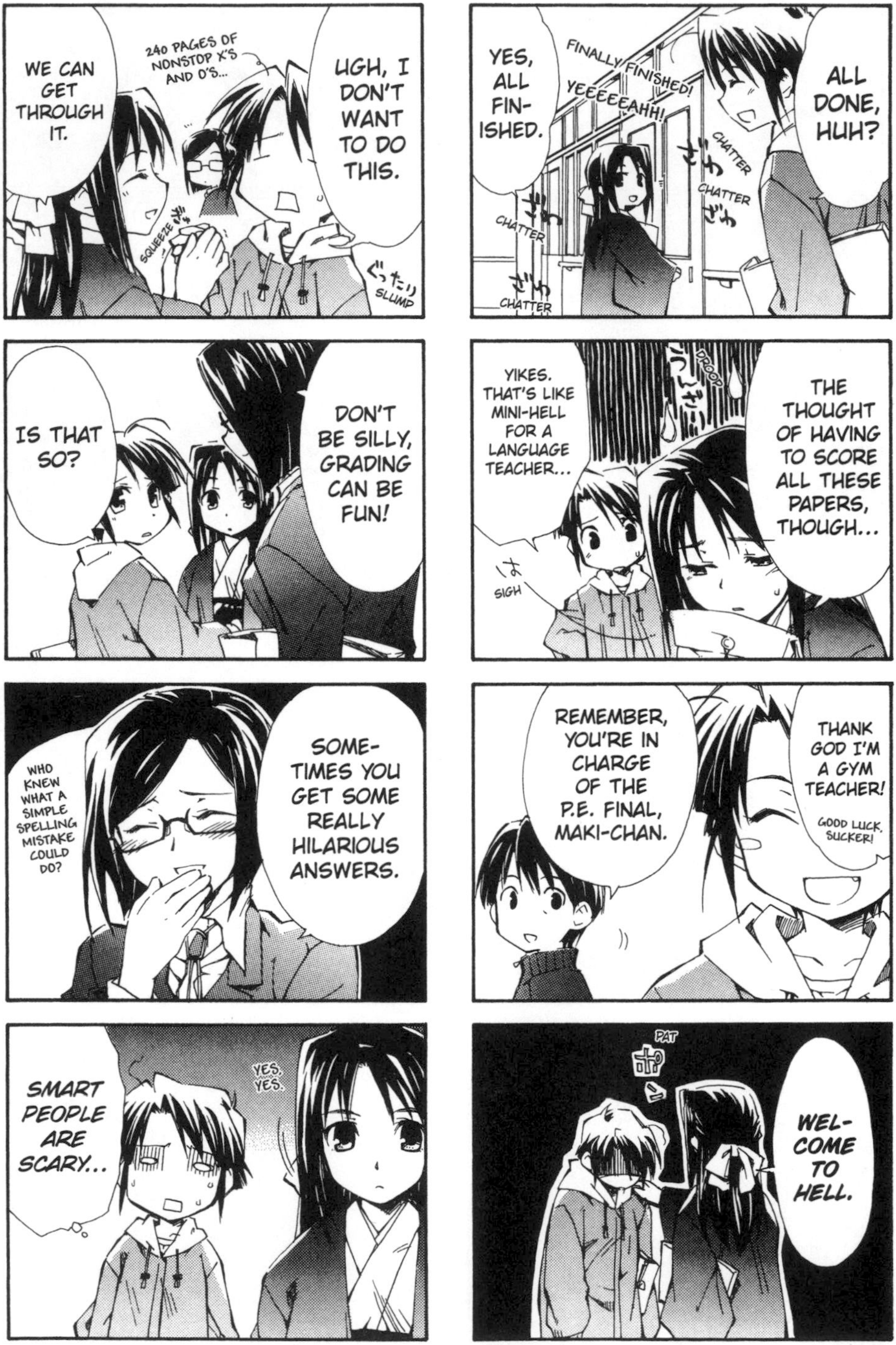
ALL DONE, HUH?
CHATTER
CHATTER
FINALLY FINISHED!
YEEEEEAHH!
YES, ALL FIN-ISHED.
CHATTER
CHATTER
THE THOUGHT OF HAVING TO SCORE ALL THESE PAPERS, THOUGH...
DROOP
YIKES. THAT'S LIKE MINI-HELL FOR A LANGUAGE TEACHER...
SIGH
THANK GOD I'M A GYM TEACHER!
GOOD LUCK, SUCKER!
REMEMBER, YOU'RE IN CHARGE OF THE P.E. FINAL, MAKI-CHAN.
PAT
WEL-COME TO HELL.
UGH, I DON'T WANT TO DO THIS.
SLUMP
240 PAGES OF NONSTOP X'S AND O'S...
WE CAN GET THROUGH IT.
SQUEEZE
DON'T BE SILLY, GRADING CAN BE FUN!
IS THAT SO?
SOME-TIMES YOU GET SOME REALLY HILARIOUS ANSWERS.
WHO KNEW WHAT A SIMPLE SPELLING MISTAKE COULD DO?
YES, YES.
SMART PEOPLE ARE SCARY...

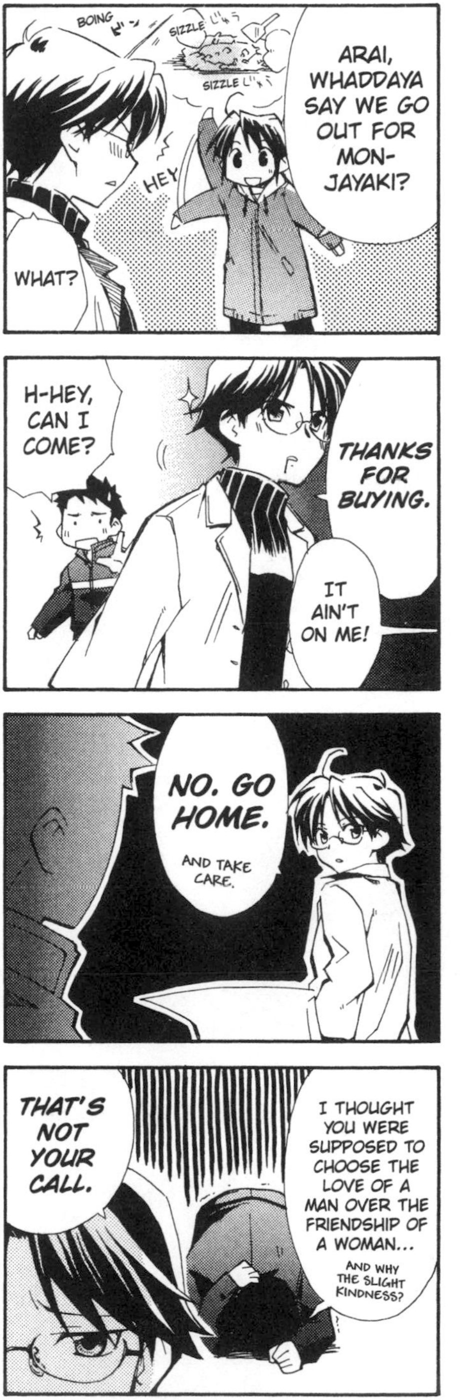
BOING
SIZZLE
SIZZLE
ARAI, WHADDAYA SAY WE GO OUT FOR MON-JAYAKI?
HEY
WHAT?
THANKS FOR BUYING.
IT AIN'T ON ME!
H-HEY, CAN I COME?
NO. GO HOME.
AND TAKE CARE.
I THOUGHT YOU WERE SUPPOSED TO CHOOSE THE LOVE OF A MAN OVER THE FRIENDSHIP OF A WOMAN...
AND WHY THE SLIGHT KINDNESS?
THAT'S NOT YOUR CALL.

ALL SIGNS: MONJAYAKI

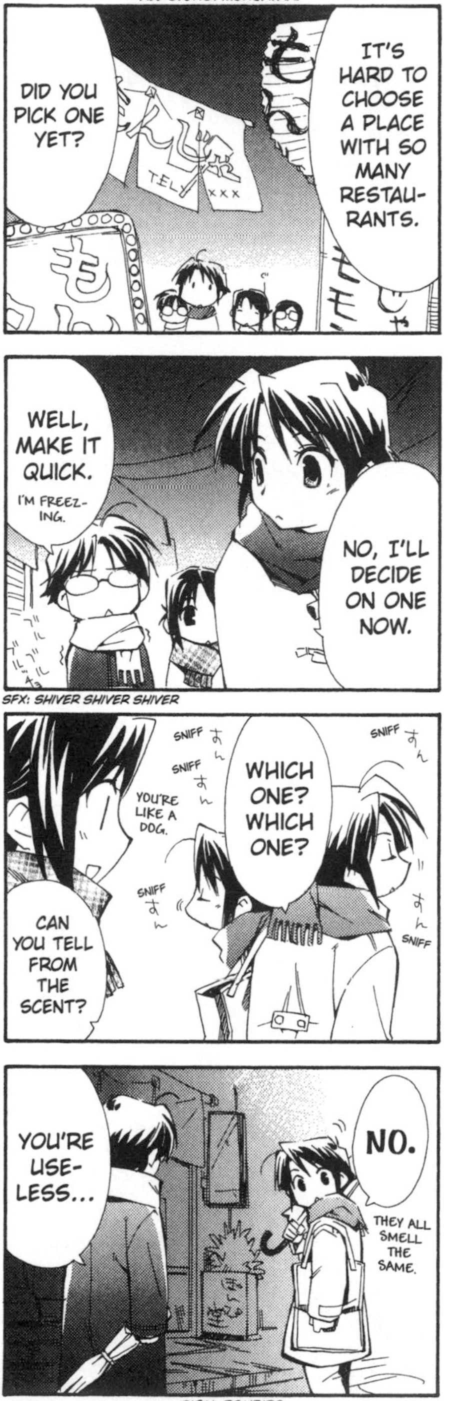
IT'S HARD TO CHOOSE A PLACE WITH SO MANY RESTAURANTS.
DID YOU PICK ONE YET?
NO, I'LL DECIDE ON ONE NOW.
WELL, MAKE IT QUICK.
I'M FREEZ-ING.
SNIFF
WHICH ONE? WHICH ONE?
SNIFF
SNIFF
YOU'RE LIKE A DOG.
SNIFF
SNIFF
CAN YOU TELL FROM THE SCENT?
NO.
THEY ALL SMELL THE SAME.
YOU'RE USE-LESS...

SFX: SHIVER SHIVER SHIVER

SIGN: PONPIDO

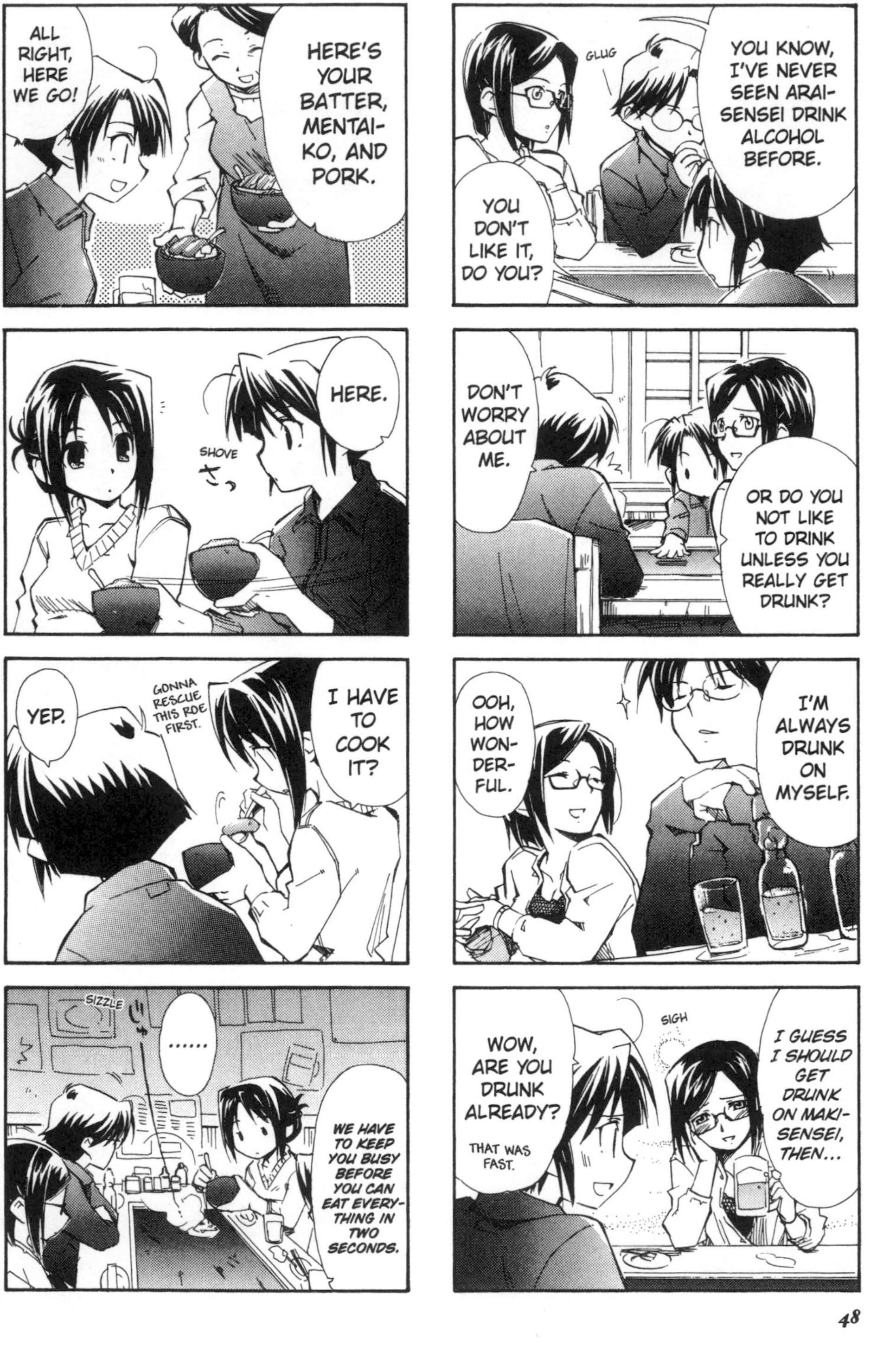
YOU KNOW, I'VE NEVER SEEN ARAI-SENSEI DRINK ALCOHOL BEFORE.
GLUG
YOU DON'T LIKE IT, DO YOU?
OR DO YOU NOT LIKE TO DRINK UNLESS YOU REALLY GET DRUNK?
DON'T WORRY ABOUT ME.
I'M ALWAYS DRUNK ON MYSELF.
OOH, HOW WON-DER-FUL.
I GUESS I SHOULD GET DRUNK ON MAKI-SENSEI, THEN...
SIGH
WOW, ARE YOU DRUNK ALREADY?
THAT WAS FAST.
HERE'S YOUR BATTER, MENTAI-KO, AND PORK.
ALL RIGHT, HERE WE GO!
HERE.
SHOVE
さっ
I HAVE TO COOK IT?
GONNA RESCUE THIS ROE FIRST.
YEP.
WE HAVE TO KEEP YOU BUSY BEFORE YOU CAN EAT EVERY-THING IN TWO SECONDS.
......
SIZZLE
じゅ

SETSUNA ARAI

CLASS: NURSING TEACHER
GENDER: MAIDEN
PERSONALITY: SNIPPY
LEVEL: 5

E: WHITE COAT
E: NDS, PLATINUM WHITE
E: PSP, BLACK
E: GLASSES

(SKIN) HEALTH POINTS: SMOOTH
MENTAL POINTS: SEEMS TO BE A COMPATRIOT
STRENGTH: LEAVE IT TO OTHERS
SPEED: LAZY
STAMINA: RATHER NOT USE IT
INTELLIGENCE: GEEK
LUCK: DO YOU EVER WIN SWEEPSTAKES?
GUTS: STUBBORN

Y: I'LL ONLY BUY THINGS NEW.

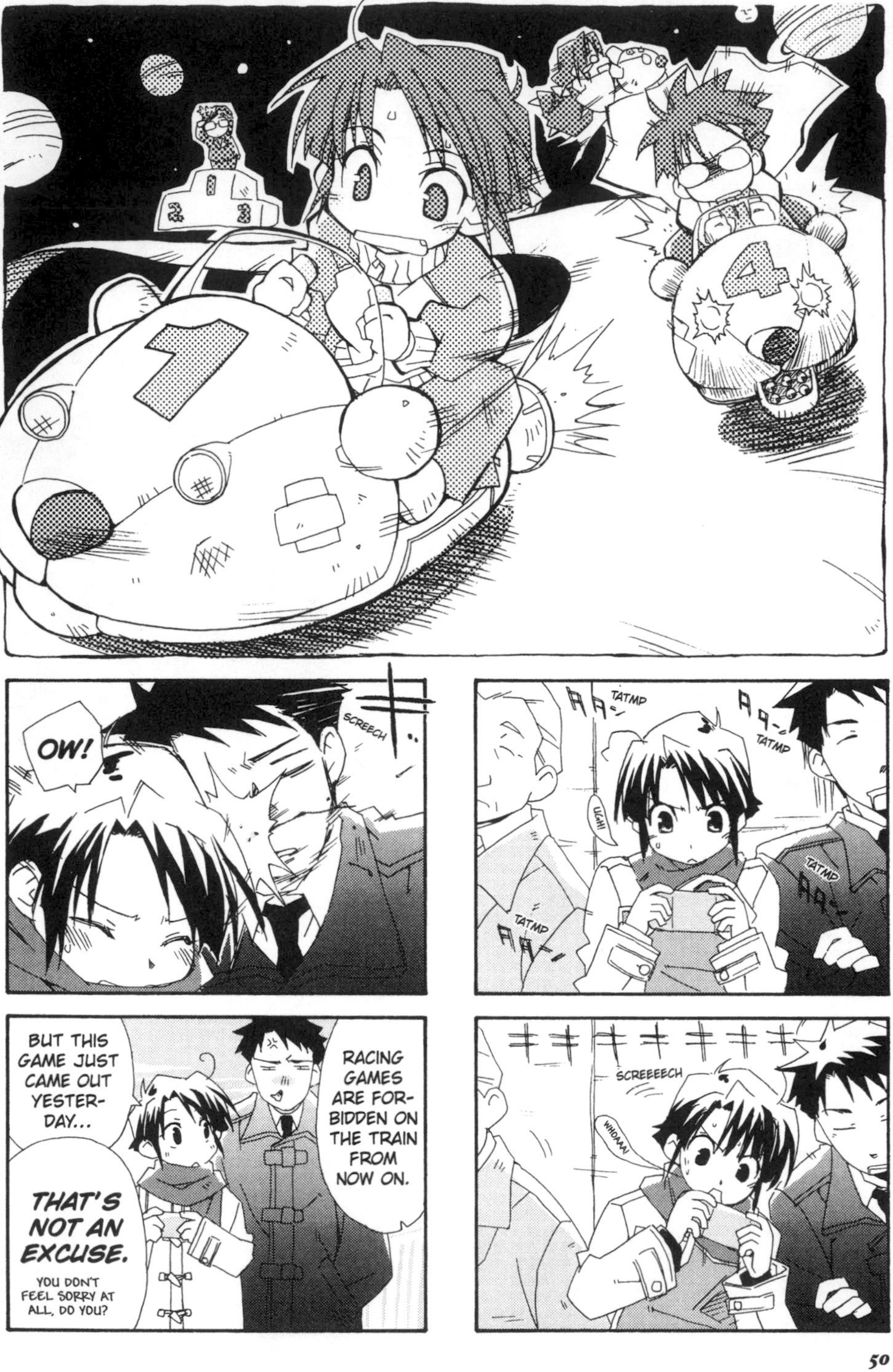

TATMP
TATMP
UGH!
TATMP
TATMP
SCREECH
OW!
SCREEEECH
WHOAAA!
RACING GAMES ARE FOR-BIDDEN ON THE TRAIN FROM NOW ON.
BUT THIS GAME JUST CAME OUT YESTER-DAY...
THAT'S NOT AN EXCUSE.
YOU DON'T FEEL SORRY AT ALL, DO YOU?

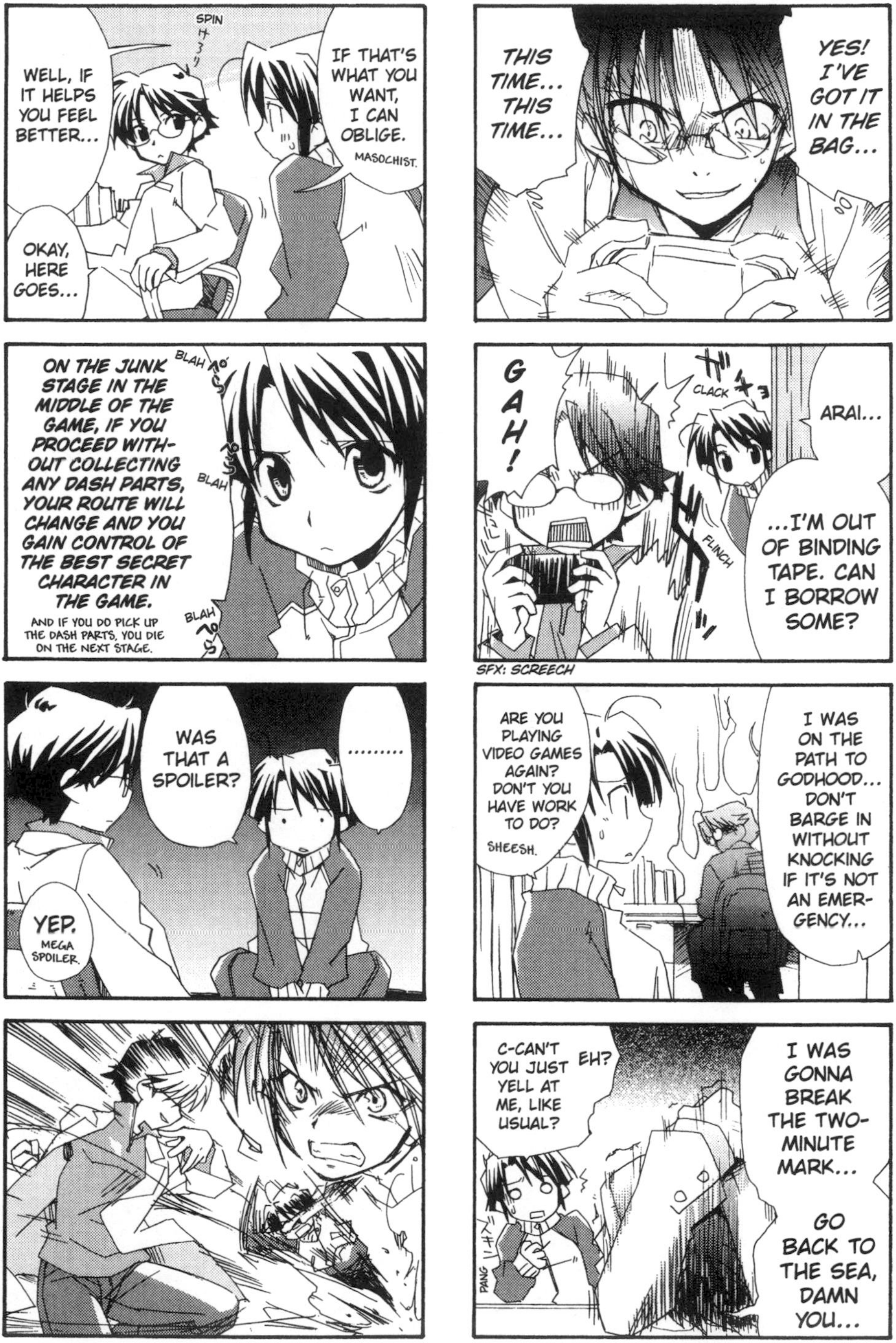
YES! I'VE GOT IT IN THE BAG...
THIS TIME... THIS TIME...
ARAI...
...I'M OUT OF BINDING TAPE. CAN I BORROW SOME?
CLACK
GAH!
FLINCH
SFX: SCREECH
I WAS ON THE PATH TO GODHOOD... DON'T BARGE IN WITHOUT KNOCKING IF IT'S NOT AN EMERGENCY...
ARE YOU PLAYING VIDEO GAMES AGAIN? DON'T YOU HAVE WORK TO DO?
SHEESH.
I WAS GONNA BREAK THE TWO-MINUTE MARK...
GO BACK TO THE SEA, DAMN YOU...
EH?
C-CAN'T YOU JUST YELL AT ME, LIKE USUAL?
PANG
IF THAT'S WHAT YOU WANT, I CAN OBLIGE.
MASOCHIST.
SPIN
WELL, IF IT HELPS YOU FEEL BETTER...
OKAY, HERE GOES...
BLAH
BLAH
BLAH
ON THE JUNK STAGE IN THE MIDDLE OF THE GAME, IF YOU PROCEED WITH-OUT COLLECTING ANY DASH PARTS, YOUR ROUTE WILL CHANGE AND YOU GAIN CONTROL OF THE BEST SECRET CHARACTER IN THE GAME.
AND IF YOU DO PICK UP THE DASH PARTS, YOU DIE ON THE NEXT STAGE.
....
WAS THAT A SPOILER?
YEP.
MEGA SPOILER.

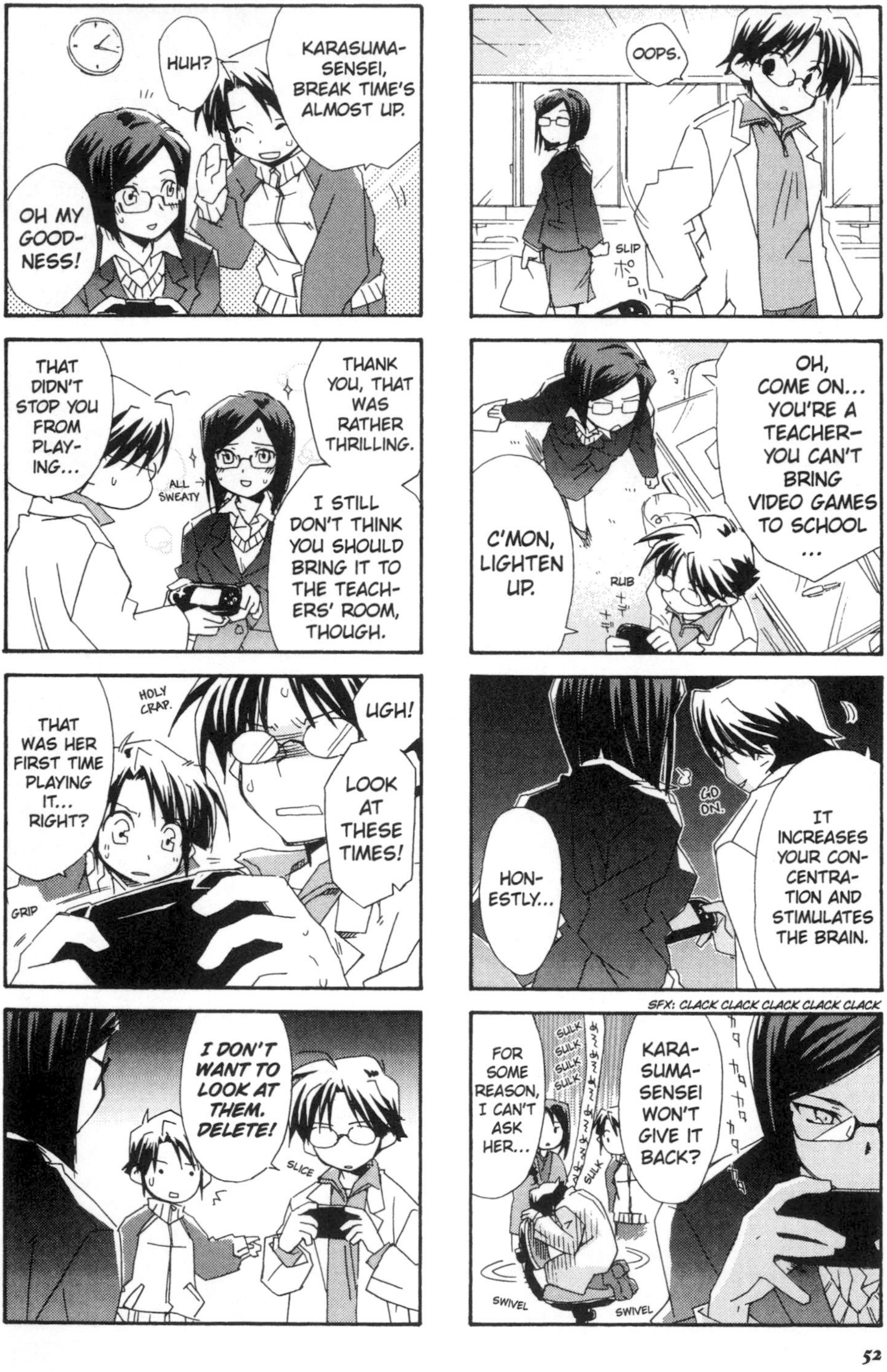
OOPS.
SLIP
OH, COME ON... YOU'RE A TEACHER— YOU CAN'T BRING VIDEO GAMES TO SCHOOL ...
C'MON, LIGHTEN UP.
RUB
GO ON.
IT INCREASES YOUR CONCENTRATION AND STIMULATES THE BRAIN.
HONESTLY...
SFX: CLACK CLACK CLACK CLACK CLACK
KARASUMA-SENSEI WON'T GIVE IT BACK?
SULK SULK SULK SULK
FOR SOME REASON, I CAN'T ASK HER...
SULK
SWIVEL
SWIVEL
KARASUMA-SENSEI, BREAK TIME'S ALMOST UP.
HUH?
OH MY GOODNESS!
THANK YOU, THAT WAS RATHER THRILLING.
I STILL DON'T THINK YOU SHOULD BRING IT TO THE TEACHERS' ROOM, THOUGH.
ALL SWEATY
THAT DIDN'T STOP YOU FROM PLAYING...
UGH!
LOOK AT THESE TIMES!
HOLY CRAP.
THAT WAS HER FIRST TIME PLAYING IT... RIGHT?
GRIP
I DON'T WANT TO LOOK AT THEM. DELETE!
SLICE

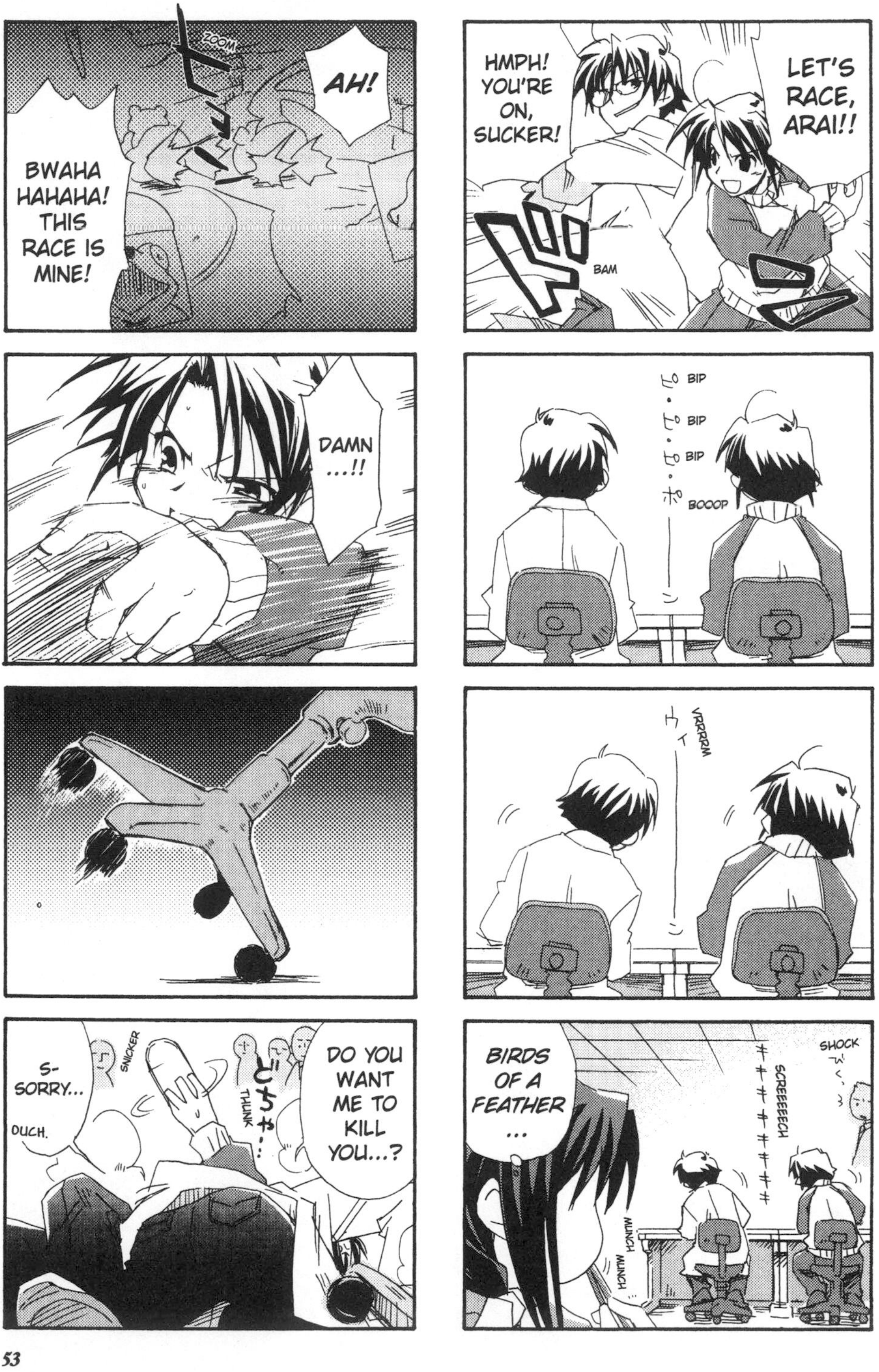
LET'S RACE, ARAI!!
HMPH! YOU'RE ON, SUCKER!
BAM
AH!
ZOOM
BWAHA HAHAHA! THIS RACE IS MINE!
BIP
BIP
BIP
BOOOP
DAMN ...!!
VRRRRM
SHOCK
SCREEEEECH
BIRDS OF A FEATHER ...
MUNCH
MUNCH
DO YOU WANT ME TO KILL YOU...?
THUNK
SNICKER
S-SORRY...
OUCH.

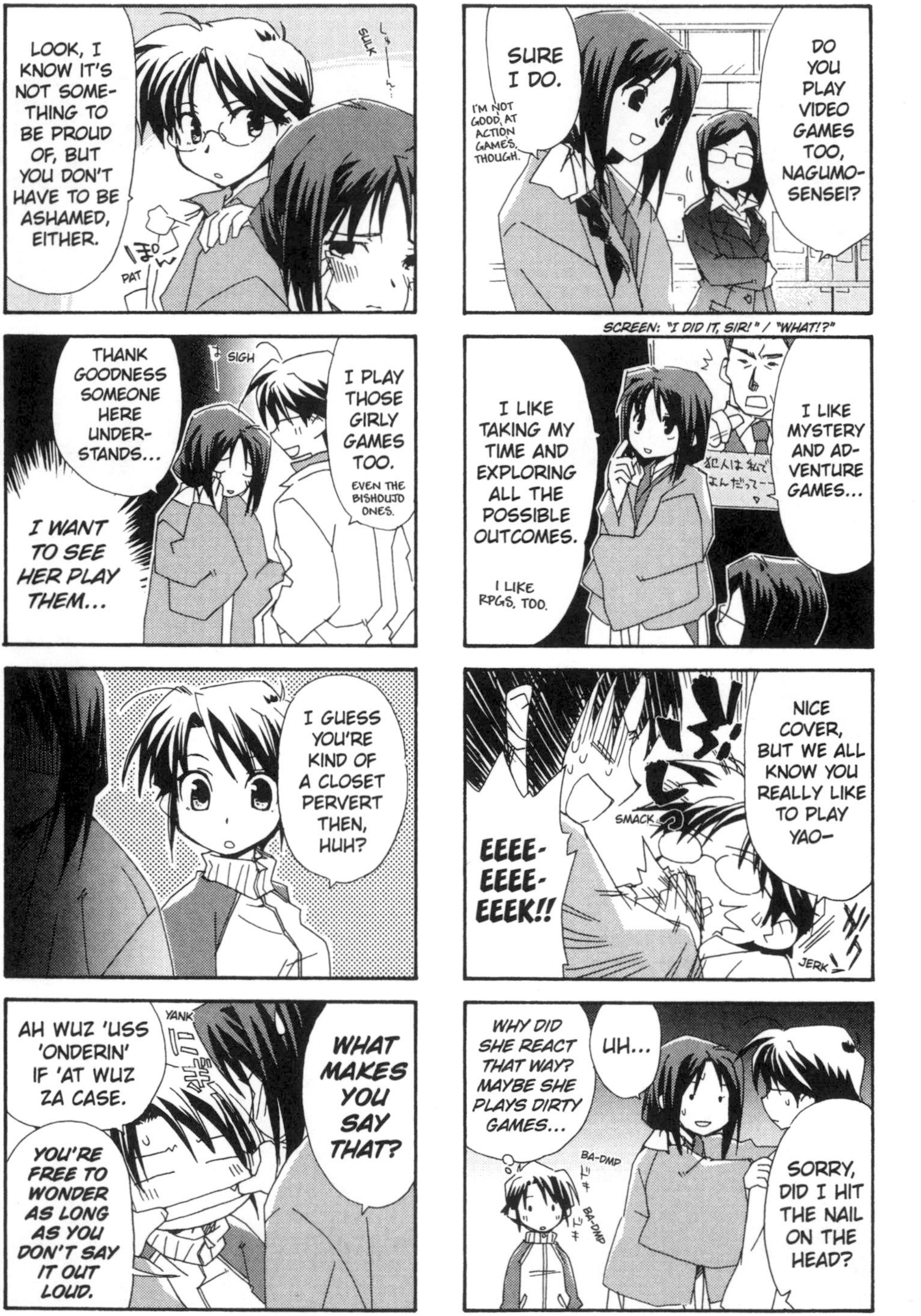
DO YOU PLAY VIDEO GAMES TOO, NAGUMO-SENSEI?
SURE I DO.
I'M NOT GOOD AT ACTION GAMES, THOUGH.
SULK
LOOK, I KNOW IT'S NOT SOMETHING TO BE PROUD OF, BUT YOU DON'T HAVE TO BE ASHAMED, EITHER.
PAT
SCREEN: "I DID IT, SIR!" / "WHAT!?"
I LIKE MYSTERY AND ADVENTURE GAMES...
I LIKE TAKING MY TIME AND EXPLORING ALL THE POSSIBLE OUTCOMES.
I LIKE RPGS, TOO.
I PLAY THOSE GIRLY GAMES TOO.
EVEN THE BISHOUJO ONES.
SIGH
THANK GOODNESS SOMEONE HERE UNDERSTANDS...
I WANT TO SEE HER PLAY THEM...
NICE COVER, BUT WE ALL KNOW YOU REALLY LIKE TO PLAY YAO-
SMACK
EEEE-EEEE-EEEK!!
JERK
I GUESS YOU'RE KIND OF A CLOSET PERVERT THEN, HUH?
SORRY, DID I HIT THE NAIL ON THE HEAD?
UH...
WHY DID SHE REACT THAT WAY? MAYBE SHE PLAYS DIRTY GAMES...
BA-DMP
BA-DMP
WHAT MAKES YOU SAY THAT?
YANK
AH WUZ 'USS 'ONDERIN' IF 'AT WUZ ZA CASE.
YOU'RE FREE TO WONDER AS LONG AS YOU DON'T SAY IT OUT LOUD.

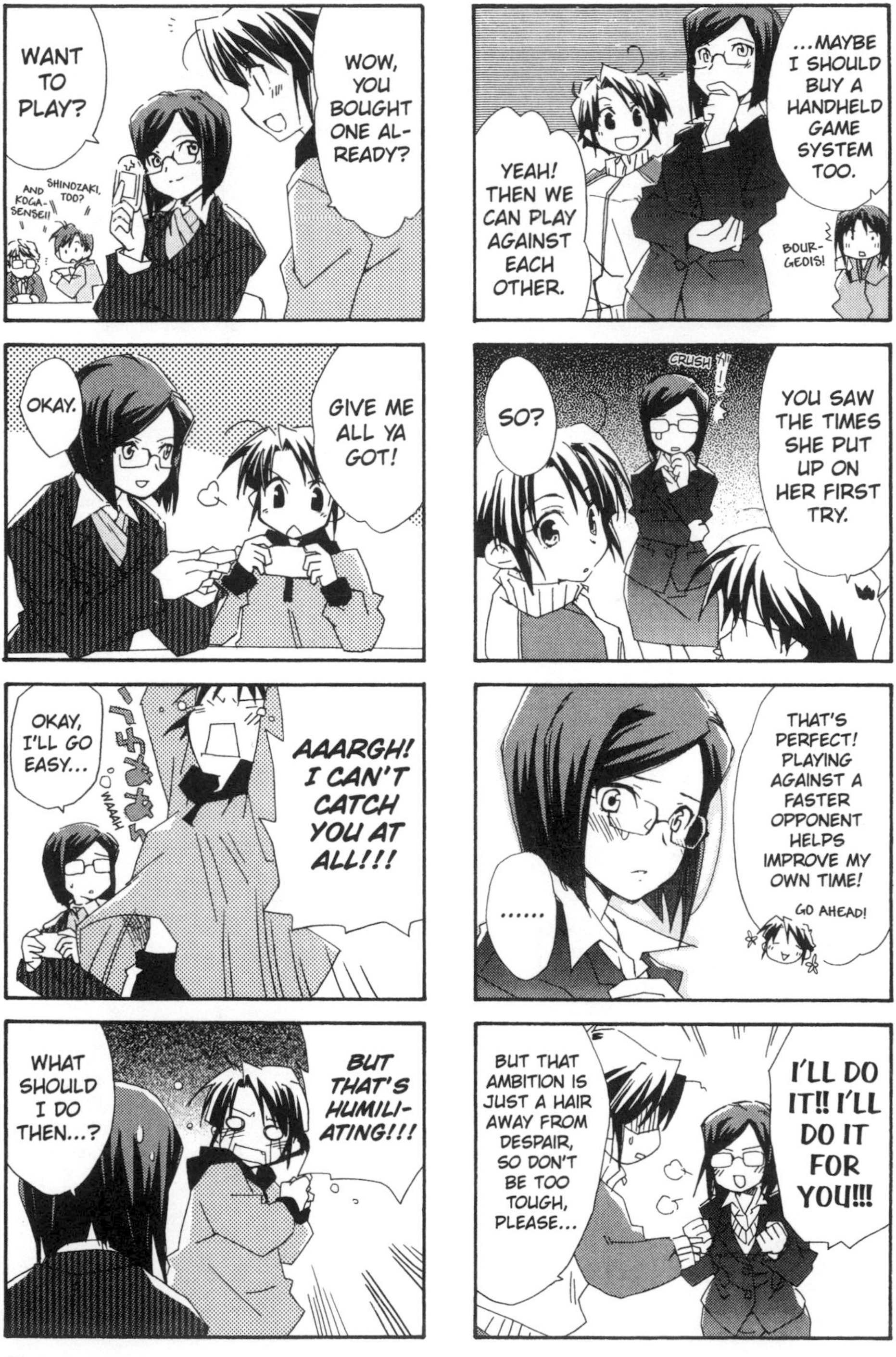
...MAYBE I SHOULD BUY A HANDHELD GAME SYSTEM TOO.
YEAH! THEN WE CAN PLAY AGAINST EACH OTHER.
BOUR-GEOIS!
WOW, YOU BOUGHT ONE AL-READY?
WANT TO PLAY?
SHINOZAKI, TOO?
AND KOGA-SENSEI!!
YOU SAW THE TIMES SHE PUT UP ON HER FIRST TRY.
CRUSH
SO?
GIVE ME ALL YA GOT!
OKAY.
THAT'S PERFECT! PLAYING AGAINST A FASTER OPPONENT HELPS IMPROVE MY OWN TIME!
GO AHEAD!
......
AAARGH! I CAN'T CATCH YOU AT ALL!!!
OKAY, I'LL GO EASY...
WAAAH
I'LL DO IT!! I'LL DO IT FOR YOU!!!
BUT THAT AMBITION IS JUST A HAIR AWAY FROM DESPAIR, SO DON'T BE TOO TOUGH, PLEASE...
BUT THAT'S HUMILI-ATING!!!
WHAT SHOULD I DO THEN...?

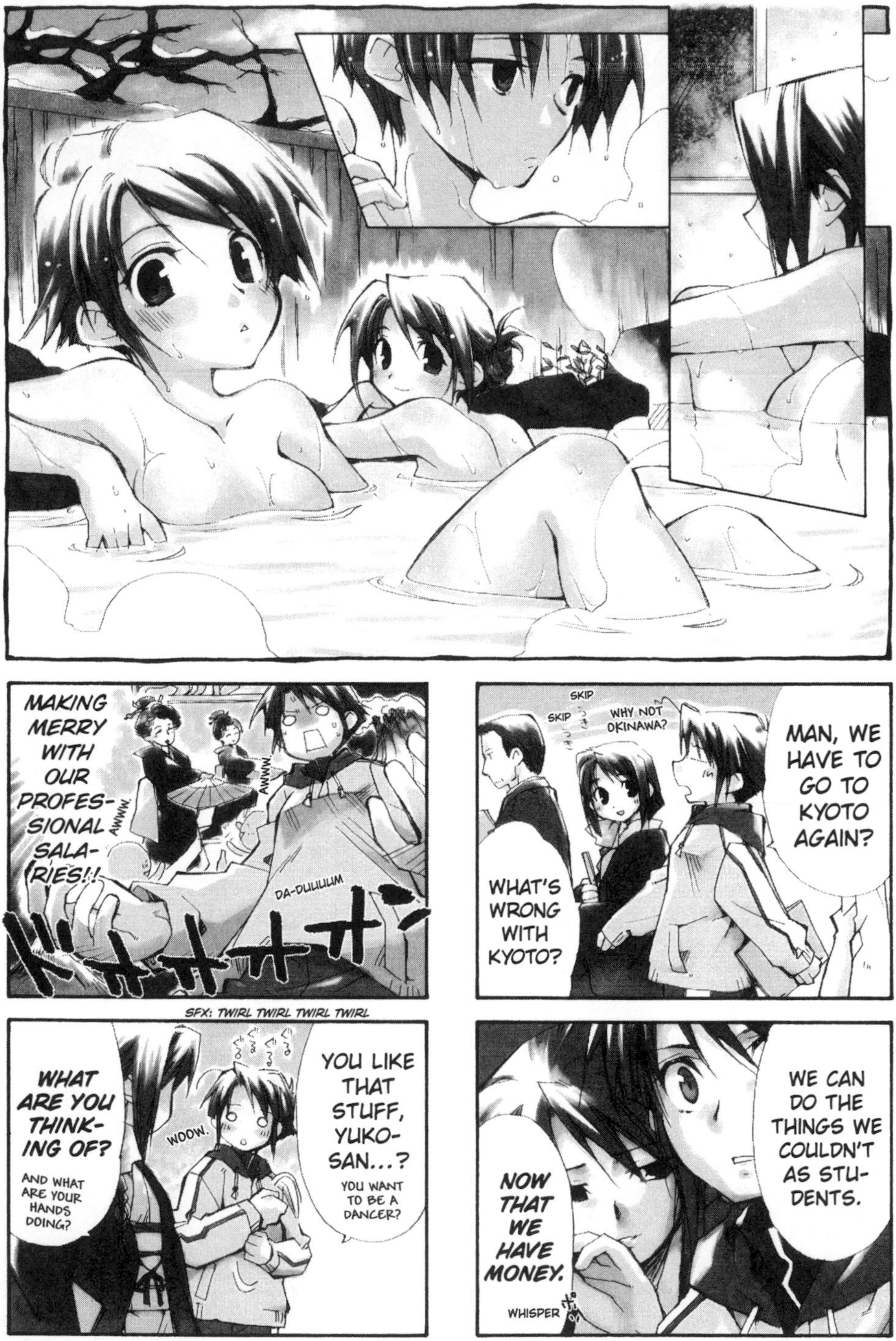
SKIP
SKIP
WHY NOT OKINAWA?
MAN, WE HAVE TO GO TO KYOTO AGAIN?
WHAT'S WRONG WITH KYOTO?
MAKING MERRY WITH OUR PROFES-SIONAL SALA-RIES!!
AWWW.
AWWW.
DA-DUUUUM
SFX: TWIRL TWIRL TWIRL TWIRL
WE CAN DO THE THINGS WE COULDN'T AS STU-DENTS.
NOW THAT WE HAVE MONEY.
WHISPER
YOU LIKE THAT STUFF, YUKO-SAN...?
YOU WANT TO BE A DANCER?
WOOW.
WHAT ARE YOU THINK-ING OF?
AND WHAT ARE YOUR HANDS DOING?

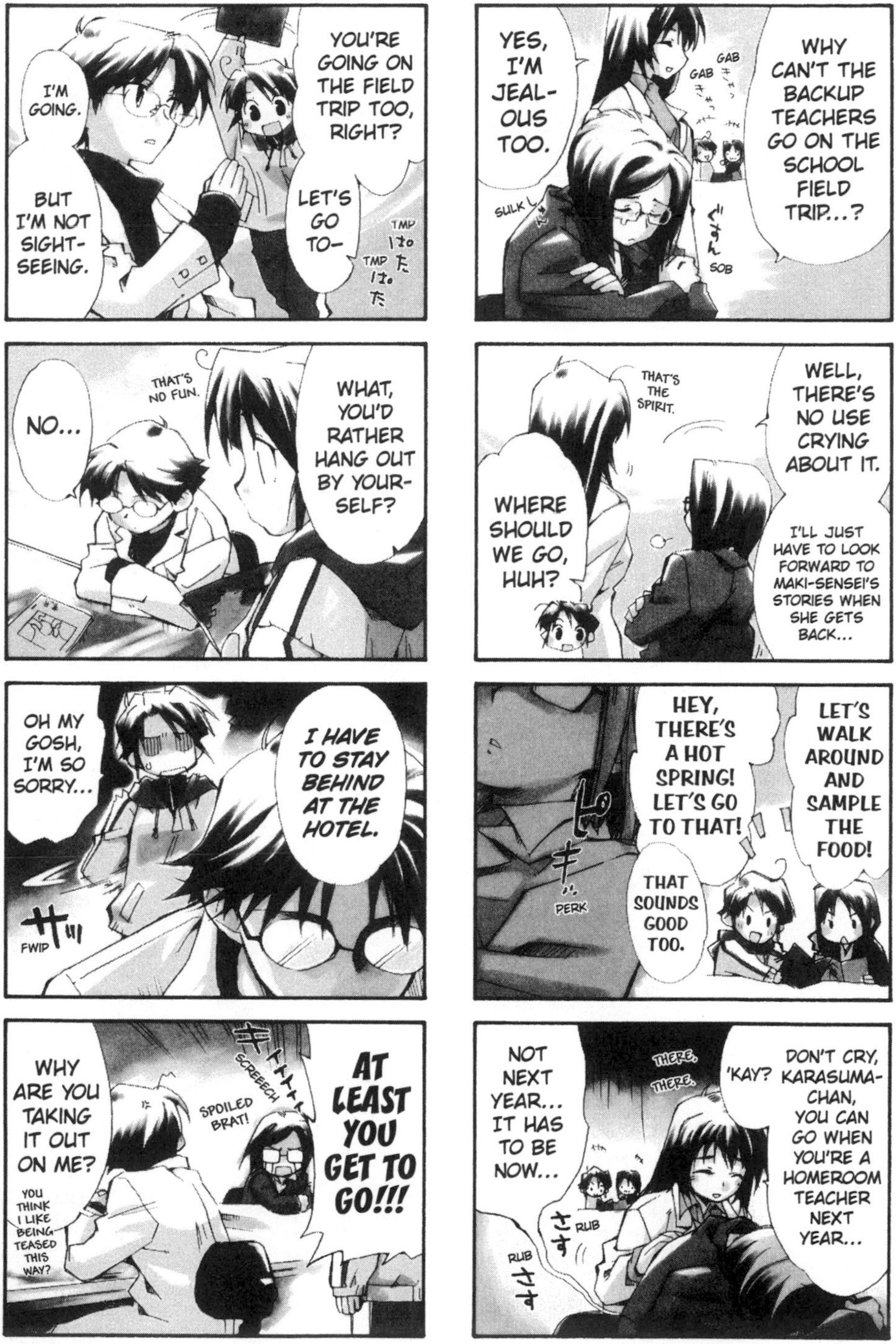

WHY CAN'T THE BACKUP TEACHERS GO ON THE SCHOOL FIELD TRIP...?
GAB GAB
YES, I'M JEALOUS TOO.
SULK
ぐすん
SOB
WELL, THERE'S NO USE CRYING ABOUT IT.
I'LL JUST HAVE TO LOOK FORWARD TO MAKI-SENSEI'S STORIES WHEN SHE GETS BACK...
THAT'S THE SPIRIT.
WHERE SHOULD WE GO, HUH?
LET'S WALK AROUND AND SAMPLE THE FOOD!
HEY, THERE'S A HOT SPRING! LET'S GO TO THAT!
THAT SOUNDS GOOD TOO.
PERK
DON'T CRY, KARASUMA-CHAN, YOU CAN GO WHEN YOU'RE A HOMEROOM TEACHER NEXT YEAR...
'KAY?
THERE, THERE.
THERE, THERE.
NOT NEXT YEAR... IT HAS TO BE NOW...
さす RUB
RUB さす
YOU'RE GOING ON THE FIELD TRIP TOO, RIGHT?
LET'S GO TO—
TMP TMP
I'M GOING.
BUT I'M NOT SIGHT-SEEING.
WHAT, YOU'D RATHER HANG OUT BY YOURSELF?
THAT'S NO FUN.
NO...
I HAVE TO STAY BEHIND AT THE HOTEL.
OH MY GOSH, I'M SO SORRY...
FWIP
AT LEAST YOU GET TO GO!!!
SCREEECH
SPOILED BRAT!
WHY ARE YOU TAKING IT OUT ON ME?
YOU THINK I LIKE BEING TEASED THIS WAY?

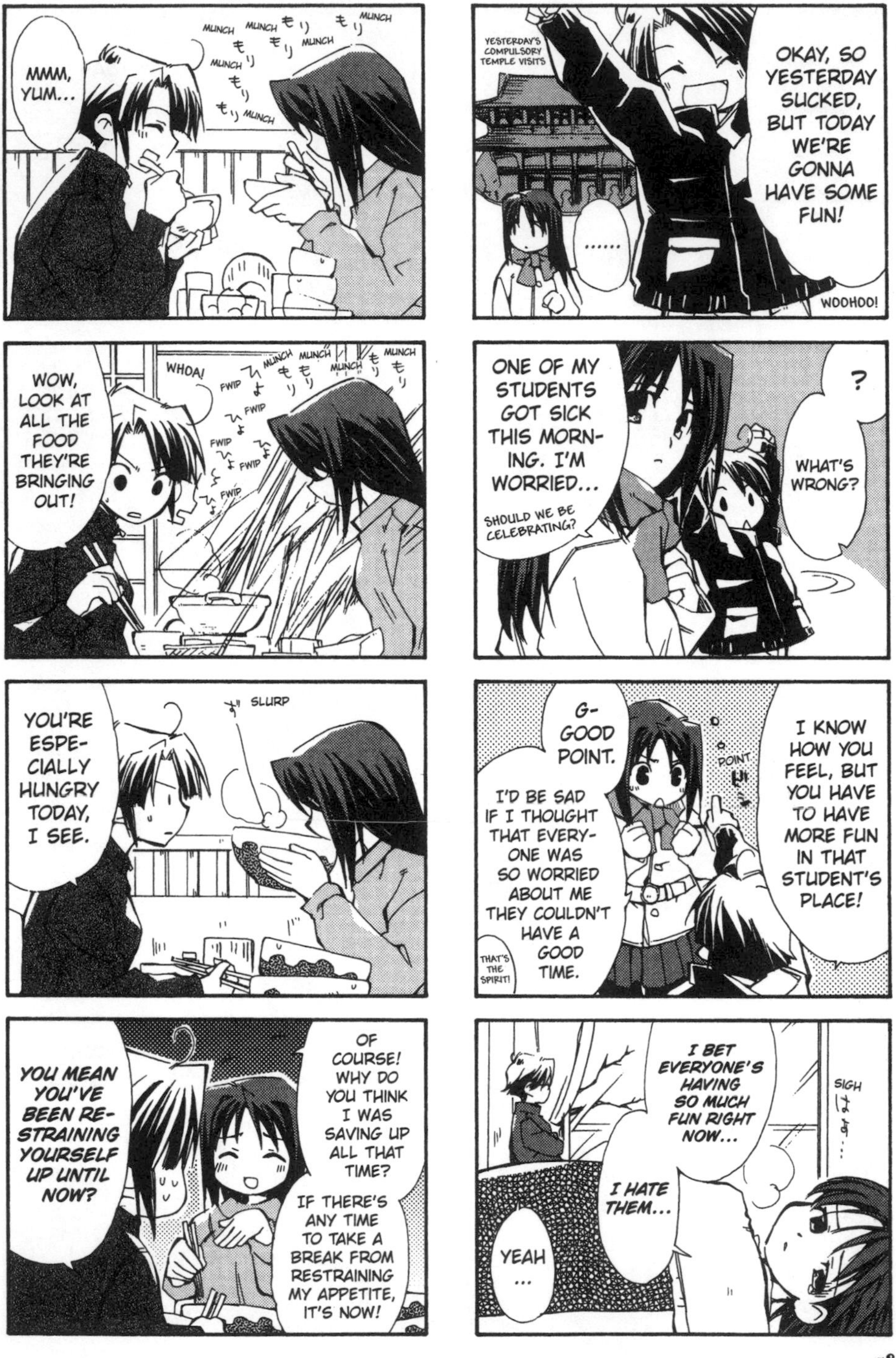

OKAY, SO YESTERDAY SUCKED, BUT TODAY WE'RE GONNA HAVE SOME FUN!
YESTERDAY'S COMPULSORY TEMPLE VISITS
......
WOOHOO!
?
WHAT'S WRONG?
ONE OF MY STUDENTS GOT SICK THIS MORNING. I'M WORRIED...
SHOULD WE BE CELEBRATING?
I KNOW HOW YOU FEEL, BUT YOU HAVE TO HAVE MORE FUN IN THAT STUDENT'S PLACE!
POINT
G-GOOD POINT.
I'D BE SAD IF I THOUGHT THAT EVERYONE WAS SO WORRIED ABOUT ME THEY COULDN'T HAVE A GOOD TIME.
THAT'S THE SPIRIT!
SIGH
はぁ…
I BET EVERYONE'S HAVING SO MUCH FUN RIGHT NOW...
I HATE THEM...
YEAH ...
MUNCH もり MUNCH もり MUNCH もり MUNCH もり MUNCH もり MUNCH
MMM, YUM...
MUNCH もり MUNCH もり MUNCH もり MUNCH もり
FWIP ひょ FWIP ひょ FWIP ひょ FWIP ひょ FWIP ひょ
WHOA!
WOW, LOOK AT ALL THE FOOD THEY'RE BRINGING OUT!
SLURP
YOU'RE ESPECIALLY HUNGRY TODAY, I SEE.
YOU MEAN YOU'VE BEEN RESTRAINING YOURSELF UP UNTIL NOW?
OF COURSE! WHY DO YOU THINK I WAS SAVING UP ALL THAT TIME?
IF THERE'S ANY TIME TO TAKE A BREAK FROM RESTRAINING MY APPETITE, IT'S NOW!

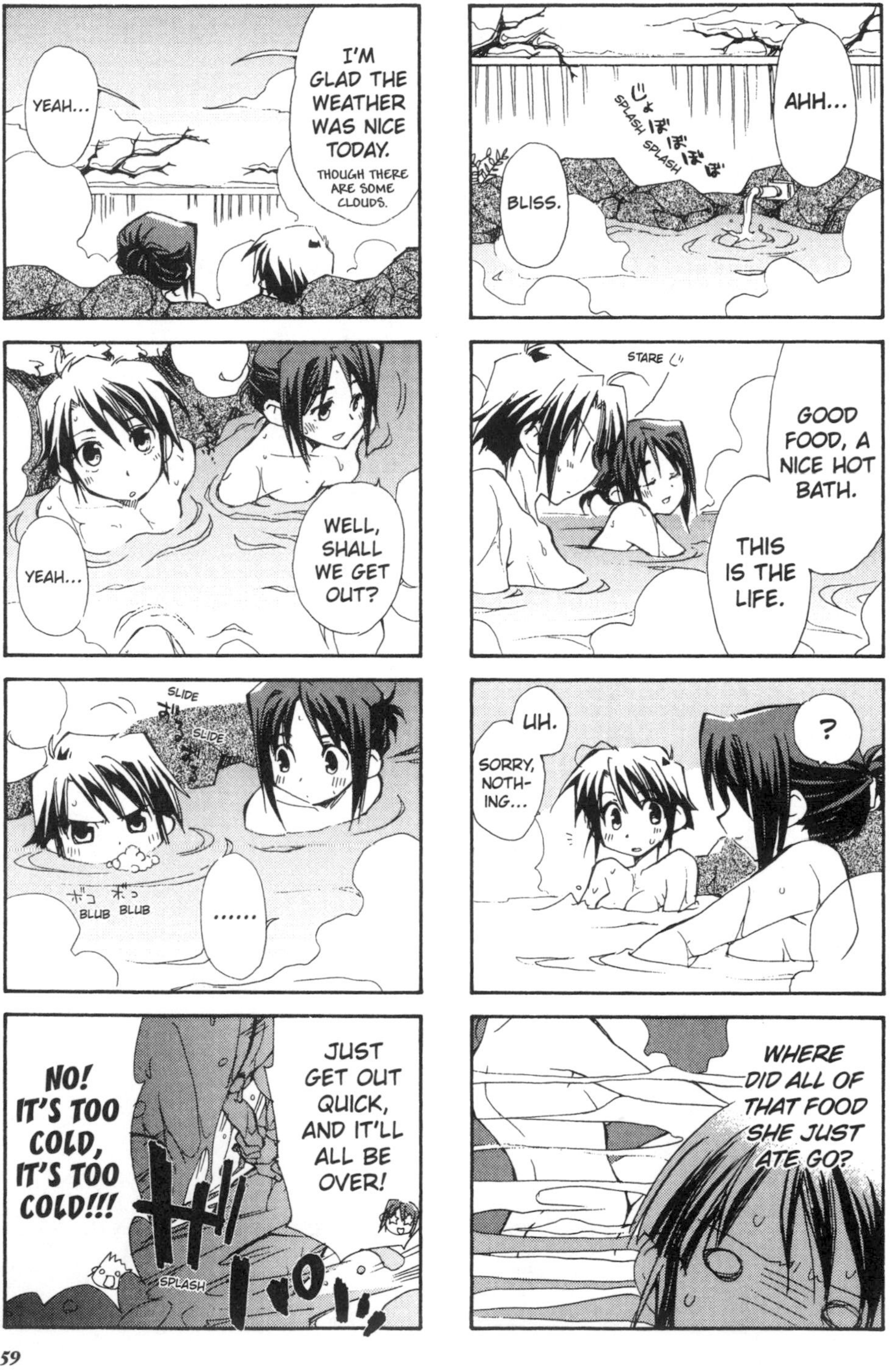
AHH...
SPLASH SPLASH
BLISS.
GOOD FOOD, A NICE HOT BATH.
STARE
THIS IS THE LIFE.
?
UH.
SORRY, NOTHING...
WHERE DID ALL OF THAT FOOD SHE JUST ATE GO?
I'M GLAD THE WEATHER WAS NICE TODAY.
THOUGH THERE ARE SOME CLOUDS.
YEAH...
WELL, SHALL WE GET OUT?
YEAH...
SLIDE
SLIDE
......
BLUB BLUB
JUST GET OUT QUICK, AND IT'LL ALL BE OVER!
NO! IT'S TOO COLD, IT'S TOO COLD!!!
SPLASH

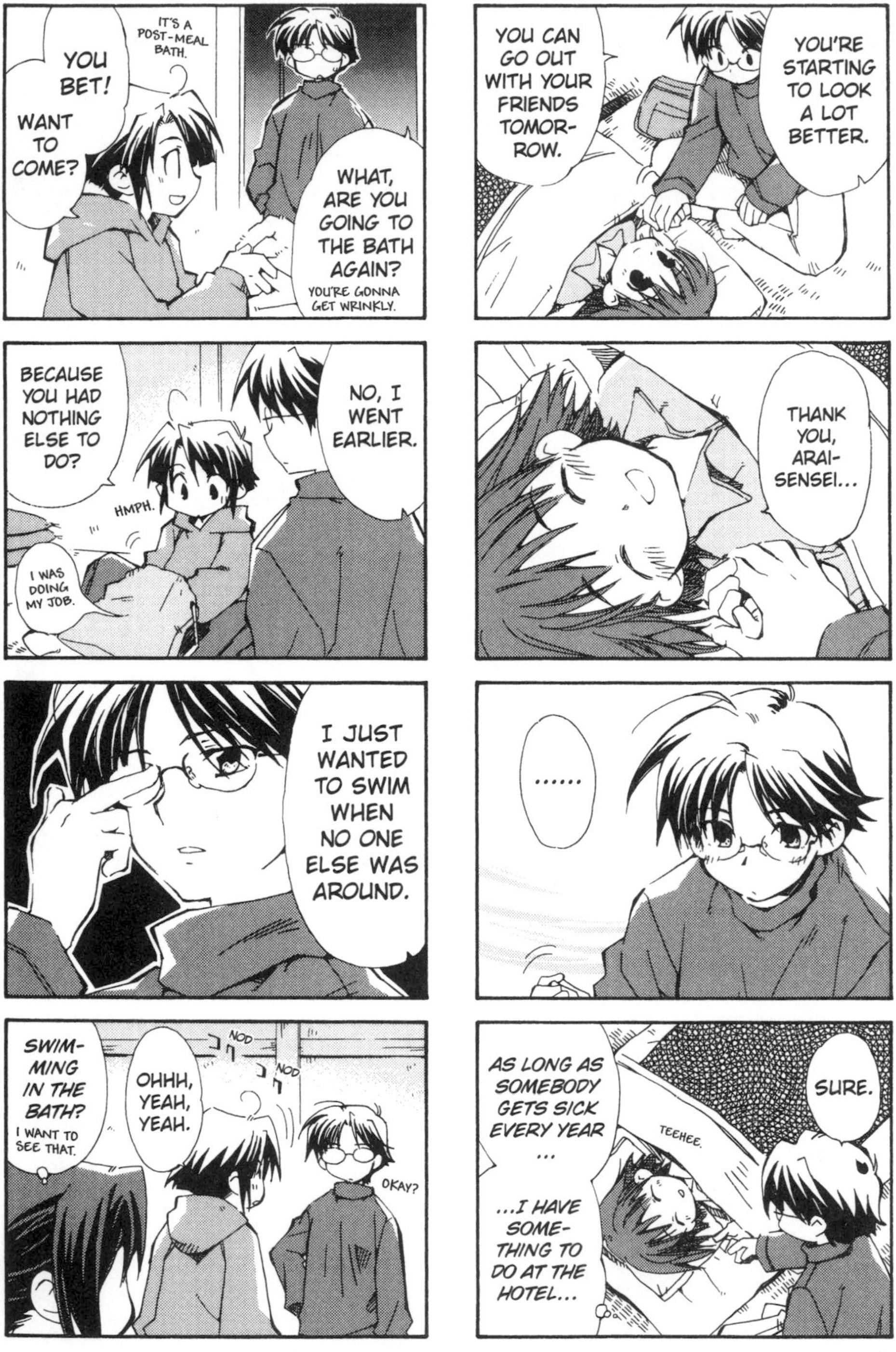
YOU'RE STARTING TO LOOK A LOT BETTER.
YOU CAN GO OUT WITH YOUR FRIENDS TOMOR-ROW.
WHAT, ARE YOU GOING TO THE BATH AGAIN?
YOU'RE GONNA GET WRINKLY.
IT'S A POST-MEAL BATH.
YOU BET!
WANT TO COME?
THANK YOU, ARAI-SENSEI...
NO, I WENT EARLIER.
BECAUSE YOU HAD NOTHING ELSE TO DO?
HMPH.
I WAS DOING MY JOB.
......
I JUST WANTED TO SWIM WHEN NO ONE ELSE WAS AROUND.
SURE.
TEEHEE.
AS LONG AS SOMEBODY GETS SICK EVERY YEAR ...
...I HAVE SOME-THING TO DO AT THE HOTEL...
NOD
NOD
OKAY?
OHHH, YEAH, YEAH.
SWIM-MING IN THE BATH?
I WANT TO SEE THAT.

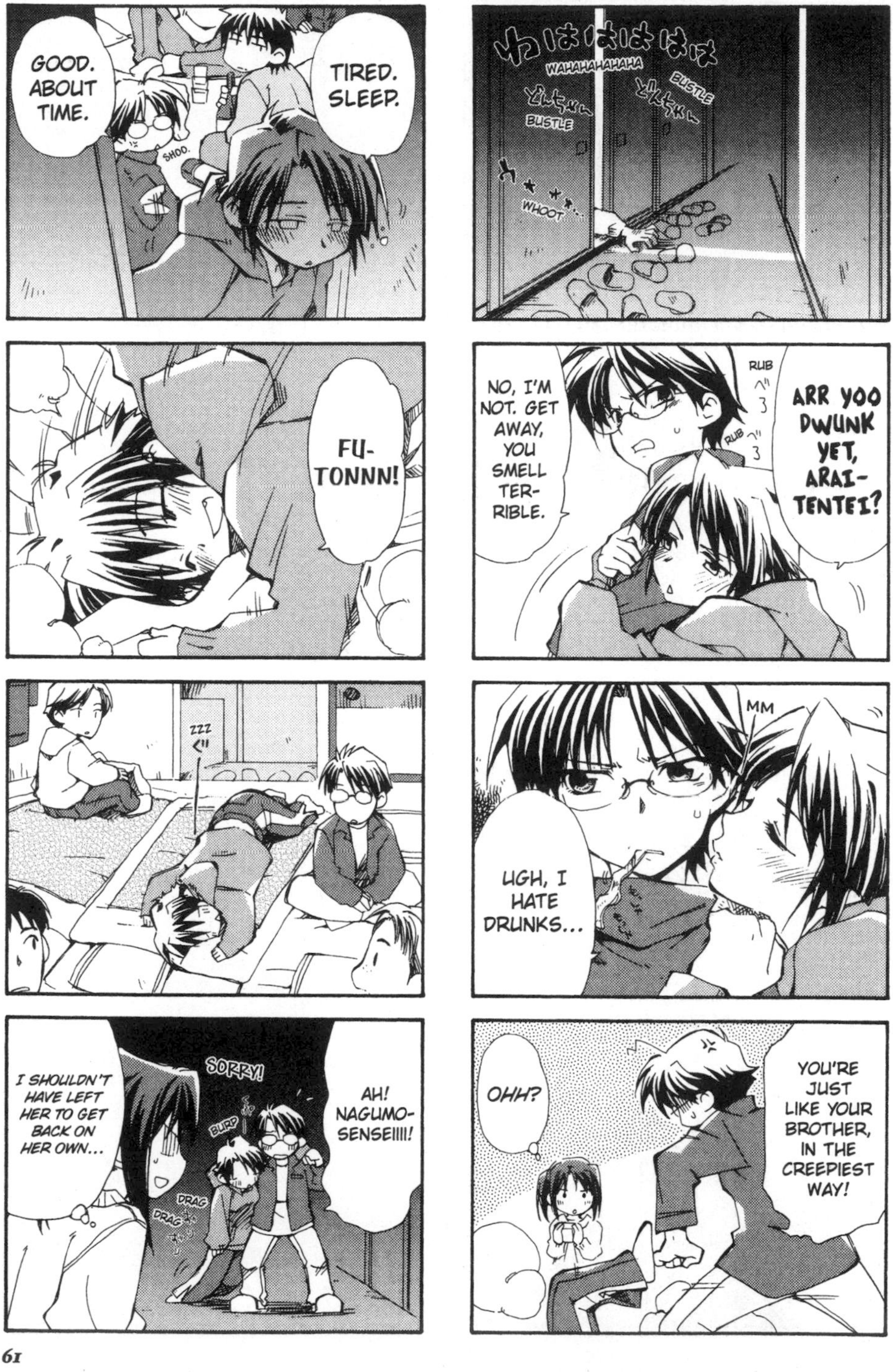
わははははは
WAHAHAHAHAHA
BUSTLE
BUSTLE
WHOOT
TIRED. SLEEP.
SHOO.
GOOD. ABOUT TIME.
ARR YOO DWUNK YET, ARAI-TENTEI?
RUB
RUB
NO, I'M NOT. GET AWAY, YOU SMELL TER-RIBLE.
FU-TONNN!
MM
UGH, I HATE DRUNKS...
ZZZ
YOU'RE JUST LIKE YOUR BROTHER, IN THE CREEPIEST WAY!
OHH?
AH! NAGUMO-SENSEI!!!!
SORRY!
BURP
DRAG
DRAG
I SHOULDN'T HAVE LEFT HER TO GET BACK ON HER OWN...

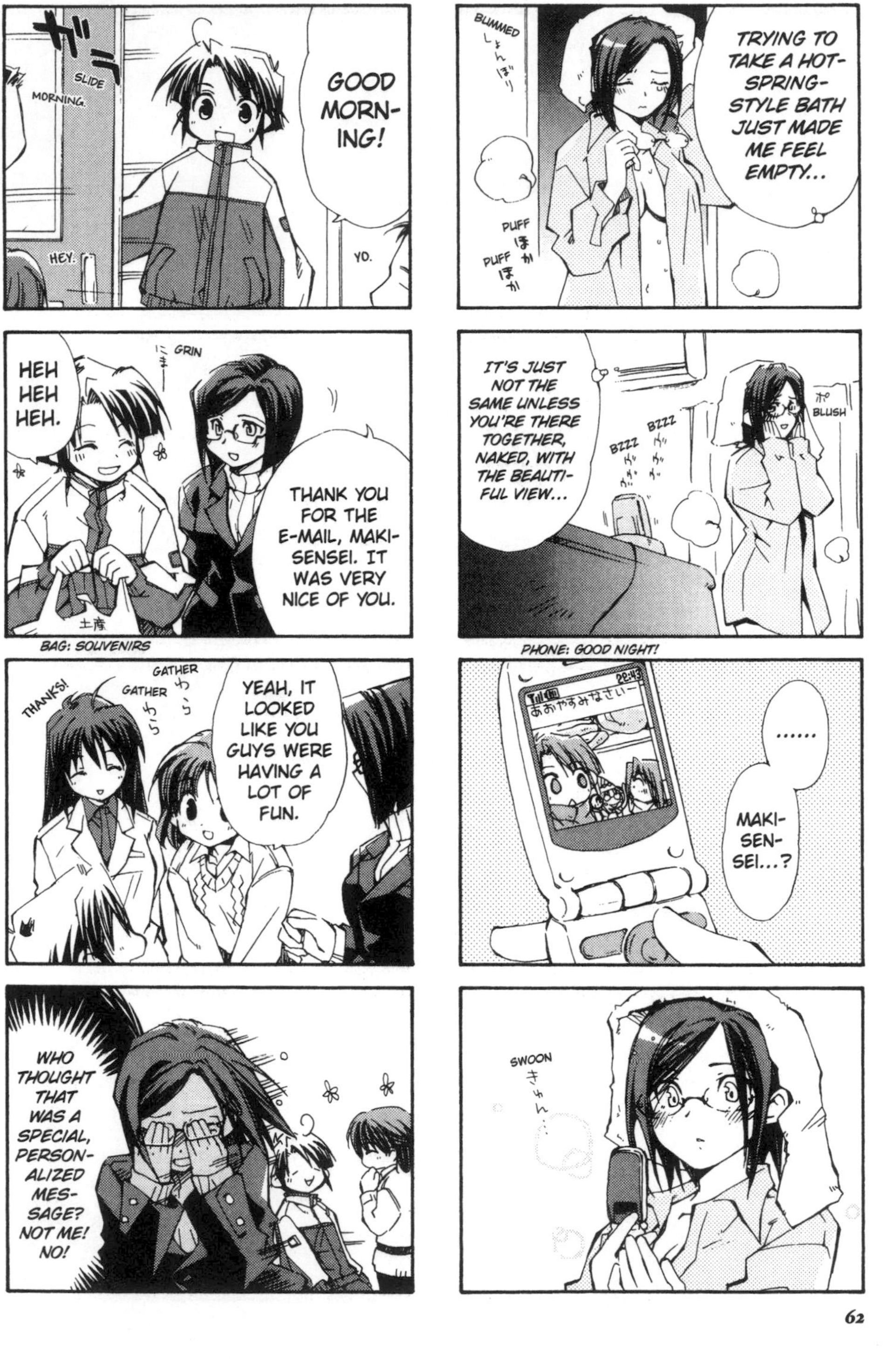
BUMMED
しょんぼり
TRYING TO TAKE A HOT-SPRING-STYLE BATH JUST MADE ME FEEL EMPTY...
PUFF ほか
PUFF ほか
IT'S JUST NOT THE SAME UNLESS YOU'RE THERE TOGETHER, NAKED, WITH THE BEAUTIFUL VIEW...
BZZZ
BZZZ
ポ BLUSH
PHONE: GOOD NIGHT!
22:43
おやすみなさいー
......
MAKI-SENSEI...?
SWOON
きゅん...
SLIDE
MORNING.
GOOD MORNING!
HEY.
YO.
HEH HEH HEH.
にまー GRIN
THANK YOU FOR THE E-MAIL, MAKI-SENSEI. IT WAS VERY NICE OF YOU.
土産
BAG: SOUVENIRS
YEAH, IT LOOKED LIKE YOU GUYS WERE HAVING A LOT OF FUN.
GATHER わら
GATHER わら
THANKS!
WHO THOUGHT THAT WAS A SPECIAL, PERSONALIZED MESSAGE? NOT ME! NO!

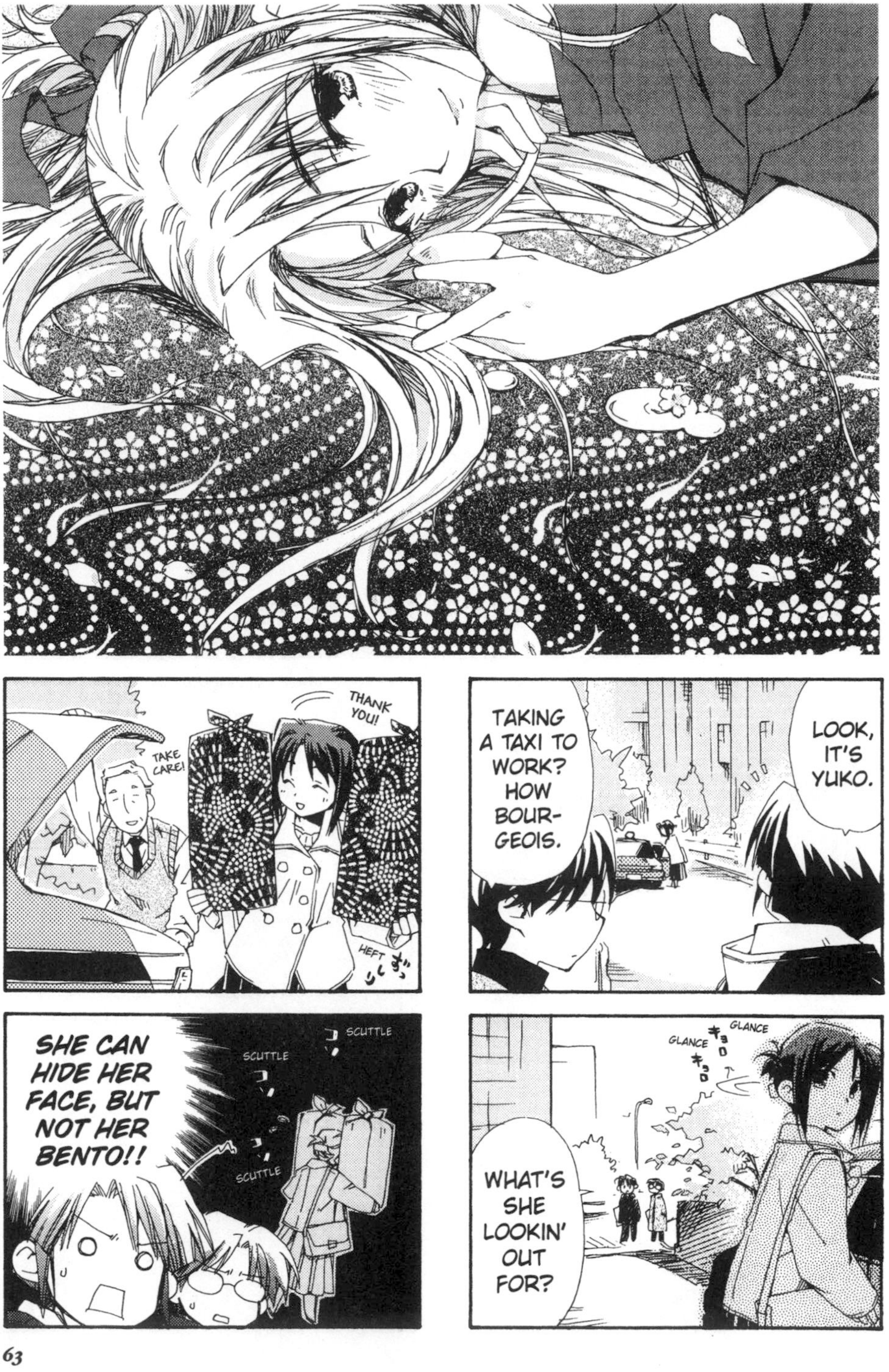
LOOK, IT'S YUKO.
TAKING A TAXI TO WORK? HOW BOURGEOIS.
THANK YOU!
TAKE CARE!
HEFT
GLANCE
GLANCE
WHAT'S SHE LOOKIN' OUT FOR?
SCUTTLE
SCUTTLE
SCUTTLE
SHE CAN HIDE HER FACE, BUT NOT HER BENTO!!

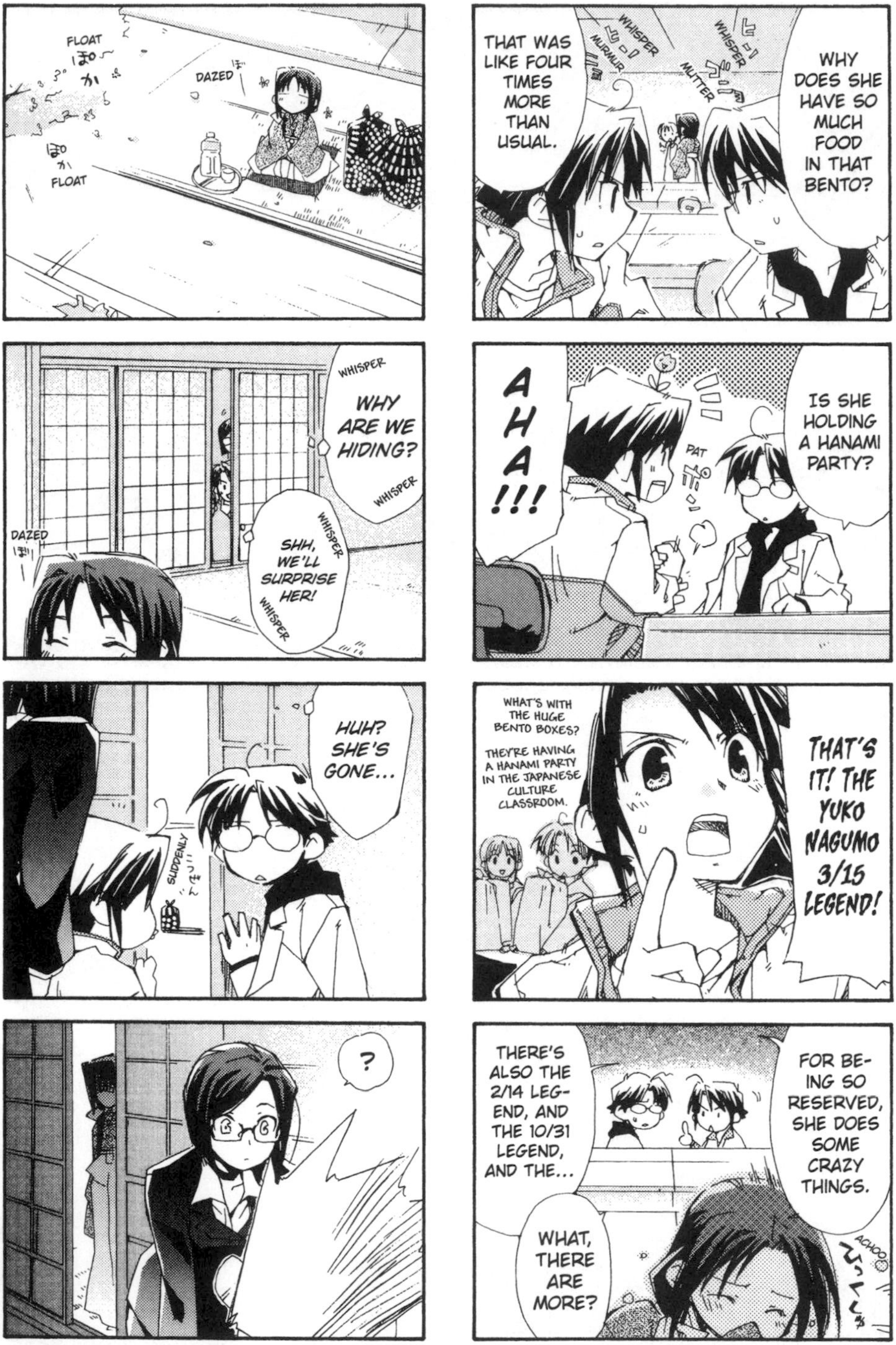
WHISPER
WHY DOES SHE HAVE SO MUCH FOOD IN THAT BENTO?
MUTTER
WHISPER
MURMUR
THAT WAS LIKE FOUR TIMES MORE THAN USUAL.
FLOAT
DAZED
FLOAT
IS SHE HOLDING A HANAMI PARTY?
PAT
AHA!!!
WHISPER
WHY ARE WE HIDING?
WHISPER
WHISPER
SHH, WE'LL SURPRISE HER!
WHISPER
DAZED
THAT'S IT! THE YUKO NAGUMO 3/15 LEGEND!
WHAT'S WITH THE HUGE BENTO BOXES?
THEY'RE HAVING A HANAMI PARTY IN THE JAPANESE CULTURE CLASSROOM.
HUH? SHE'S GONE...
SUDDENLY
FOR BEING SO RESERVED, SHE DOES SOME CRAZY THINGS.
THERE'S ALSO THE 2/14 LEGEND, AND THE 10/31 LEGEND, AND THE...
ACHOO
WHAT, THERE ARE MORE?
?

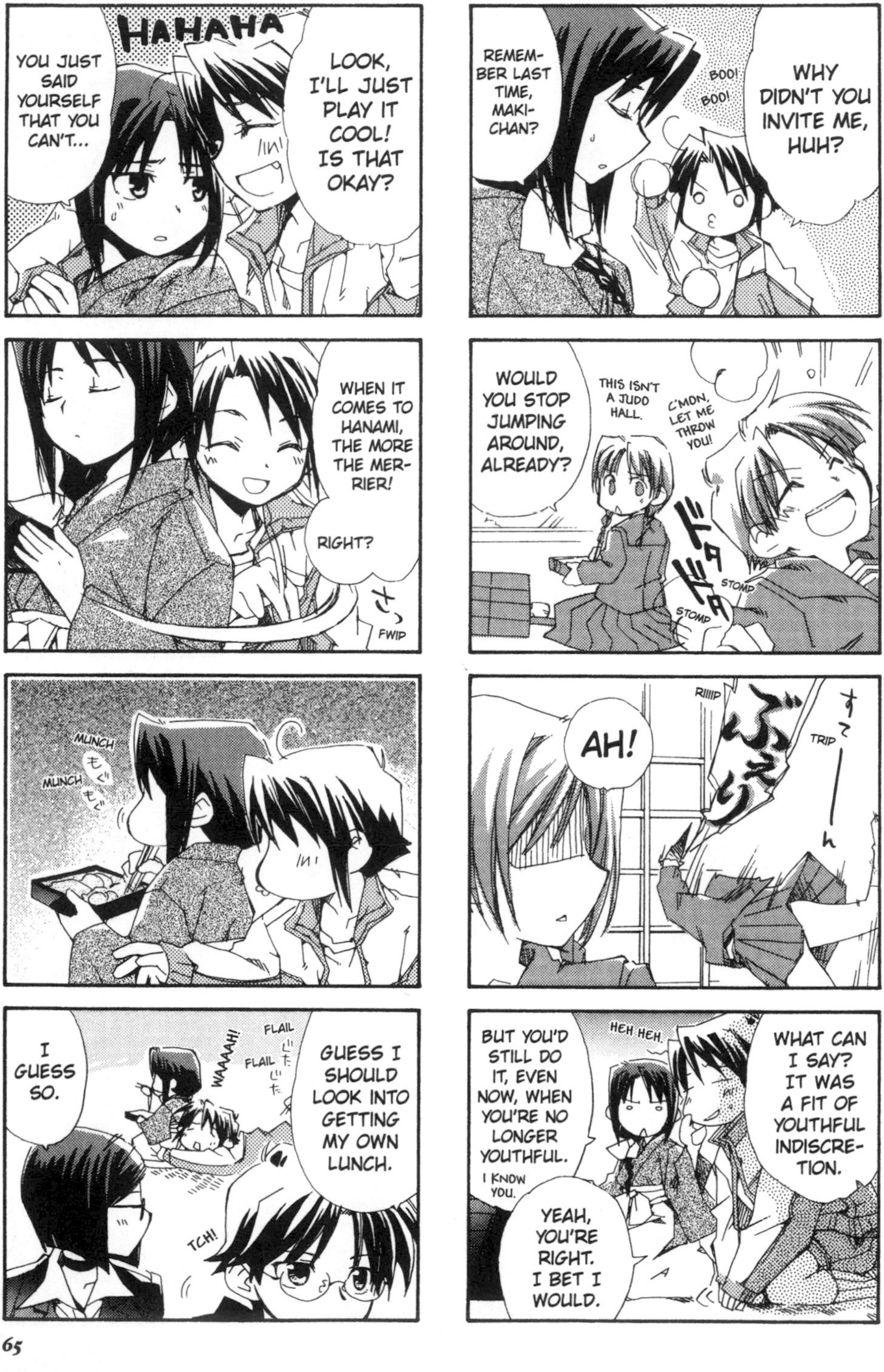
WHY DIDN'T YOU INVITE ME, HUH?
BOO!
BOO!
REMEMBER LAST TIME, MAKI-CHAN?
C'MON, LET ME THROW YOU!
STOMP
STOMP
THIS ISN'T A JUDO HALL.
WOULD YOU STOP JUMPING AROUND, ALREADY?
TRIP
RIIIP
AH!
WHAT CAN I SAY? IT WAS A FIT OF YOUTHFUL INDISCRETION.
HEH HEH.
BUT YOU'D STILL DO IT, EVEN NOW, WHEN YOU'RE NO LONGER YOUTHFUL.
I KNOW YOU.
YEAH, YOU'RE RIGHT. I BET I WOULD.
LOOK, I'LL JUST PLAY IT COOL! IS THAT OKAY?
HAHAHA
YOU JUST SAID YOURSELF THAT YOU CAN'T...
WHEN IT COMES TO HANAMI, THE MORE THE MERRIER!
RIGHT?
FWIP
MUNCH
MUNCH
GUESS I SHOULD LOOK INTO GETTING MY OWN LUNCH.
FLAIL
FLAIL
WAAAAH!
I GUESS SO.
TCH!

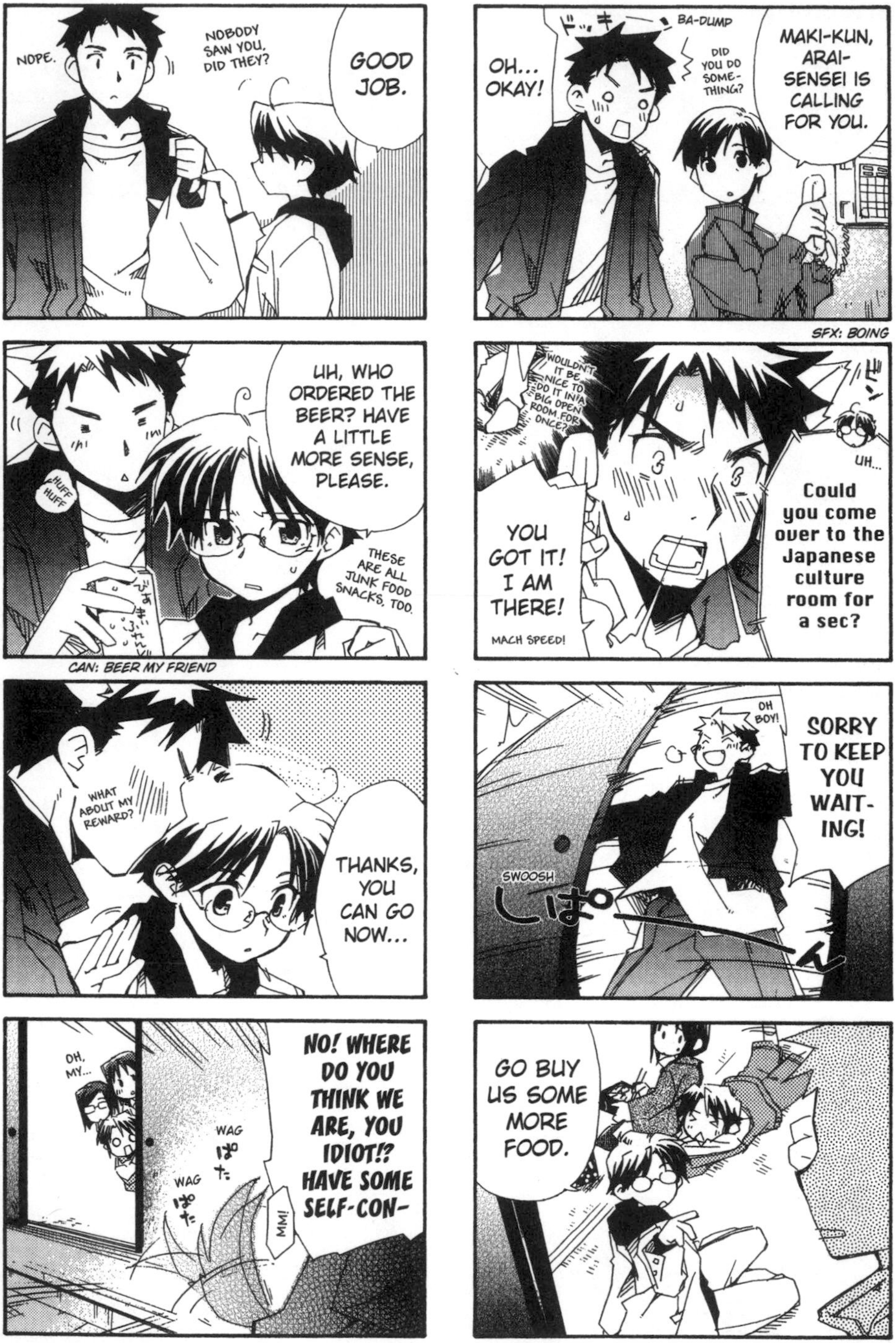
MAKI-KUN, ARAI-SENSEI IS CALLING FOR YOU.
DID YOU DO SOME-THING?
BA-DUMP
ドッキ
OH... OKAY!
SFX: BOING
Could you come over to the Japanese culture room for a sec?
UH...
WOULDN'T IT BE NICE TO DO IT IN A BIG OPEN ROOM FOR ONCE?
YOU GOT IT! I AM THERE!
MACH SPEED!
SORRY TO KEEP YOU WAIT-ING!
OH BOY!
SWOOSH
しぱ―――ん
GO BUY US SOME MORE FOOD.
GOOD JOB.
NOBODY SAW YOU, DID THEY?
NOPE.
UH, WHO ORDERED THE BEER? HAVE A LITTLE MORE SENSE, PLEASE.
THESE ARE ALL JUNK FOOD SNACKS, TOO.
HUFF HUFF
CAN: BEER MY FRIEND
THANKS, YOU CAN GO NOW...
WHAT ABOUT MY REWARD?
NO! WHERE DO YOU THINK WE ARE, YOU IDIOT!? HAVE SOME SELF-CON-
MM!
WAG ぱた
WAG ぱた
OH, MY...

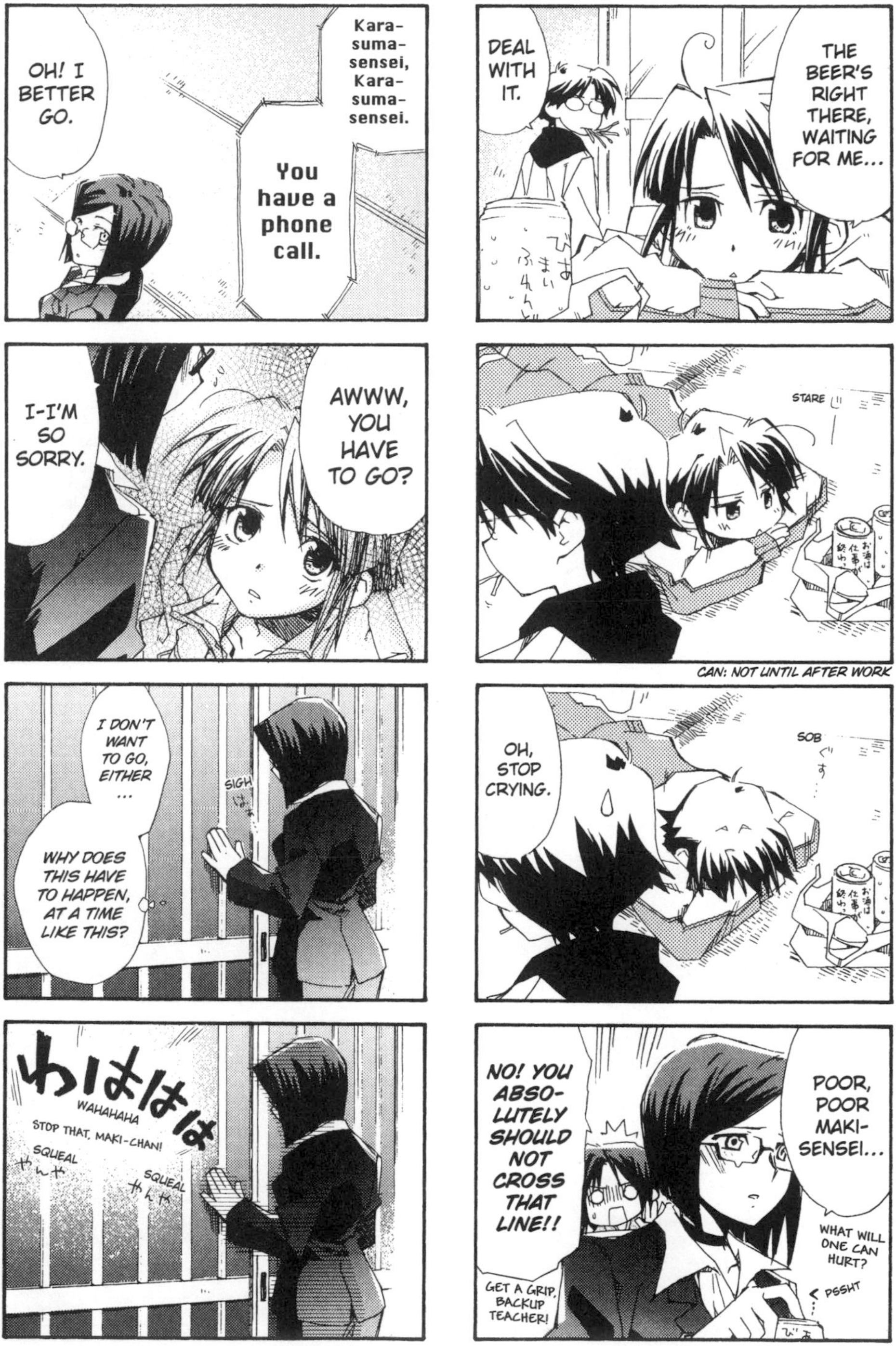
THE BEER'S RIGHT THERE, WAITING FOR ME...
DEAL WITH IT.
STARE
CAN: NOT UNTIL AFTER WORK
SOB
OH, STOP CRYING.
POOR, POOR MAKI-SENSEI...
WHAT WILL ONE CAN HURT?
PSSHT
NO! YOU ABSOLUTELY SHOULD NOT CROSS THAT LINE!!
GET A GRIP, BACKUP TEACHER!
Kara-suma-sensei, Kara-suma-sensei.
You have a phone call.
OH! I BETTER GO.
AWWW, YOU HAVE TO GO?
I-I'M SO SORRY.
I DON'T WANT TO GO, EITHER...
WHY DOES THIS HAVE TO HAPPEN, AT A TIME LIKE THIS?
SIGH
わははは
WAHAHAHA
STOP THAT, MAKI-CHAN!
SQUEAL
やんや
SQUEAL
やんや

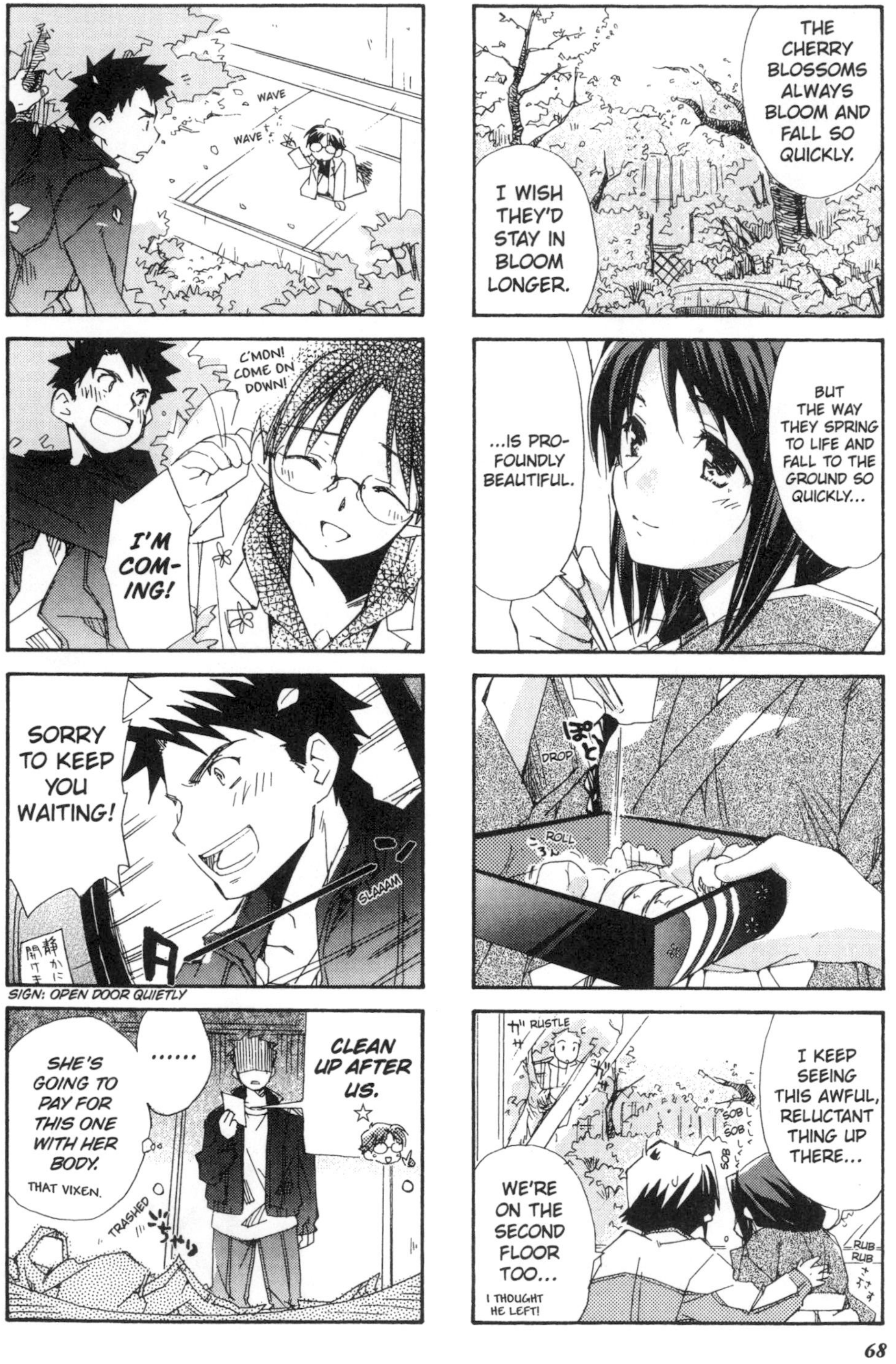
THE CHERRY BLOSSOMS ALWAYS BLOOM AND FALL SO QUICKLY.
I WISH THEY'D STAY IN BLOOM LONGER.
BUT THE WAY THEY SPRING TO LIFE AND FALL TO THE GROUND SO QUICKLY...
...IS PRO-FOUNDLY BEAUTIFUL.
ぽと
DROP
ROLL
ころん
ガ RUSTLE
I KEEP SEEING THIS AWFUL, RELUCTANT THING UP THERE...
SOB SOB しくしく
SOB
WE'RE ON THE SECOND FLOOR TOO...
I THOUGHT HE LEFT!
RUB RUB
WAVE
WAVE
C'MON! COME ON DOWN!
I'M COMING!
SORRY TO KEEP YOU WAITING!
SLAAAM
静かに開けま
SIGN: OPEN DOOR QUIETLY
CLEAN UP AFTER US. ☆
......
SHE'S GOING TO PAY FOR THIS ONE WITH HER BODY.
THAT VIXEN.
TRASHED

YUKO NAGUMO

CLASS: LANGUAGE TEACHER
GENDER: FEMALE
PERSONALITY: GLUTTON
LEVEL: 3

E: HAKAMA
E: SHINMEIKAI JAPANESE DICTIONARY, 4TH ED.
E: MULTI-LEVEL BENTO
E: MATERIAL MEMO

(SKIN) HEALTH POINTS: PUFFY
MENTAL POINTS: THE FU SYMBOL
STRENGTH: GETS IT DONE WITH ATTITUDE
SPEED: EARLY PRINTING DISCOUNT
STAMINA: ALL ABOUT ENERGY DRINKS
INTELLIGENCE: MASTER OF IMAGINATION
LUCK: PLEASE TRY AGAIN
GUTS: GETS IT DONE

Y: NO ADDITIONAL INCOME

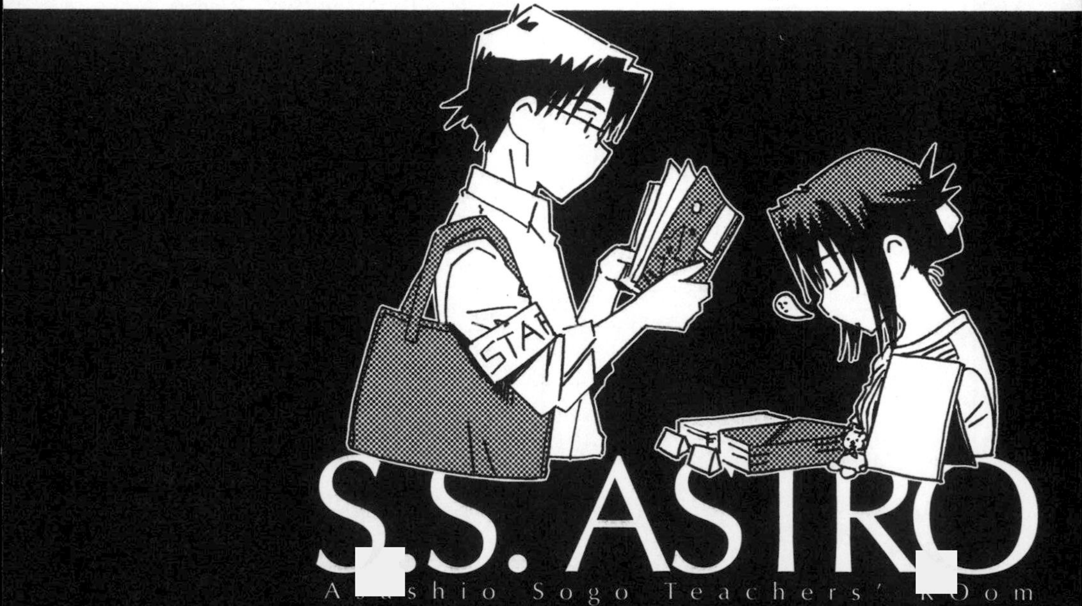
STAF
S.S. ASTRO
A[redacted]shio Sogo Teachers'[redacted]Oom

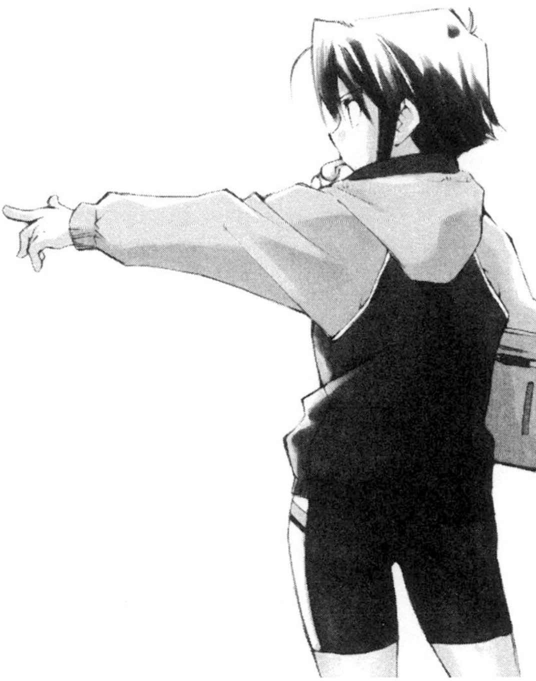

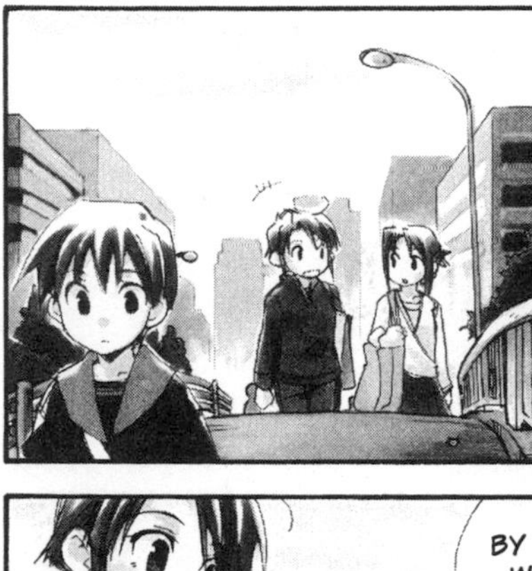

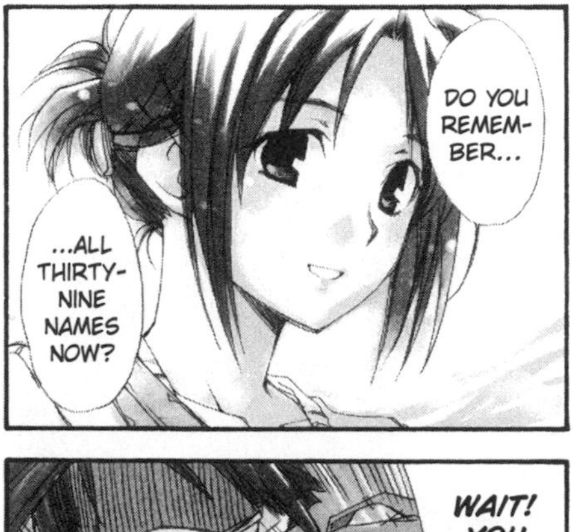
DO YOU REMEMBER...
...ALL THIRTY-NINE NAMES NOW?

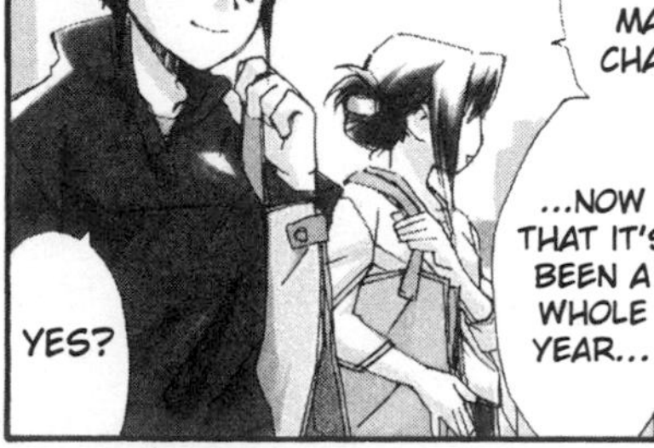
BY THE WAY, MAKI-CHAN...
...NOW THAT IT'S BEEN A WHOLE YEAR...
YES?

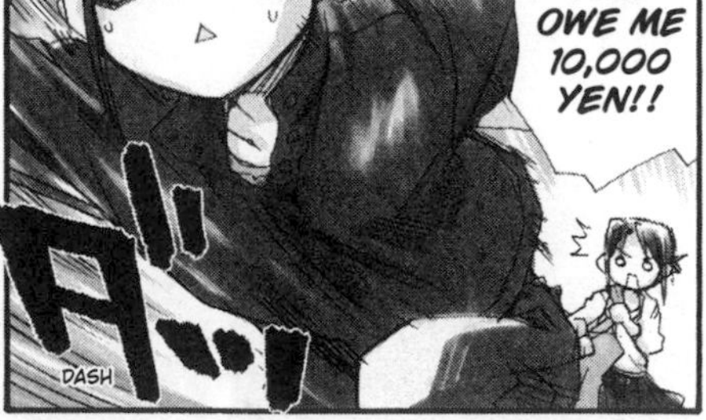
WAIT! YOU OWE ME 10,000 YEN!!
DASH

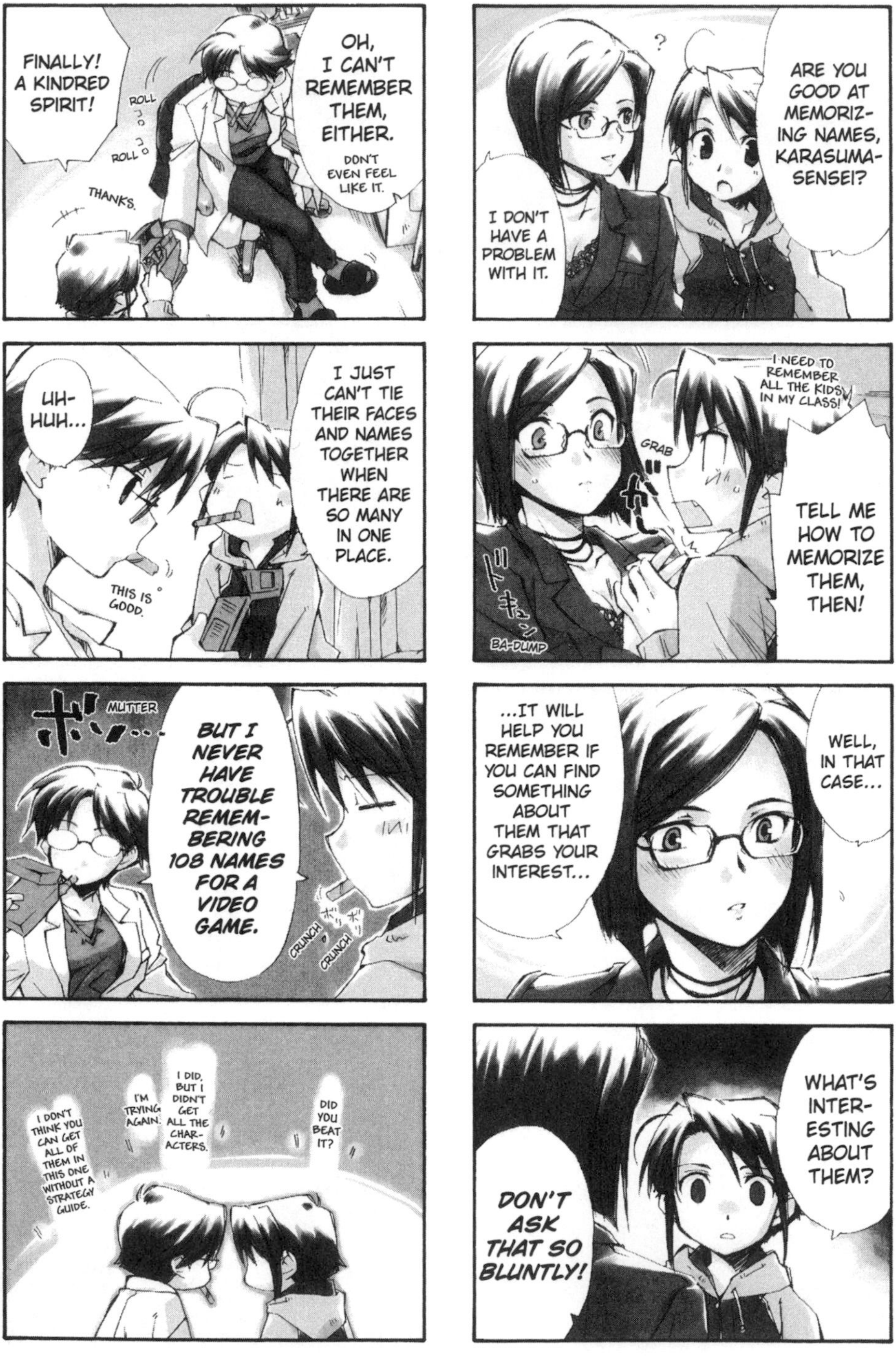
ARE YOU GOOD AT MEMORIZING NAMES, KARASUMA-SENSEI?
I DON'T HAVE A PROBLEM WITH IT.
OH, I CAN'T REMEMBER THEM, EITHER.
DON'T EVEN FEEL LIKE IT.
FINALLY! A KINDRED SPIRIT!
ROLL
ROLL
THANKS.
I NEED TO REMEMBER ALL THE KIDS IN MY CLASS!
GRAB
TELL ME HOW TO MEMORIZE THEM, THEN!
BA-DUMP
I JUST CAN'T TIE THEIR FACES AND NAMES TOGETHER WHEN THERE ARE SO MANY IN ONE PLACE.
UH-HUH...
THIS IS GOOD.
WELL, IN THAT CASE...
...IT WILL HELP YOU REMEMBER IF YOU CAN FIND SOMETHING ABOUT THEM THAT GRABS YOUR INTEREST...
MUTTER
BUT I NEVER HAVE TROUBLE REMEMBERING 108 NAMES FOR A VIDEO GAME.
CRUNCH
CRUNCH
WHAT'S INTERESTING ABOUT THEM?
DON'T ASK THAT SO BLUNTLY!
DID YOU BEAT IT?
I DID, BUT I DIDN'T GET ALL THE CHARACTERS.
I'M TRYING AGAIN.
I DON'T THINK YOU CAN GET ALL OF THEM IN THIS ONE WITHOUT A STRATEGY GUIDE.

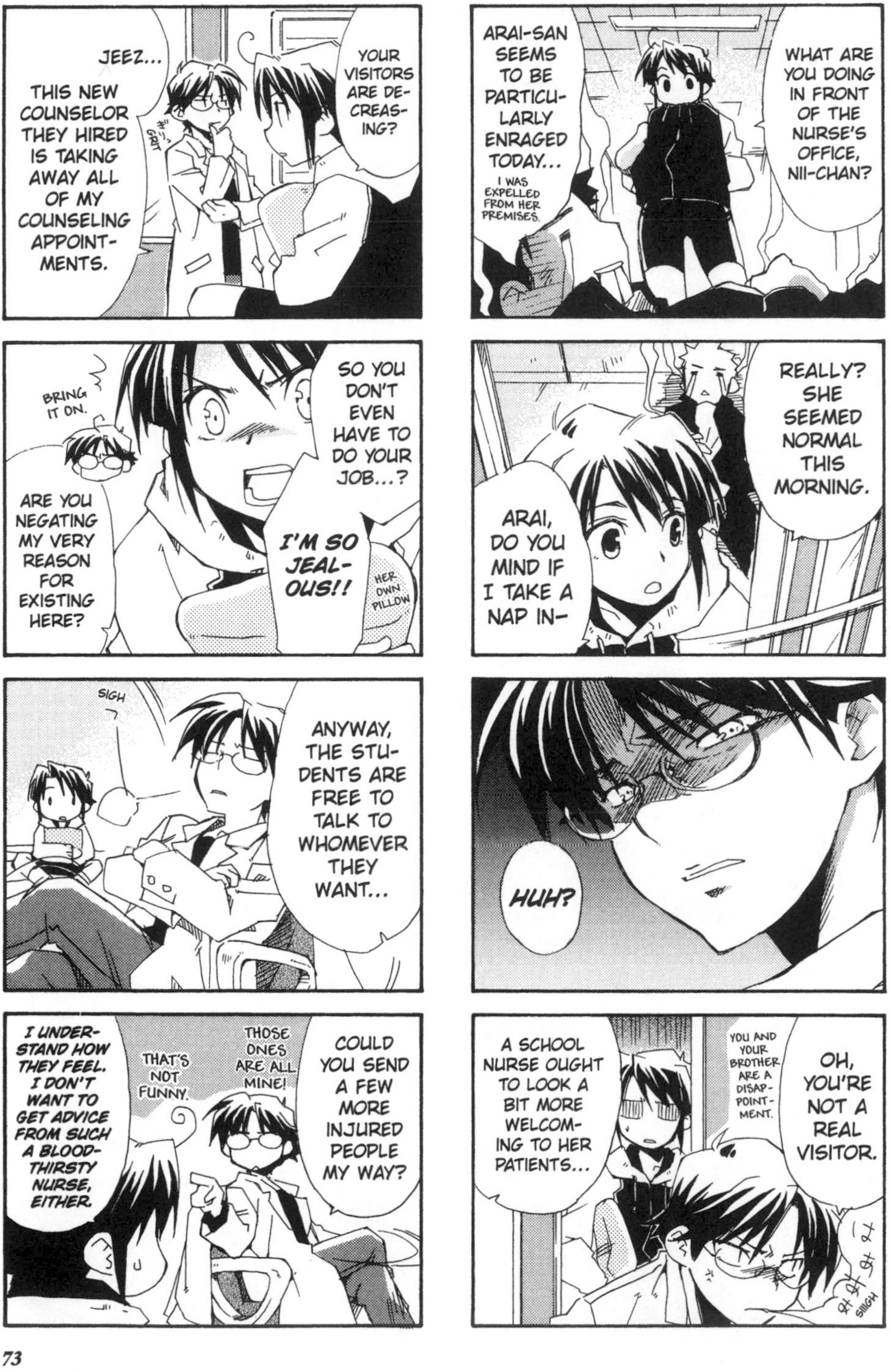
WHAT ARE YOU DOING IN FRONT OF THE NURSE'S OFFICE, NII-CHAN?
ARAI-SAN SEEMS TO BE PARTICULARLY ENRAGED TODAY...
I WAS EXPELLED FROM HER PREMISES.
REALLY? SHE SEEMED NORMAL THIS MORNING.
ARAI, DO YOU MIND IF I TAKE A NAP IN-
HUH?
OH, YOU'RE NOT A REAL VISITOR.
YOU AND YOUR BROTHER ARE A DISAPPOINTMENT.
A SCHOOL NURSE OUGHT TO LOOK A BIT MORE WELCOMING TO HER PATIENTS...
SIIIGH
YOUR VISITORS ARE DECREASING?
JEEZ... THIS NEW COUNSELOR THEY HIRED IS TAKING AWAY ALL OF MY COUNSELING APPOINTMENTS.
GRIT
SO YOU DON'T EVEN HAVE TO DO YOUR JOB...?
BRING IT ON.
ARE YOU NEGATING MY VERY REASON FOR EXISTING HERE?
I'M SO JEALOUS!!
HER OWN PILLOW
ANYWAY, THE STUDENTS ARE FREE TO TALK TO WHOMEVER THEY WANT...
SIGH
COULD YOU SEND A FEW MORE INJURED PEOPLE MY WAY?
THOSE ONES ARE ALL MINE!
THAT'S NOT FUNNY.
I UNDERSTAND HOW THEY FEEL. I DON'T WANT TO GET ADVICE FROM SUCH A BLOODTHIRSTY NURSE, EITHER.

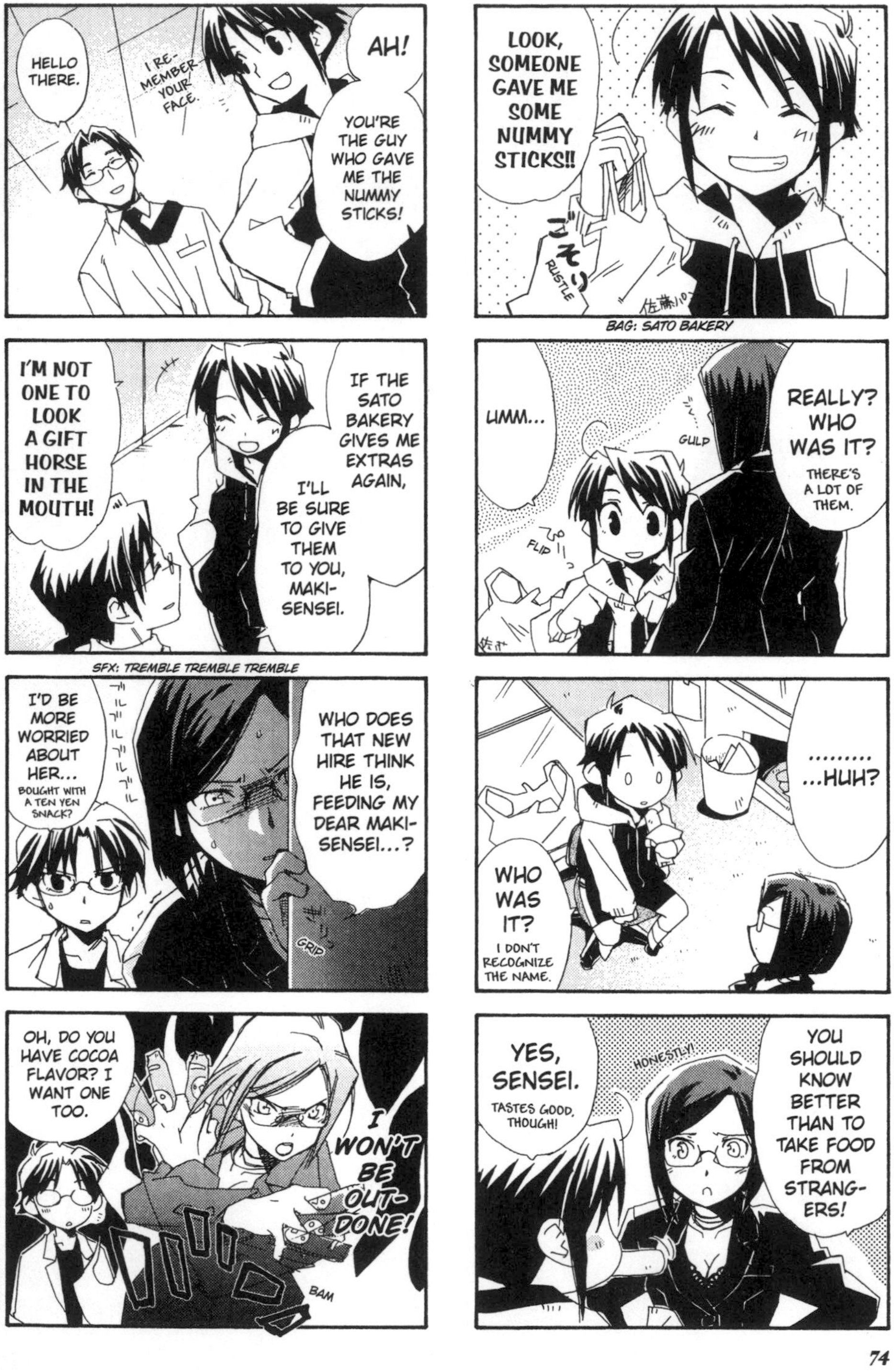
LOOK, SOMEONE GAVE ME SOME NUMMY STICKS!!
RUSTLE
BAG: SATO BAKERY
REALLY? WHO WAS IT?
THERE'S A LOT OF THEM.
GULP
UMM...
FLIP
....HUH?
WHO WAS IT?
I DON'T RECOGNIZE THE NAME.
YOU SHOULD KNOW BETTER THAN TO TAKE FOOD FROM STRANG-ERS!
HONESTLY!
YES, SENSEI.
TASTES GOOD, THOUGH!
AH!
YOU'RE THE GUY WHO GAVE ME THE NUMMY STICKS!
I RE-MEMBER YOUR FACE.
HELLO THERE.
IF THE SATO BAKERY GIVES ME EXTRAS AGAIN,
I'LL BE SURE TO GIVE THEM TO YOU, MAKI-SENSEI.
I'M NOT ONE TO LOOK A GIFT HORSE IN THE MOUTH!
SFX: TREMBLE TREMBLE TREMBLE
WHO DOES THAT NEW HIRE THINK HE IS, FEEDING MY DEAR MAKI-SENSEI...?
GRIP
I'D BE MORE WORRIED ABOUT HER...
BOUGHT WITH A TEN YEN SNACK?
I WON'T BE OUT-DONE!
BAM
OH, DO YOU HAVE COCOA FLAVOR? I WANT ONE TOO.

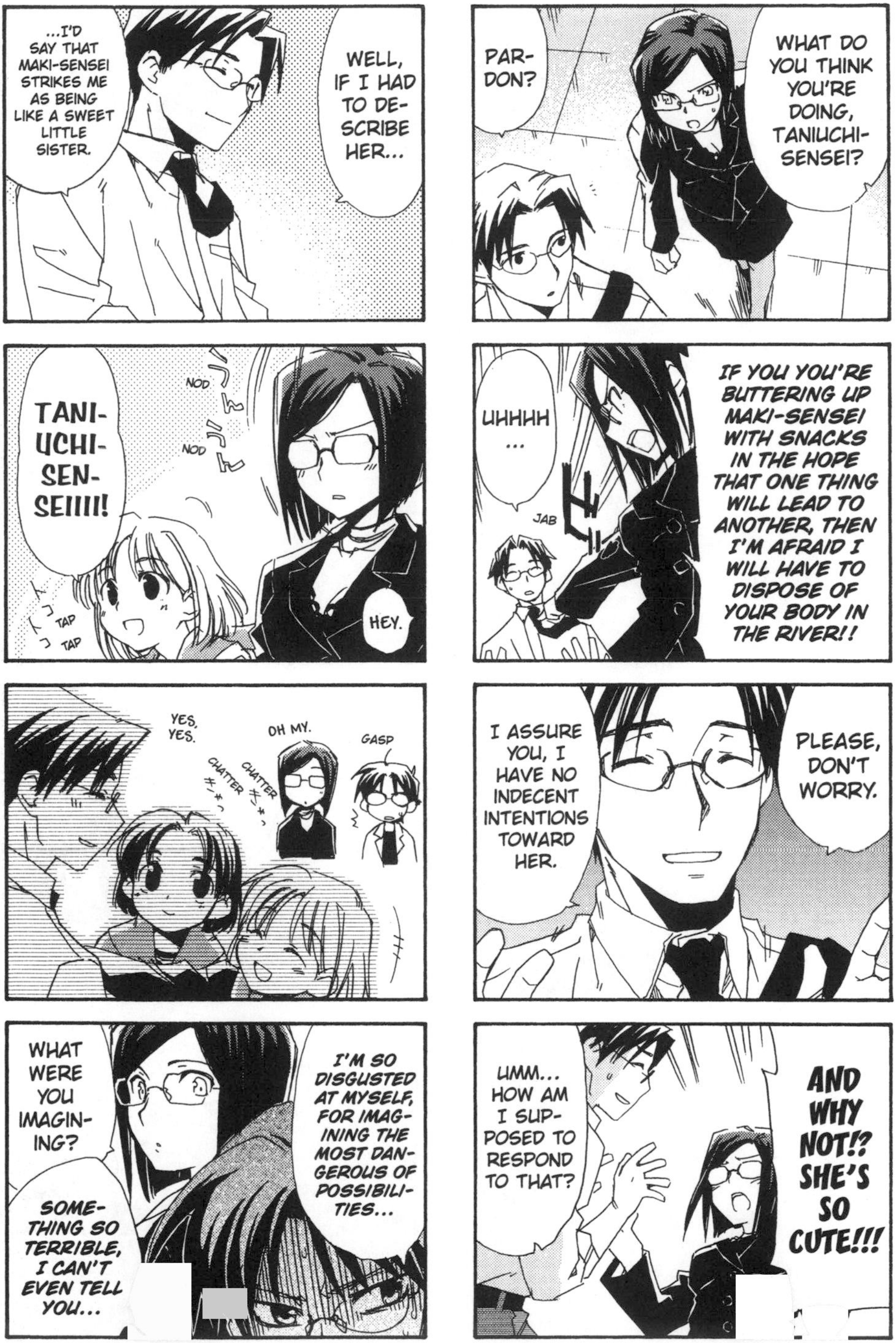
WHAT DO YOU THINK YOU'RE DOING, TANIUCHI-SENSEI?
PAR-DON?
IF YOU YOU'RE BUTTERING UP MAKI-SENSEI WITH SNACKS IN THE HOPE THAT ONE THING WILL LEAD TO ANOTHER, THEN I'M AFRAID I WILL HAVE TO DISPOSE OF YOUR BODY IN THE RIVER!!
UHHHH ...
JAB
PLEASE, DON'T WORRY.
I ASSURE YOU, I HAVE NO INDECENT INTENTIONS TOWARD HER.
AND WHY NOT!? SHE'S SO CUTE!!!
UMM... HOW AM I SUP-POSED TO RESPOND TO THAT?
WELL, IF I HAD TO DE-SCRIBE HER...
...I'D SAY THAT MAKI-SENSEI STRIKES ME AS BEING LIKE A SWEET LITTLE SISTER.
NOD
NOD
TANI-UCHI-SEN-SEIIIII!
HEY.
TAP
TAP
GASP
OH MY.
CHATTER
CHATTER
YES, YES.
I'M SO DISGUSTED AT MYSELF, FOR IMAGIN-ING THE MOST DAN-GEROUS OF POSSIBILI-TIES...
WHAT WERE YOU IMAGIN-ING?
SOME-THING SO TERRIBLE, I CAN'T EVEN TELL YOU...

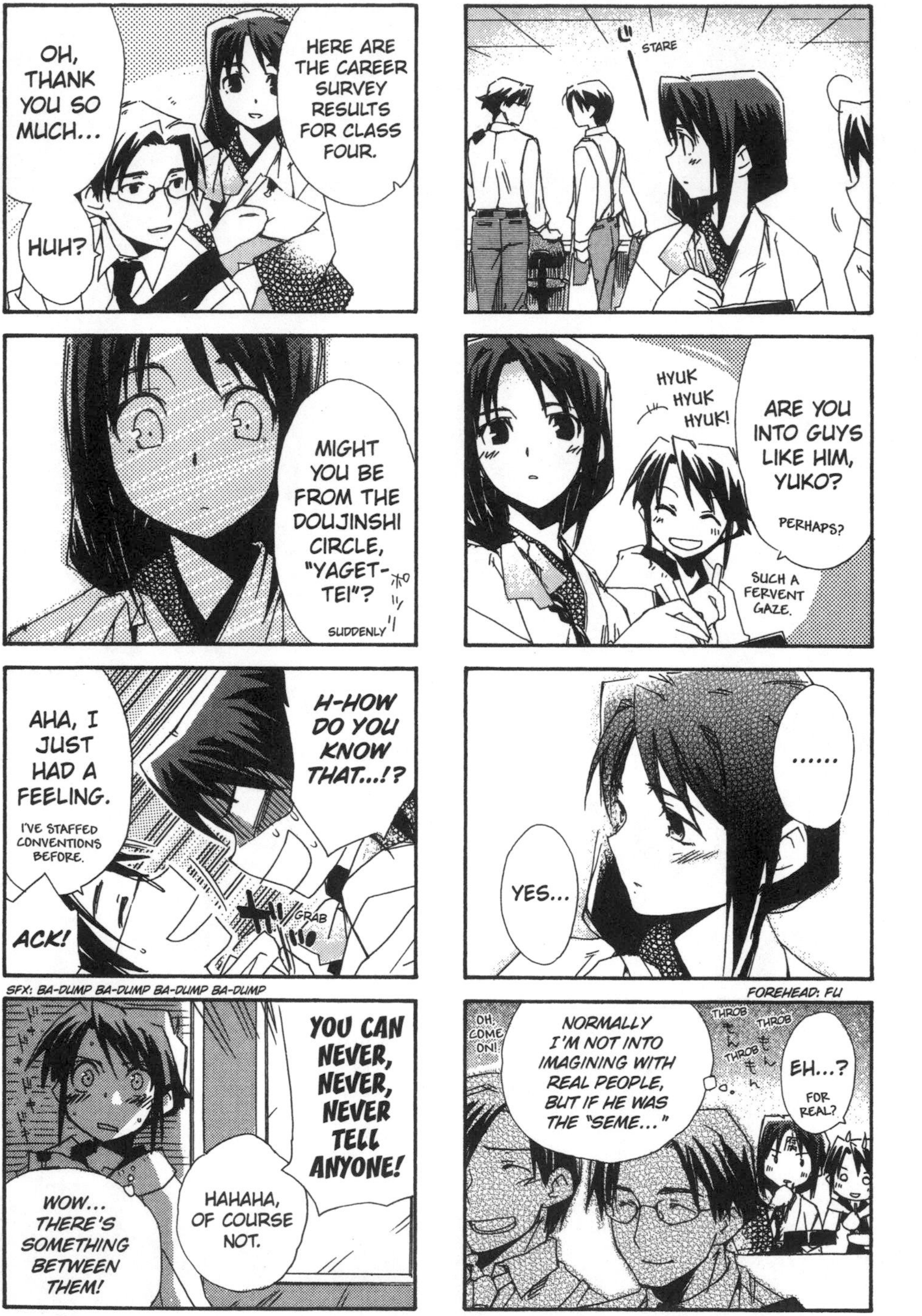

STARE
HYUK HYUK HYUK!
ARE YOU INTO GUYS LIKE HIM, YUKO?
PERHAPS?
SUCH A FERVENT GAZE.
......
YES...
FOREHEAD: FU
EH...?
FOR REAL?
THROB THROB THROB
NORMALLY I'M NOT INTO IMAGINING WITH REAL PEOPLE, BUT IF HE WAS THE "SEME..."
OH, COME ON!
HERE ARE THE CAREER SURVEY RESULTS FOR CLASS FOUR.
OH, THANK YOU SO MUCH...
HUH?
MIGHT YOU BE FROM THE DOUJINSHI CIRCLE, "YAGET-TEI"?
SUDDENLY
H-HOW DO YOU KNOW THAT...!?
AHA, I JUST HAD A FEELING.
I'VE STAFFED CONVENTIONS BEFORE.
GRAB
ACK!
SFX: BA-DUMP BA-DUMP BA-DUMP BA-DUMP
YOU CAN NEVER, NEVER, NEVER TELL ANYONE!
HAHAHA, OF COURSE NOT.
WOW... THERE'S SOMETHING BETWEEN THEM!

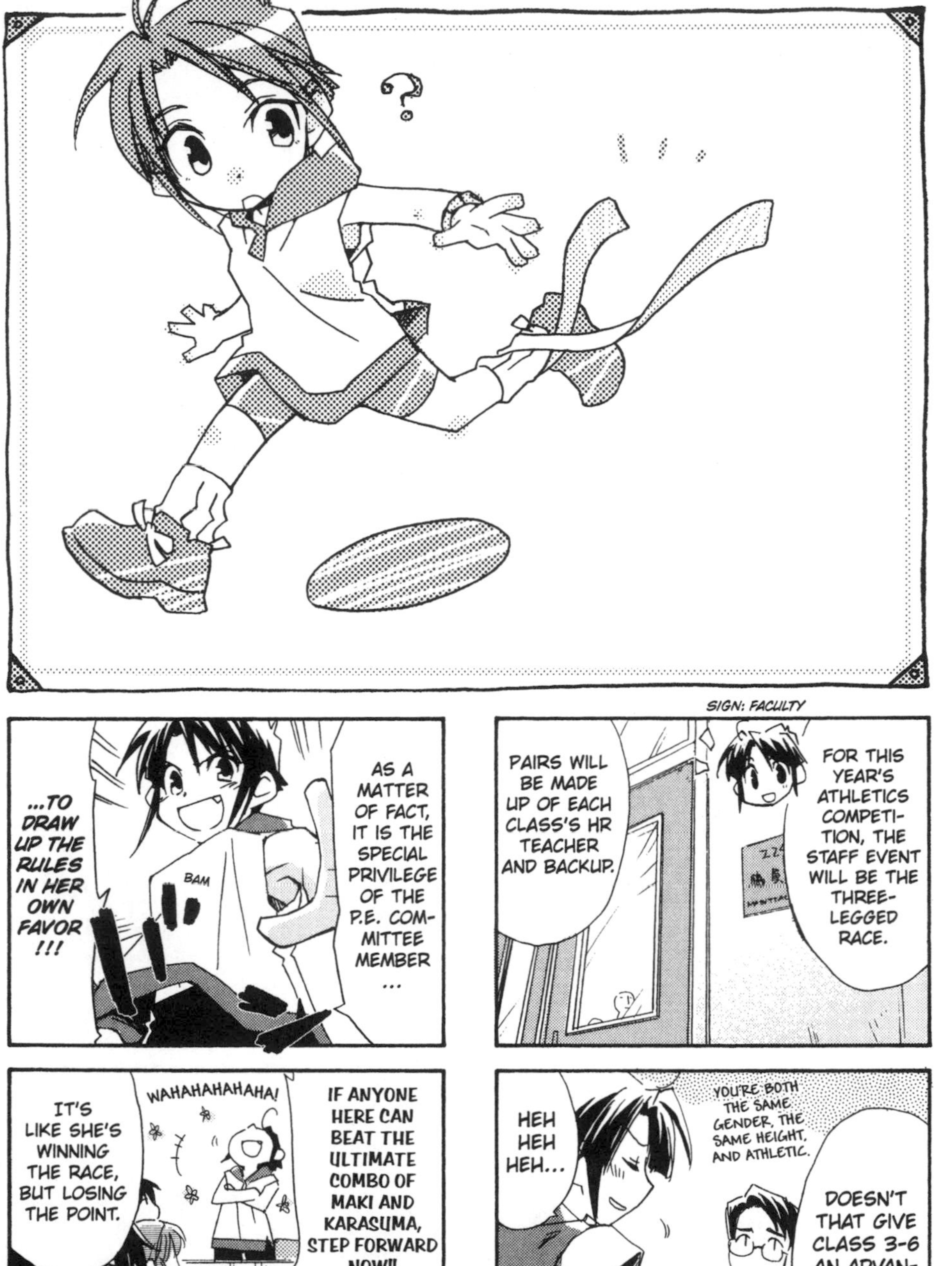
?
SIGN: FACULTY
FOR THIS YEAR'S ATHLETICS COMPETITION, THE STAFF EVENT WILL BE THE THREE-LEGGED RACE.
PAIRS WILL BE MADE UP OF EACH CLASS'S HR TEACHER AND BACKUP.
AS A MATTER OF FACT, IT IS THE SPECIAL PRIVILEGE OF THE P.E. COMMITTEE MEMBER...
BAM
...TO DRAW UP THE RULES IN HER OWN FAVOR!!!
DOESN'T THAT GIVE CLASS 3-6 AN ADVANTAGE OVER EVERYONE ELSE?
YOU'RE BOTH THE SAME GENDER, THE SAME HEIGHT, AND ATHLETIC.
HEH HEH HEH...
IF ANYONE HERE CAN BEAT THE ULTIMATE COMBO OF MAKI AND KARASUMA, STEP FORWARD NOW!!
WAHAHAHAHAHA!
IT'S LIKE SHE'S WINNING THE RACE, BUT LOSING THE POINT.
YOU'RE RIGHT.

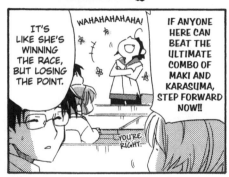

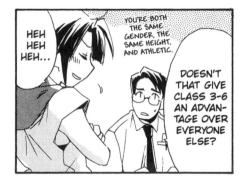

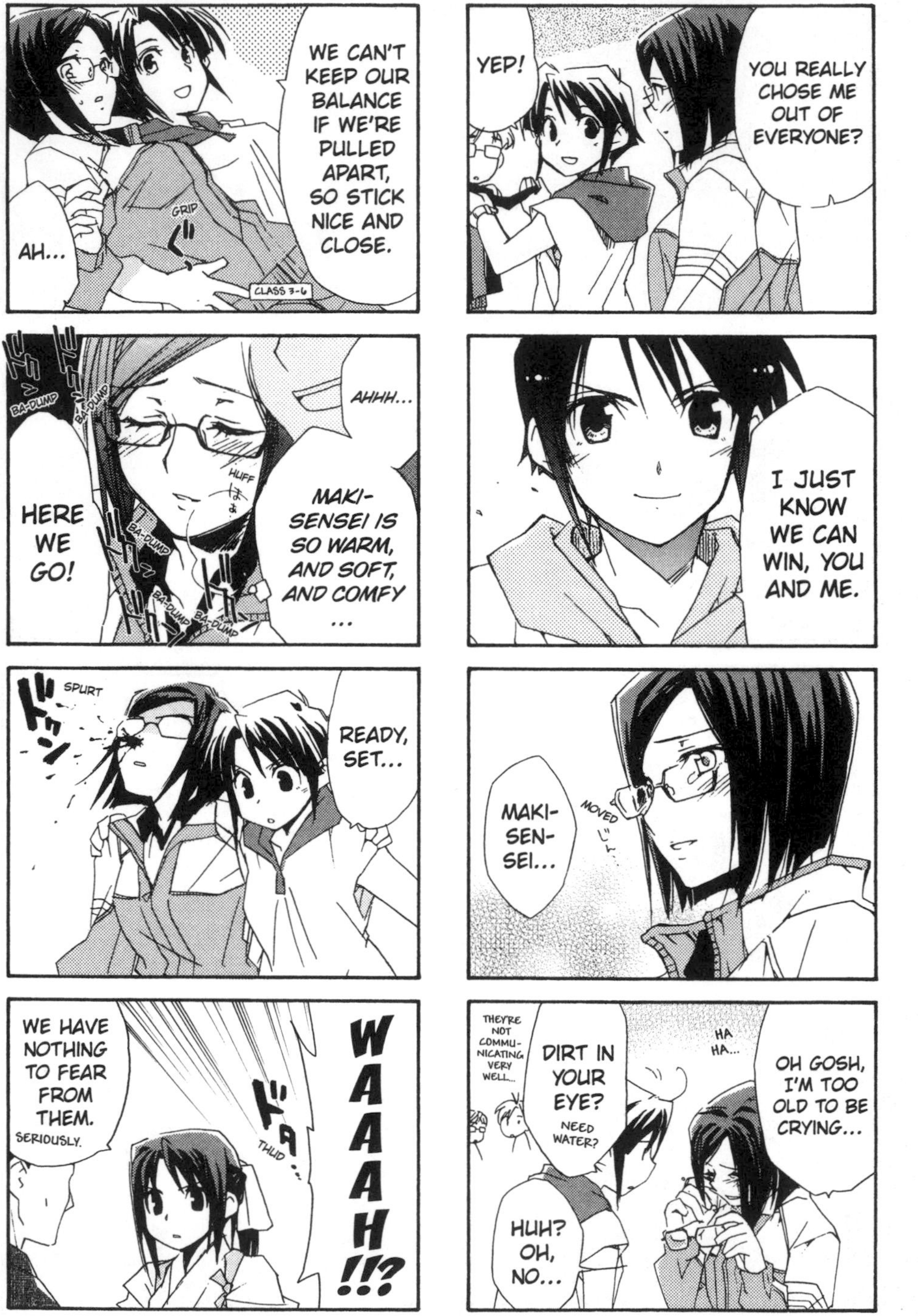
YOU REALLY CHOSE ME OUT OF EVERYONE?
YEP!
I JUST KNOW WE CAN WIN, YOU AND ME.
MAKI-SEN-SEI...
MOVED
OH GOSH, I'M TOO OLD TO BE CRYING...
HA HA...
DIRT IN YOUR EYE?
NEED WATER?
THEY'RE NOT COMMUNICATING VERY WELL...
HUH? OH, NO...
WE CAN'T KEEP OUR BALANCE IF WE'RE PULLED APART, SO STICK NICE AND CLOSE.
GRIP
CLASS 3-6
AH...
AHHH...
MAKI-SENSEI IS SO WARM, AND SOFT, AND COMFY ...
HUFF
BA-DUMP
BA-DUMP
BA-DUMP
BA-DUMP
BA-DUMP
HERE WE GO!
READY, SET...
SPURT
WAAAAH!!?
THUD
WE HAVE NOTHING TO FEAR FROM THEM.
SERIOUSLY.

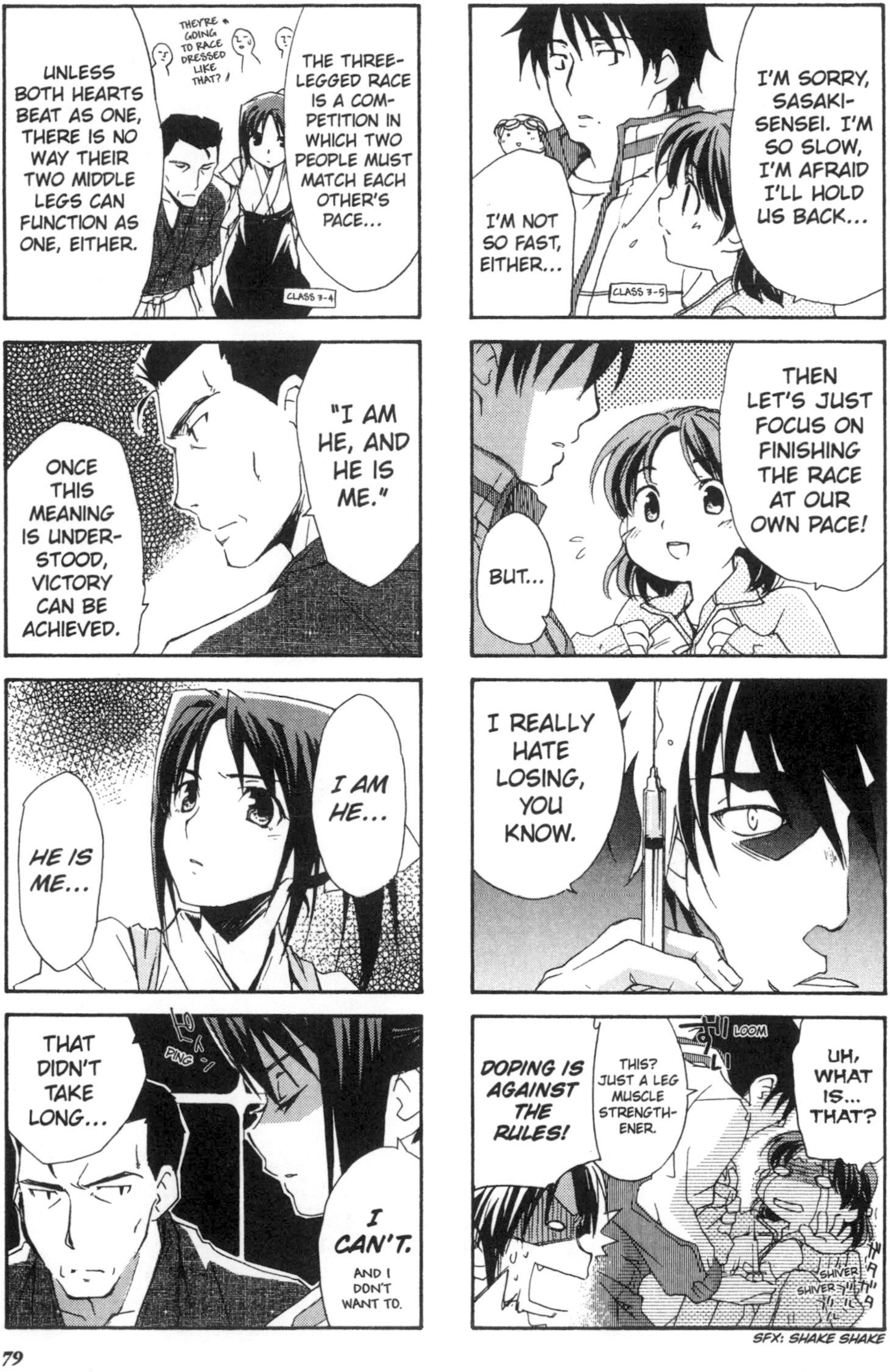
I'M SORRY, SASAKI-SENSEI. I'M SO SLOW, I'M AFRAID I'LL HOLD US BACK...
I'M NOT SO FAST, EITHER...
CLASS 3-5
THEN LET'S JUST FOCUS ON FINISHING THE RACE AT OUR OWN PACE!
BUT...
I REALLY HATE LOSING, YOU KNOW.
UH, WHAT IS... THAT?
LOOM
THIS? JUST A LEG MUSCLE STRENGTHENER.
DOPING IS AGAINST THE RULES!
SHIVER
SHIVER
THE THREE-LEGGED RACE IS A COMPETITION IN WHICH TWO PEOPLE MUST MATCH EACH OTHER'S PACE...
THEY'RE GOING TO RACE DRESSED LIKE THAT?
UNLESS BOTH HEARTS BEAT AS ONE, THERE IS NO WAY THEIR TWO MIDDLE LEGS CAN FUNCTION AS ONE, EITHER.
CLASS 3-4
"I AM HE, AND HE IS ME."
ONCE THIS MEANING IS UNDERSTOOD, VICTORY CAN BE ACHIEVED.
I AM HE...
HE IS ME...
PING
THAT DIDN'T TAKE LONG...
I CAN'T.
AND I DON'T WANT TO.

SFX: SHAKE SHAKE

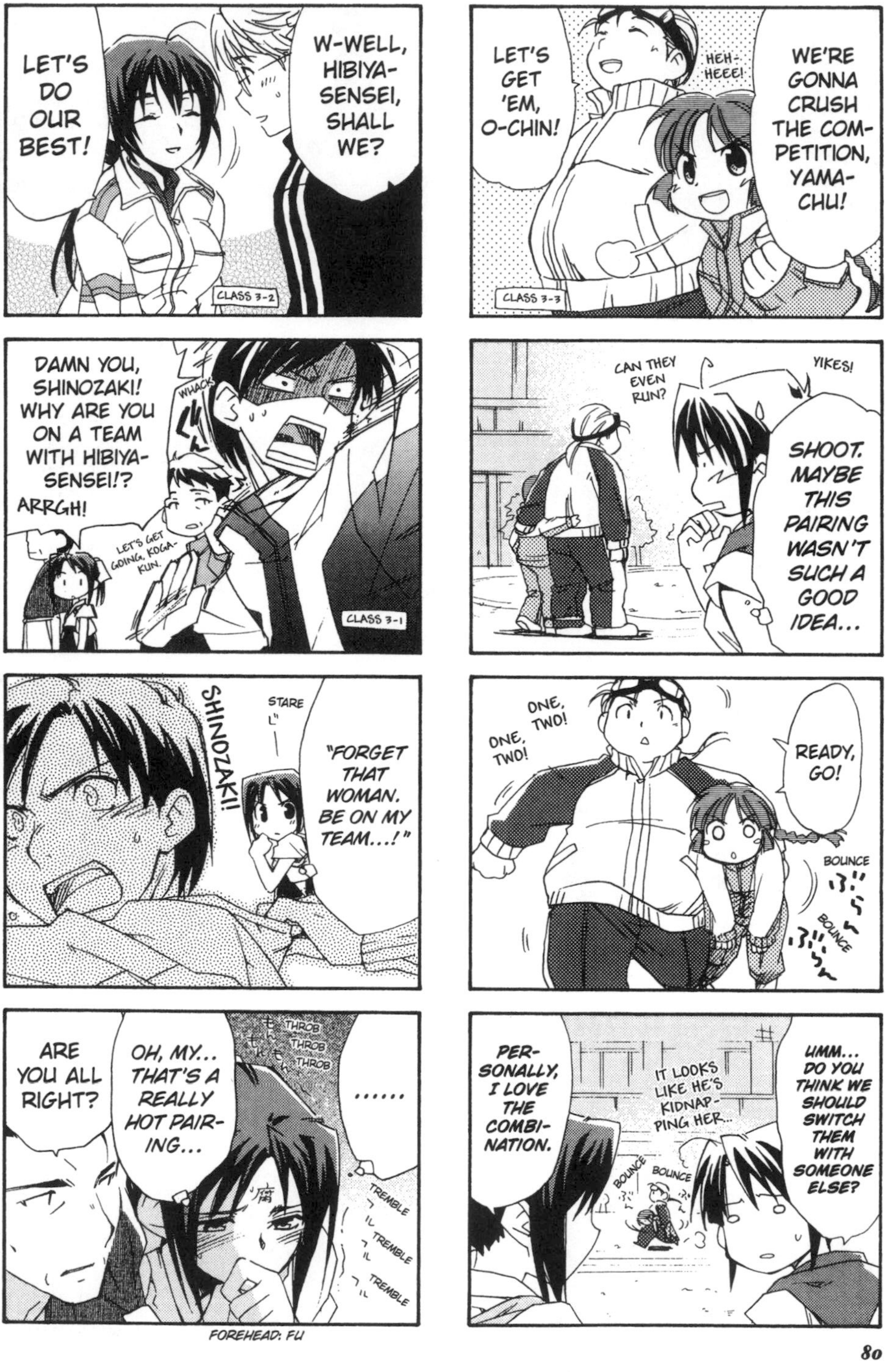
WE'RE GONNA CRUSH THE COMPETITION, YAMA-CHU!
HEH-HEEE!
LET'S GET 'EM, O-CHIN!
CLASS 3-3
YIKES!
SHOOT. MAYBE THIS PAIRING WASN'T SUCH A GOOD IDEA...
CAN THEY EVEN RUN?
READY, GO!
ONE, TWO!
ONE, TWO!
BOUNCE
BOUNCE
UMM... DO YOU THINK WE SHOULD SWITCH THEM WITH SOMEONE ELSE?
BOUNCE
BOUNCE
IT LOOKS LIKE HE'S KIDNAPPING HER...
PERSONALLY, I LOVE THE COMBINATION.
W-WELL, HIBIYA-SENSEI, SHALL WE?
LET'S DO OUR BEST!
CLASS 3-2
DAMN YOU, SHINOZAKI! WHY ARE YOU ON A TEAM WITH HIBIYA-SENSEI!?
WHACK
ARRGH!
LET'S GET GOING, KOGA-KUN.
CLASS 3-1
STARE
"FORGET THAT WOMAN. BE ON MY TEAM...!"
SHINOZAKI!!
......
THROB
THROB
THROB
OH, MY... THAT'S A REALLY HOT PAIRING...
ARE YOU ALL RIGHT?
TREMBLE
TREMBLE
TREMBLE

FOREHEAD: FU

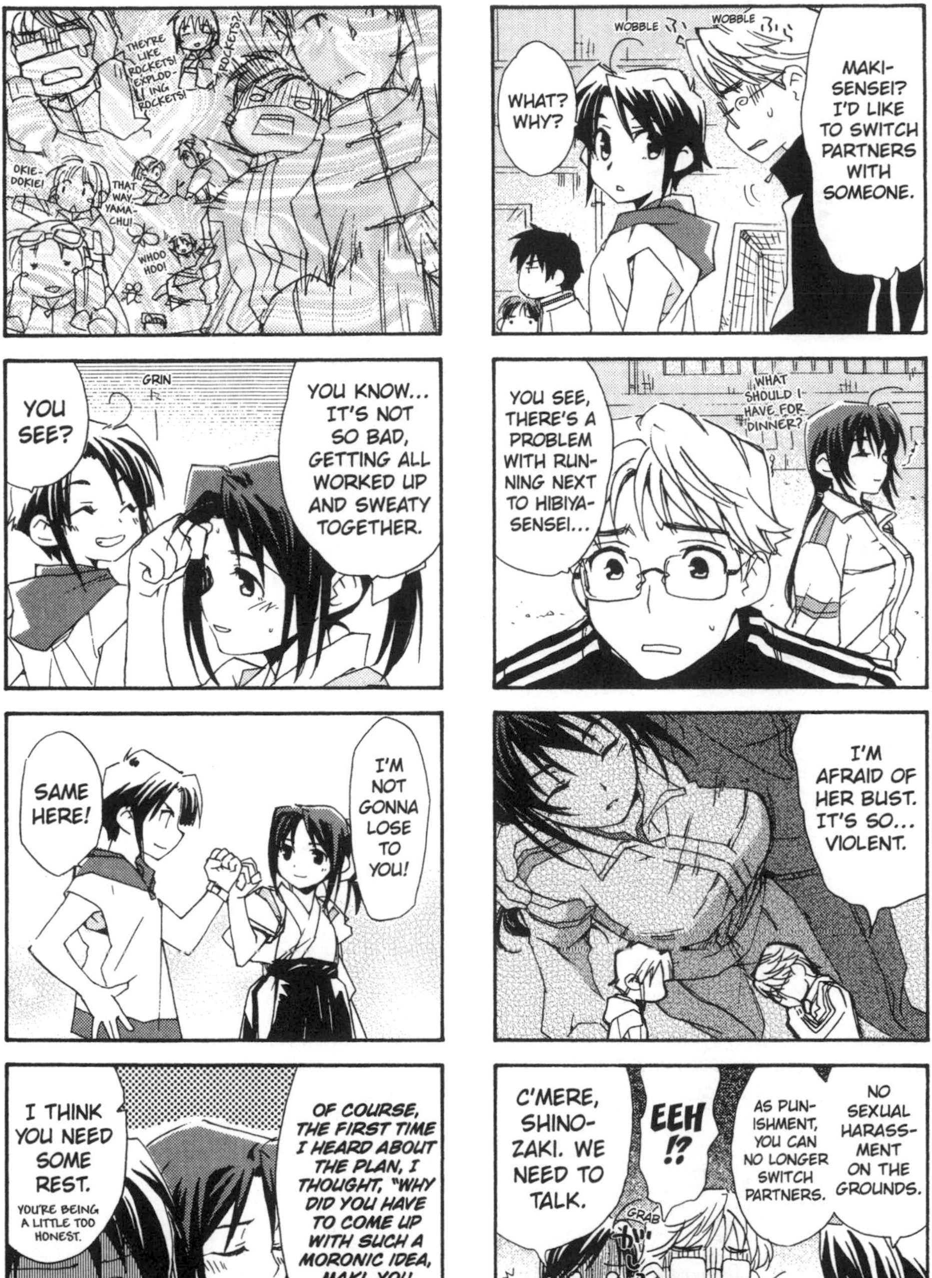
WOBBLE
WOBBLE
MAKI-SENSEI? I'D LIKE TO SWITCH PARTNERS WITH SOMEONE.
WHAT? WHY?
WHAT SHOULD I HAVE FOR DINNER?
YOU SEE, THERE'S A PROBLEM WITH RUNNING NEXT TO HIBIYA-SENSEI...
I'M AFRAID OF HER BUST. IT'S SO... VIOLENT.
NO SEXUAL HARASSMENT ON THE GROUNDS.
AS PUNISHMENT, YOU CAN NO LONGER SWITCH PARTNERS.
EEH !?
C'MERE, SHINOZAKI. WE NEED TO TALK.
GRAB
UWAAAH!
ROCKETS?
THEY'RE LIKE ROCKETS! EXPLODING ROCKETS!
THAT WAY, YAMA-CHU!
OKIE-DOKIE!
WHOO HOO!
YOU KNOW... IT'S NOT SO BAD, GETTING ALL WORKED UP AND SWEATY TOGETHER.
GRIN
YOU SEE?
I'M NOT GONNA LOSE TO YOU!
SAME HERE!
OF COURSE, THE FIRST TIME I HEARD ABOUT THE PLAN, I THOUGHT, "WHY DID YOU HAVE TO COME UP WITH SUCH A MORONIC IDEA, MAKI, YOU GODDAMN IDIOT?"
SIGH
I THINK YOU NEED SOME REST.
YOU'RE BEING A LITTLE TOO HONEST.

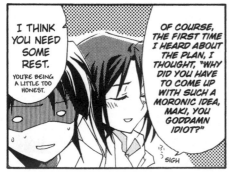

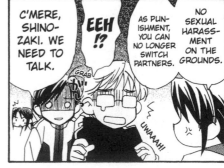

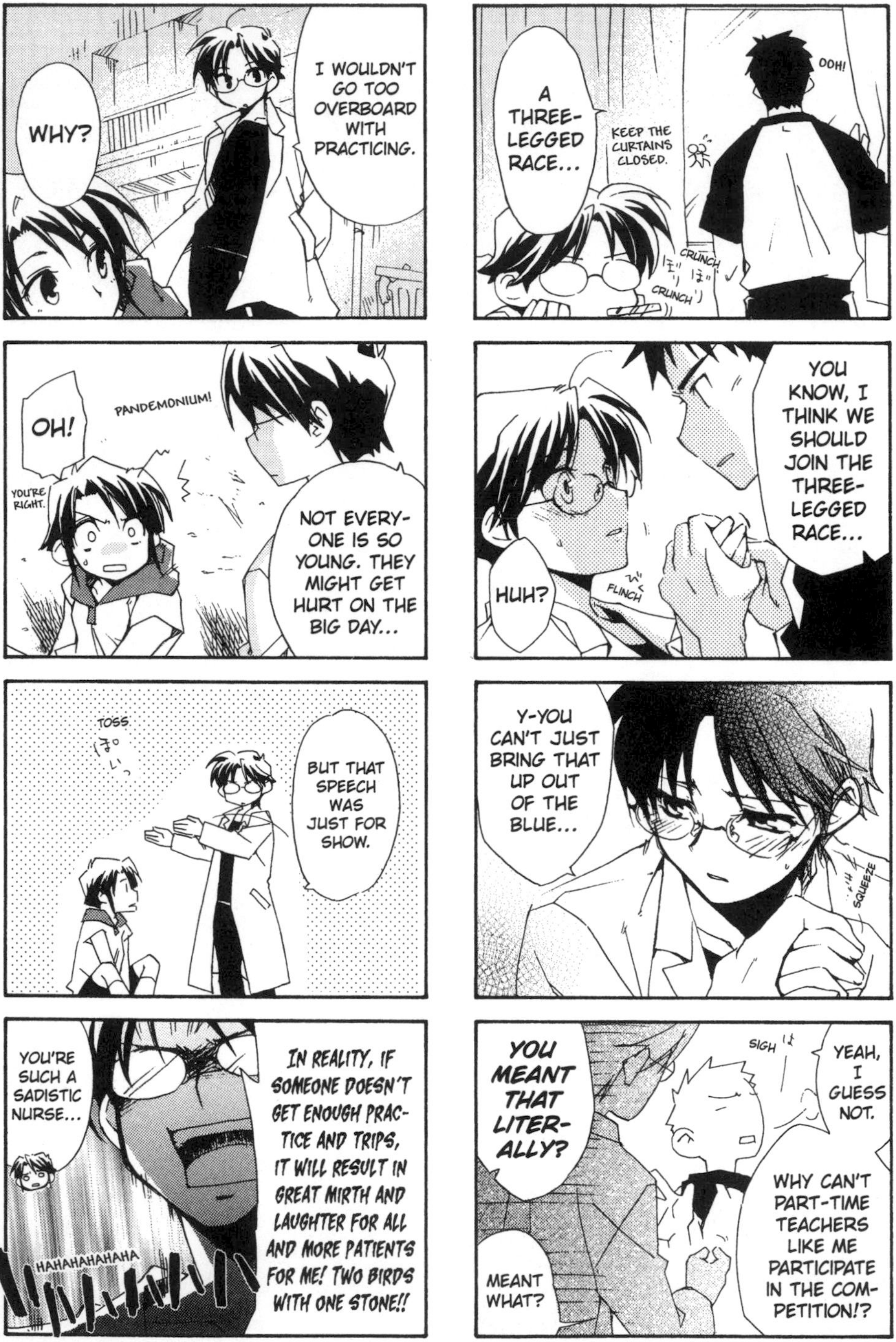
OOH!
A THREE-LEGGED RACE...
KEEP THE CURTAINS CLOSED.
CRUNCH
CRUNCH
YOU KNOW, I THINK WE SHOULD JOIN THE THREE-LEGGED RACE...
FLINCH
HUH?
Y-YOU CAN'T JUST BRING THAT UP OUT OF THE BLUE...
SQUEEZE
YEAH, I GUESS NOT.
SIGH
YOU MEANT THAT LITERALLY?
WHY CAN'T PART-TIME TEACHERS LIKE ME PARTICIPATE IN THE COMPETITION!?
MEANT WHAT?
I WOULDN'T GO TOO OVERBOARD WITH PRACTICING.
WHY?
PANDEMONIUM!
NOT EVERYONE IS SO YOUNG. THEY MIGHT GET HURT ON THE BIG DAY...
OH!
YOU'RE RIGHT.
BUT THAT SPEECH WAS JUST FOR SHOW.
TOSS
IN REALITY, IF SOMEONE DOESN'T GET ENOUGH PRACTICE AND TRIPS, IT WILL RESULT IN GREAT MIRTH AND LAUGHTER FOR ALL AND MORE PATIENTS FOR ME! TWO BIRDS WITH ONE STONE!!
YOU'RE SUCH A SADISTIC NURSE...
HAHAHAHAHAHA

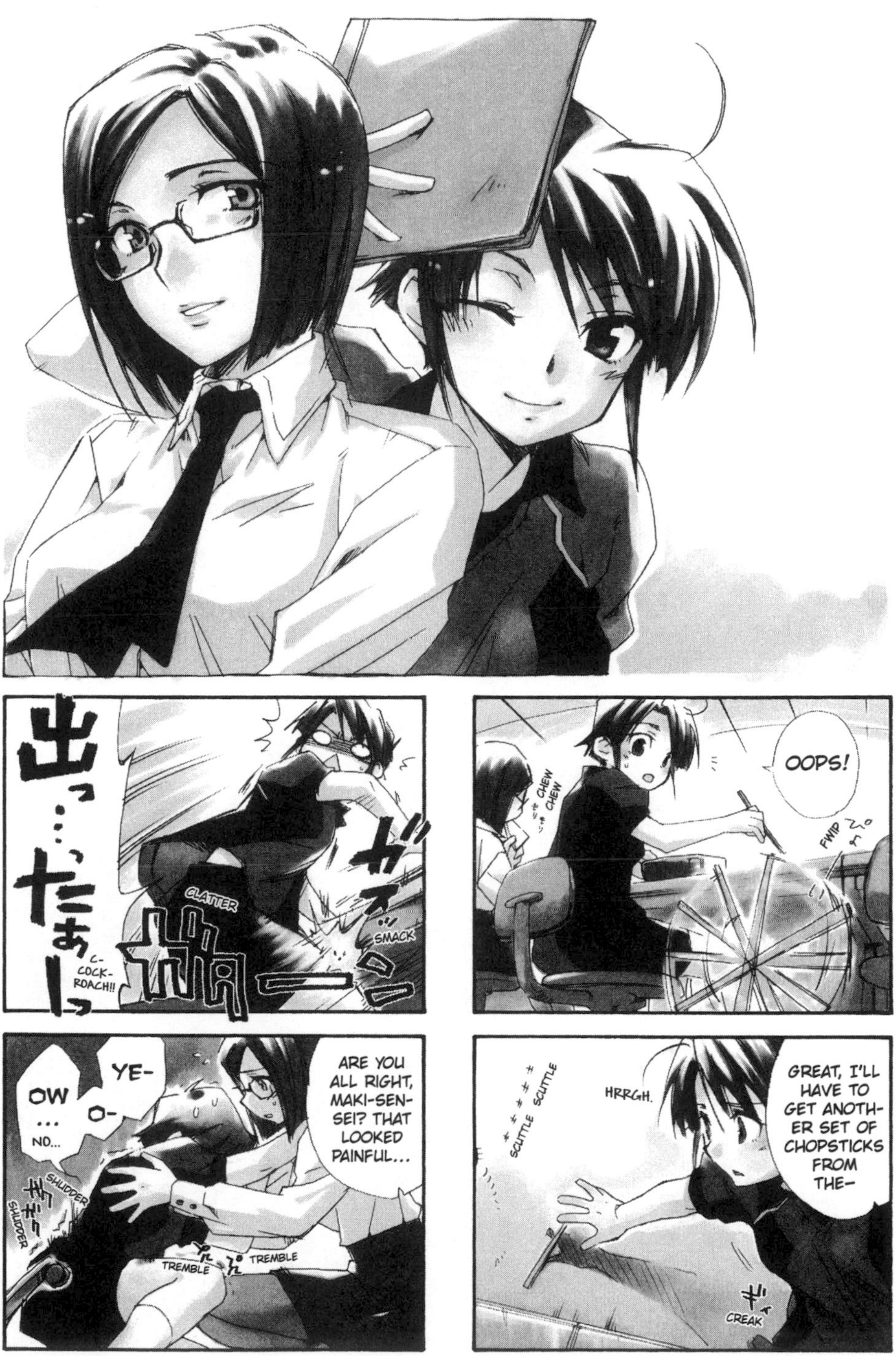

CHEW CHEW
OOPS!
FWIP
CLATTER
SMACK
C-COCK-ROACH!!
HRRGH.
GREAT, I'LL HAVE TO GET ANOTHER SET OF CHOPSTICKS FROM THE-
SCUTTLE SCUTTLE
CREAK
ARE YOU ALL RIGHT, MAKI-SENSEI? THAT LOOKED PAINFUL...
YE- O-
OW... NO...
SHUDDER SHUDDER
TREMBLE TREMBLE

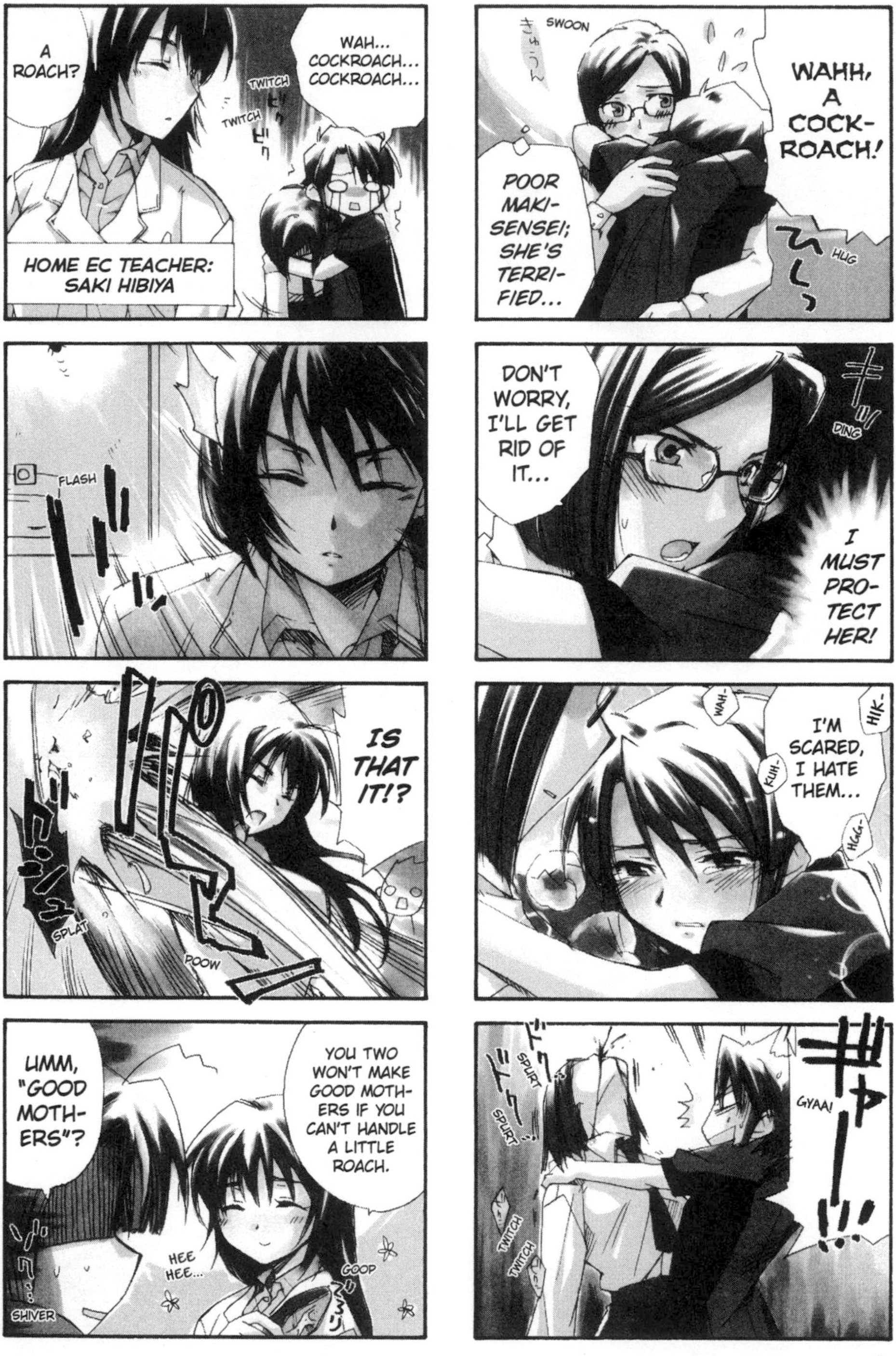
SWOON
WAHH, A COCKROACH!
POOR MAKI-SENSEI; SHE'S TERRIFIED...
HUG
DON'T WORRY, I'LL GET RID OF IT...
DING
I MUST PROTECT HER!
HIK-
I'M SCARED, I HATE THEM...
WAH-
KUH-
HGG-
GYAA!
SPURT
SPURT
TWITCH
TWITCH
A ROACH?
WAH... COCKROACH... COCKROACH...
TWITCH
TWITCH
HOME EC TEACHER: SAKI HIBIYA
FLASH
IS THAT IT!?
SPLAT
POOW
YOU TWO WON'T MAKE GOOD MOTHERS IF YOU CAN'T HANDLE A LITTLE ROACH.
UMM, "GOOD MOTHERS"?
HEE HEE...
GOOP
SHIVER

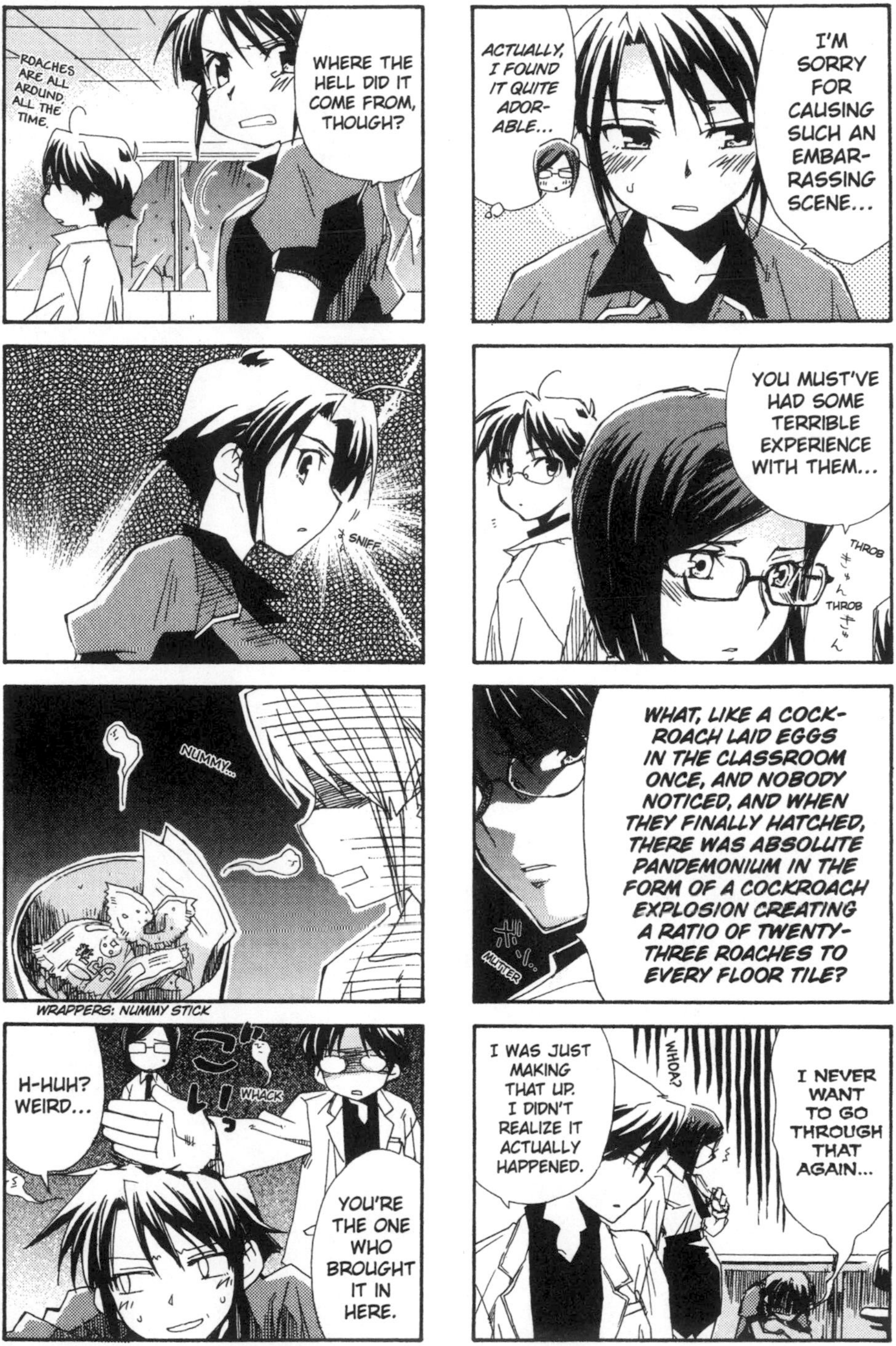
I'M SORRY FOR CAUSING SUCH AN EMBARRASSING SCENE...
ACTUALLY, I FOUND IT QUITE ADORABLE...
YOU MUST'VE HAD SOME TERRIBLE EXPERIENCE WITH THEM...
THROB
THROB
WHAT, LIKE A COCKROACH LAID EGGS IN THE CLASSROOM ONCE, AND NOBODY NOTICED, AND WHEN THEY FINALLY HATCHED, THERE WAS ABSOLUTE PANDEMONIUM IN THE FORM OF A COCKROACH EXPLOSION CREATING A RATIO OF TWENTY-THREE ROACHES TO EVERY FLOOR TILE?
MUTTER
I NEVER WANT TO GO THROUGH THAT AGAIN...
WHOA?
I WAS JUST MAKING THAT UP. I DIDN'T REALIZE IT ACTUALLY HAPPENED.
WHERE THE HELL DID IT COME FROM, THOUGH?
ROACHES ARE ALL AROUND ALL THE TIME.
SNIFF
NUMMY...
WRAPPERS: NUMMY STICK
WHACK
H-HUH? WEIRD...
YOU'RE THE ONE WHO BROUGHT IT IN HERE.

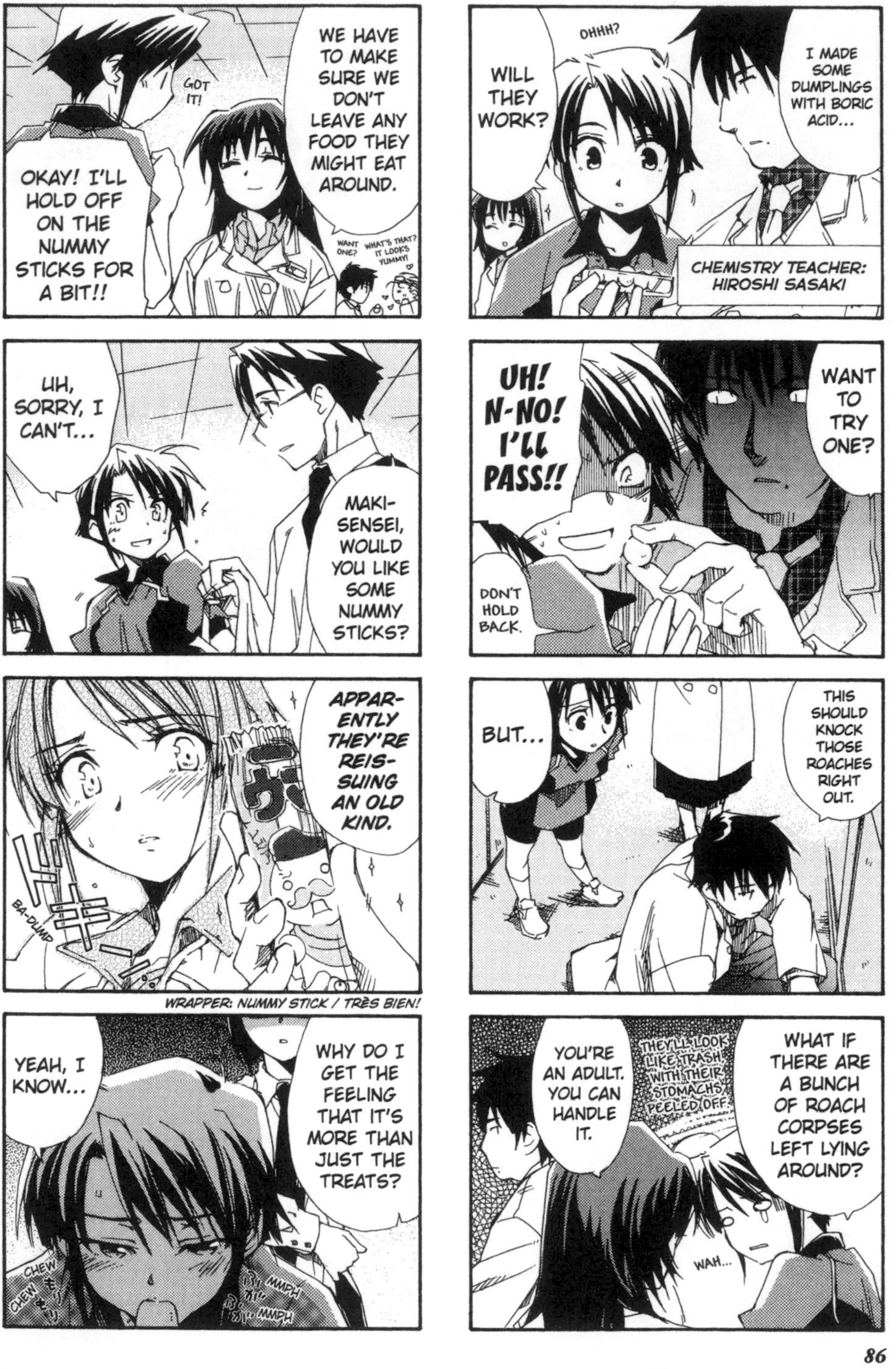
OHHH?
I MADE SOME DUMPLINGS WITH BORIC ACID...
WILL THEY WORK?
CHEMISTRY TEACHER: HIROSHI SASAKI
WANT TO TRY ONE?
UH! N-NO! I'LL PASS!!
DON'T HOLD BACK.
THIS SHOULD KNOCK THOSE ROACHES RIGHT OUT.
BUT...
WHAT IF THERE ARE A BUNCH OF ROACH CORPSES LEFT LYING AROUND?
THEY'LL LOOK LIKE TRASH WITH THEIR STOMACHS PEELED OFF.
YOU'RE AN ADULT. YOU CAN HANDLE IT.
WAH...
WE HAVE TO MAKE SURE WE DON'T LEAVE ANY FOOD THEY MIGHT EAT AROUND.
GOT IT!
OKAY! I'LL HOLD OFF ON THE NUMMY STICKS FOR A BIT!!
WHAT'S THAT? IT LOOKS YUMMY!
WANT ONE?
MAKI-SENSEI, WOULD YOU LIKE SOME NUMMY STICKS?
UH, SORRY, I CAN'T...
APPARENTLY THEY'RE REISSUING AN OLD KIND.
BA-DUMP
WRAPPER: NUMMY STICK / TRÈS BIEN!
WHY DO I GET THE FEELING THAT IT'S MORE THAN JUST THE TREATS?
YEAH, I KNOW...
MMPH MMPH
CHEW CHEW

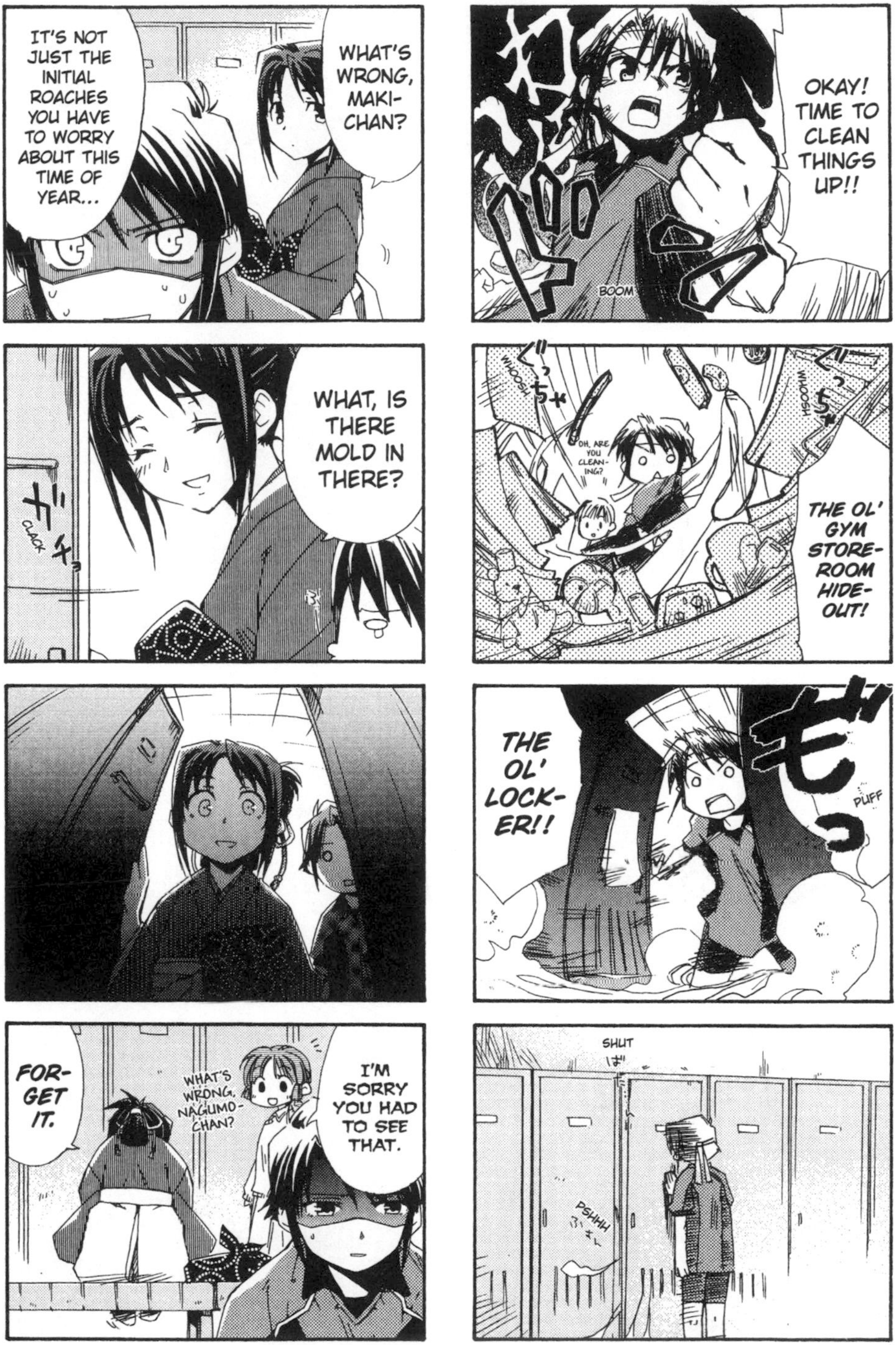
OKAY! TIME TO CLEAN THINGS UP!!
BOOM
WHOOSH
WHOOSH
OH, ARE YOU CLEANING?!
THE OL' GYM STOREROOM HIDEOUT!
THE OL' LOCKER!!
PUFF
SHUT
PSHHH
WHAT'S WRONG, MAKI-CHAN?
IT'S NOT JUST THE INITIAL ROACHES YOU HAVE TO WORRY ABOUT THIS TIME OF YEAR...
WHAT, IS THERE MOLD IN THERE?
CLACK
I'M SORRY YOU HAD TO SEE THAT.
WHAT'S WRONG, NAGUMO-CHAN?
FORGET IT.

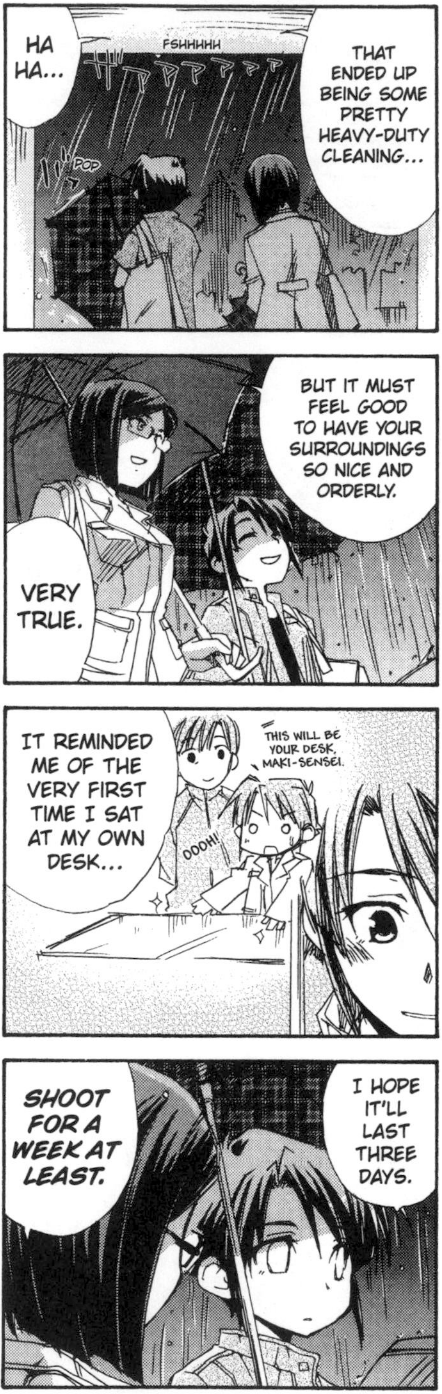
THAT ENDED UP BEING SOME PRETTY HEAVY-DUTY CLEANING...
FSHHHHH
HA HA...
POP
BUT IT MUST FEEL GOOD TO HAVE YOUR SURROUNDINGS SO NICE AND ORDERLY.
VERY TRUE.
THIS WILL BE YOUR DESK, MAKI-SENSEI.
IT REMINDED ME OF THE VERY FIRST TIME I SAT AT MY OWN DESK...
OOOH!
I HOPE IT'LL LAST THREE DAYS.
SHOOT FOR A WEEK AT LEAST.
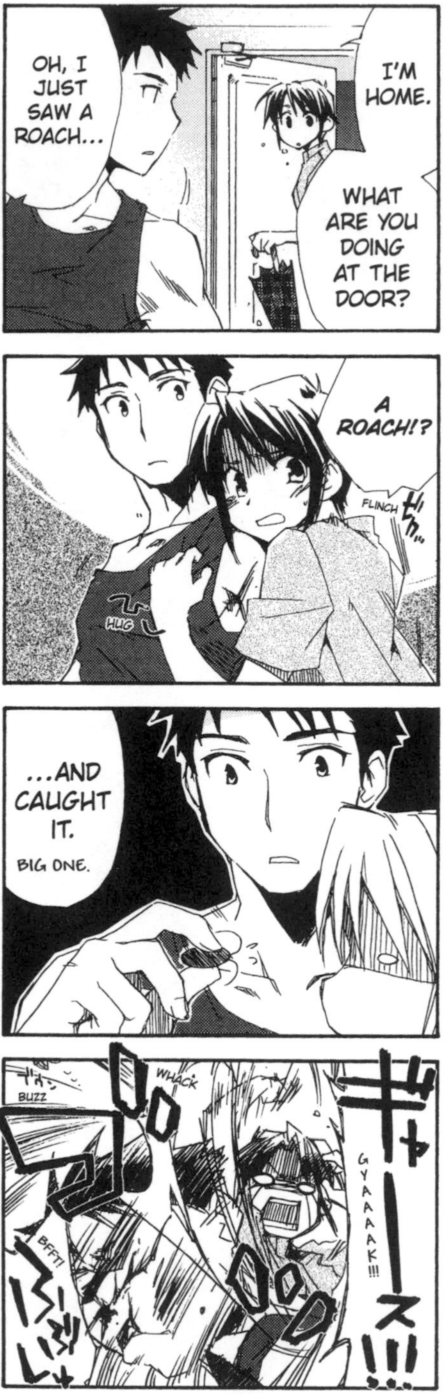
I'M HOME.
WHAT ARE YOU DOING AT THE DOOR?
OH, I JUST SAW A ROACH...
A ROACH!?
FLINCH
HUG
...AND CAUGHT IT.
BIG ONE.
GYAAAAK!!!
WHACK
BUZZ
BFFT!

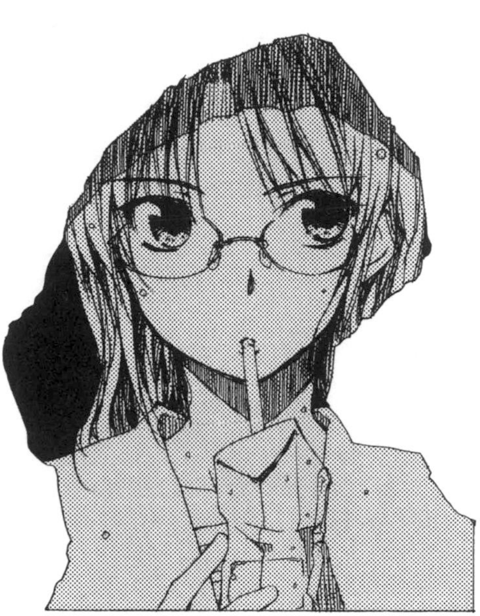

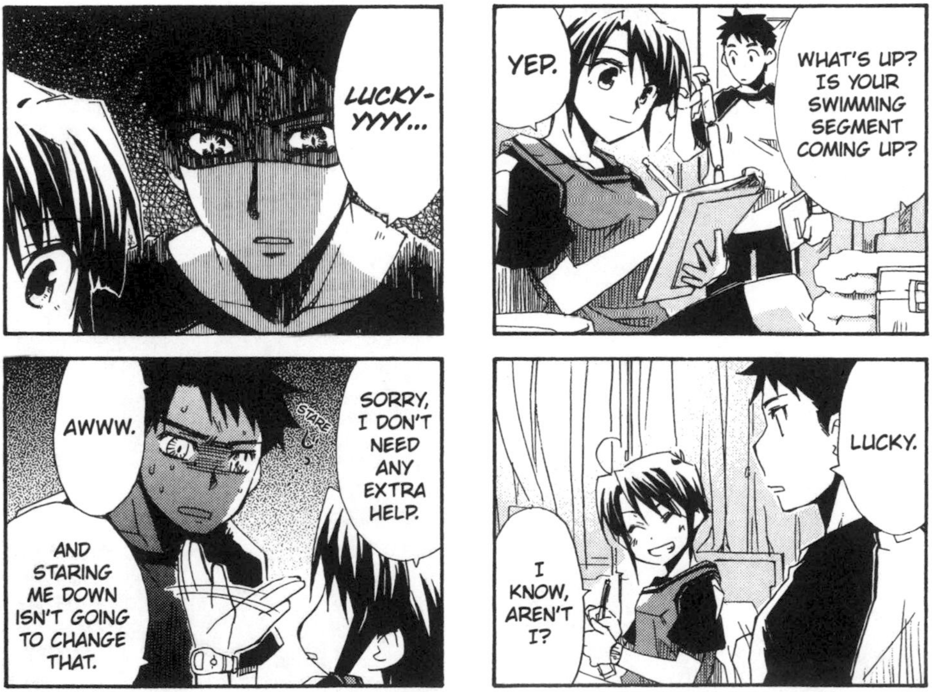
WHAT'S UP? IS YOUR SWIMMING SEGMENT COMING UP?
YEP.
LUCKY-YYYY...
LUCKY.
I KNOW, AREN'T I?
SORRY, I DON'T NEED ANY EXTRA HELP.
STARE
AWWW.
AND STARING ME DOWN ISN'T GOING TO CHANGE THAT.

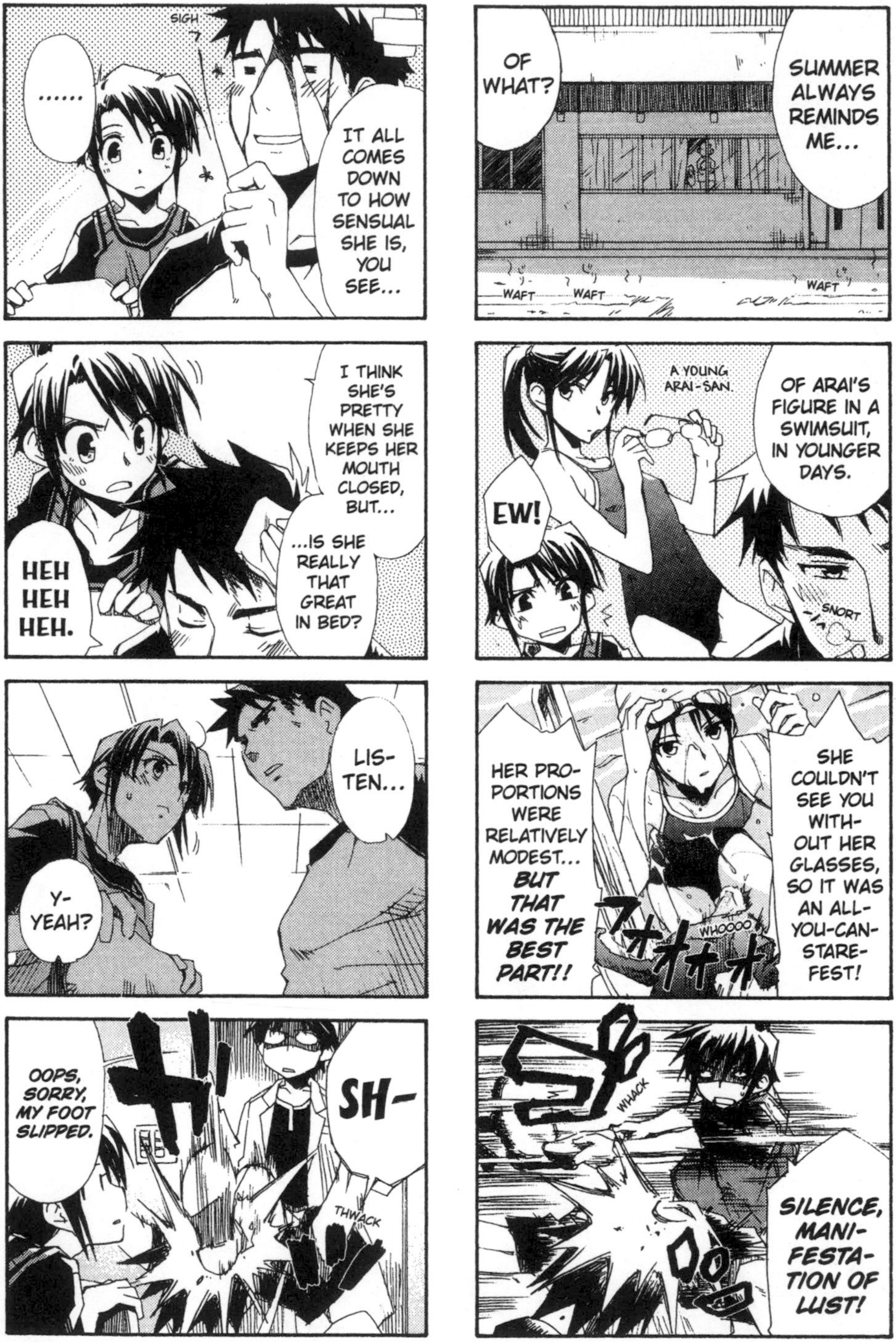
SUMMER ALWAYS REMINDS ME...
OF WHAT?
WAFT
WAFT
WAFT
SIGH
IT ALL COMES DOWN TO HOW SENSUAL SHE IS, YOU SEE...
......
OF ARAI'S FIGURE IN A SWIMSUIT, IN YOUNGER DAYS.
A YOUNG ARAI-SAN.
EW!
SNORT
I THINK SHE'S PRETTY WHEN SHE KEEPS HER MOUTH CLOSED, BUT...
...IS SHE REALLY THAT GREAT IN BED?
HEH HEH HEH.
SHE COULDN'T SEE YOU WITHOUT HER GLASSES, SO IT WAS AN ALL-YOU-CAN-STARE-FEST!
HER PROPORTIONS WERE RELATIVELY MODEST... BUT THAT WAS THE BEST PART!!
WHOOOO
LISTEN...
Y-YEAH?
WHACK
SILENCE, MANIFESTATION OF LUST!
SH-
OOPS, SORRY, MY FOOT SLIPPED.
THWACK

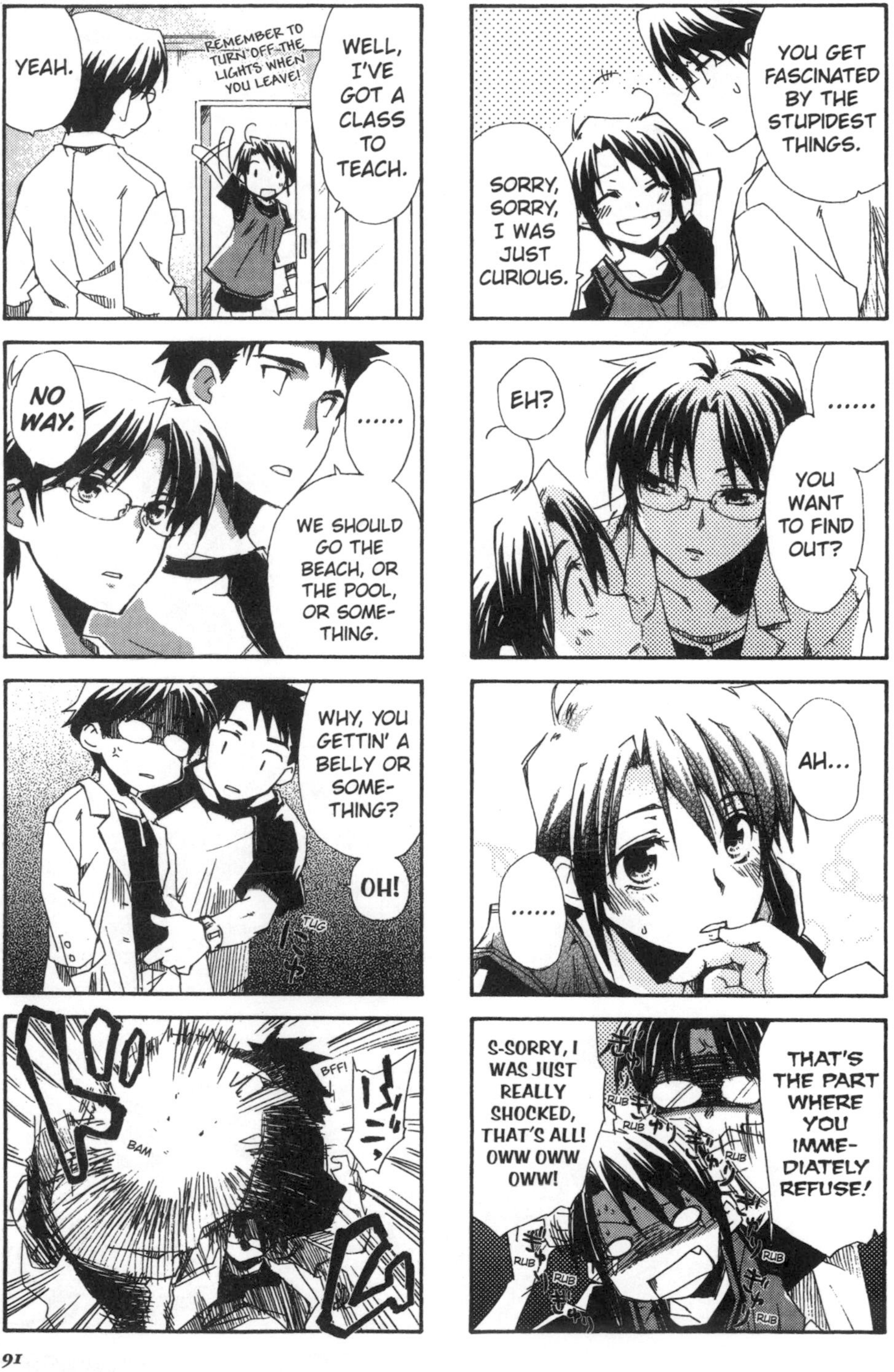
YOU GET FASCINATED BY THE STUPIDEST THINGS.
SORRY, SORRY, I WAS JUST CURIOUS.
WELL, I'VE GOT A CLASS TO TEACH.
REMEMBER TO TURN OFF THE LIGHTS WHEN YOU LEAVE!
YEAH.
......
YOU WANT TO FIND OUT?
EH?
......
WE SHOULD GO THE BEACH, OR THE POOL, OR SOME-THING.
NO WAY.
AH...
......
WHY, YOU GETTIN' A BELLY OR SOME-THING?
OH!
TUG
THAT'S THE PART WHERE YOU IMME-DIATELY REFUSE!
S-SORRY, I WAS JUST REALLY SHOCKED, THAT'S ALL! OWW OWW OWW!
RUB
RUB
RUB
RUB
RUB
RUB
RUB
BFF!
BAM

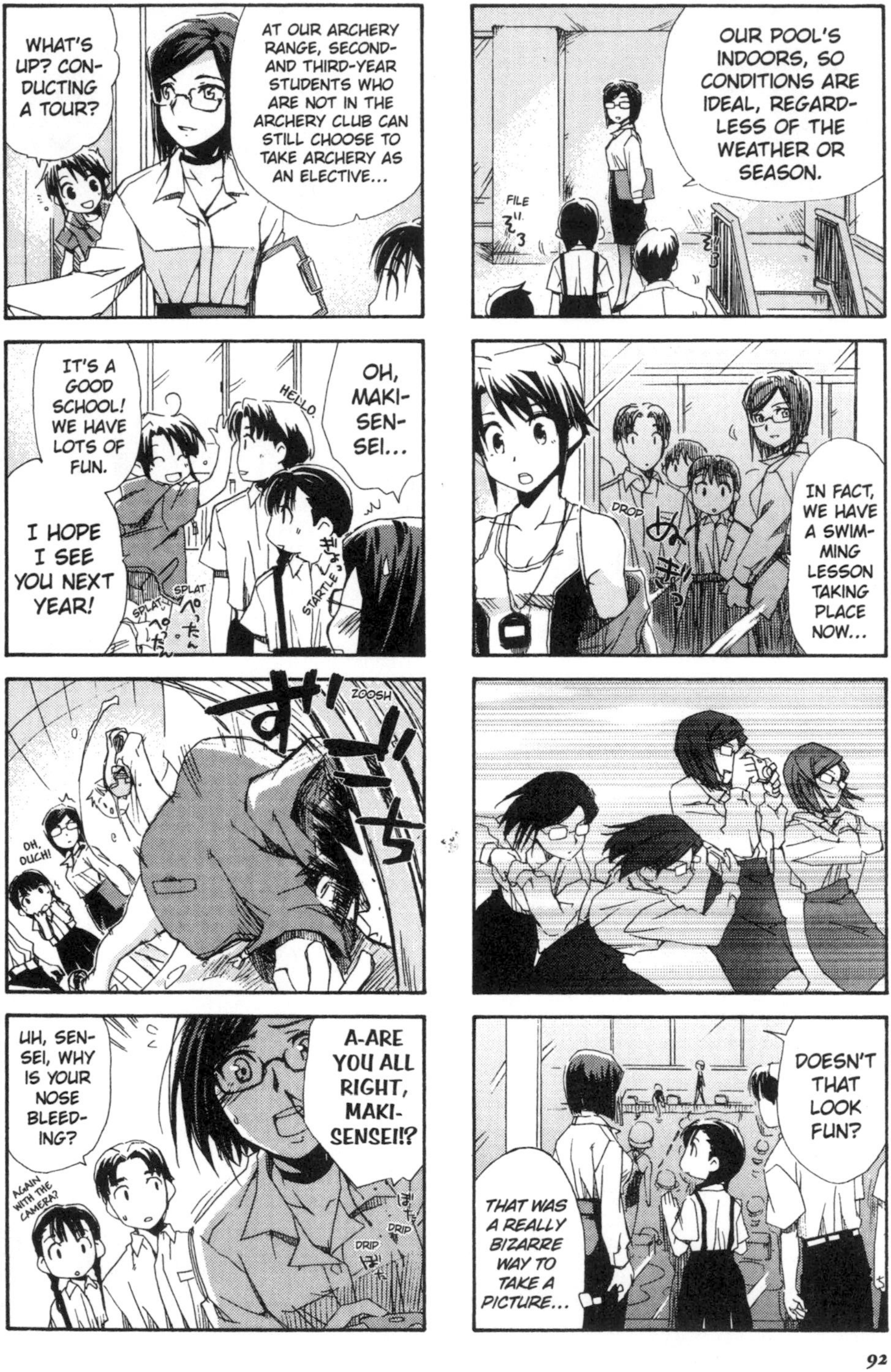
OUR POOL'S INDOORS, SO CONDITIONS ARE IDEAL, REGARDLESS OF THE WEATHER OR SEASON.
FILE
AT OUR ARCHERY RANGE, SECOND- AND THIRD-YEAR STUDENTS WHO ARE NOT IN THE ARCHERY CLUB CAN STILL CHOOSE TO TAKE ARCHERY AS AN ELECTIVE...
WHAT'S UP? CONDUCTING A TOUR?
IN FACT, WE HAVE A SWIMMING LESSON TAKING PLACE NOW...
DROP
OH, MAKI-SENSEI...
HELLO.
STARTLE
IT'S A GOOD SCHOOL! WE HAVE LOTS OF FUN.
I HOPE I SEE YOU NEXT YEAR!
SPLAT
SPLAT
ZOOSH
OH, OUCH!
DOESN'T THAT LOOK FUN?
THAT WAS A REALLY BIZARRE WAY TO TAKE A PICTURE...
A-ARE YOU ALL RIGHT, MAKI-SENSEI!?
DRIP
DRIP
UH, SENSEI, WHY IS YOUR NOSE BLEEDING?
AGAIN WITH THE CAMERA?

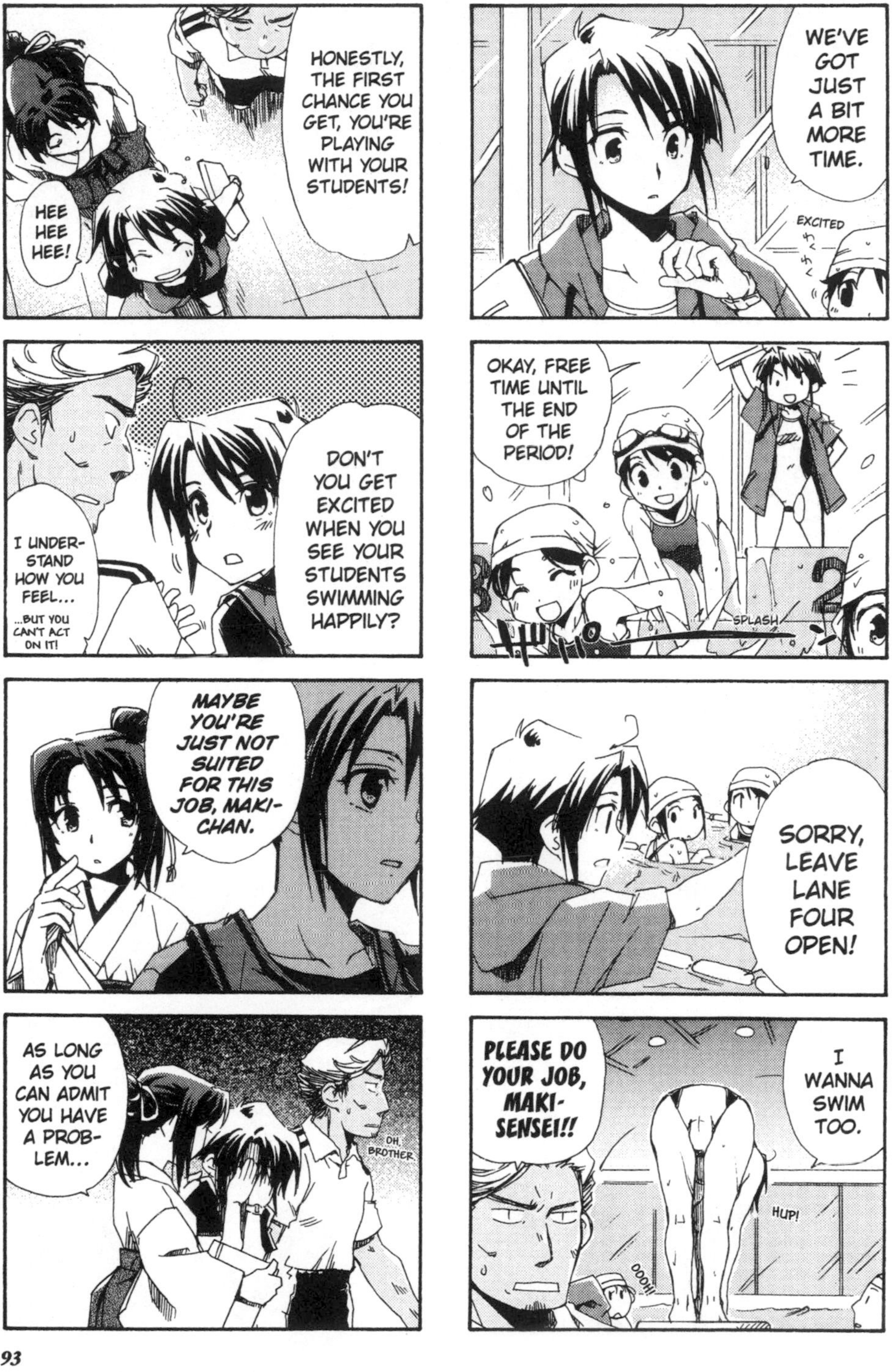
WE'VE GOT JUST A BIT MORE TIME.
EXCITED
HONESTLY, THE FIRST CHANCE YOU GET, YOU'RE PLAYING WITH YOUR STUDENTS!
HEE HEE HEE!
OKAY, FREE TIME UNTIL THE END OF THE PERIOD!
SPLASH
DON'T YOU GET EXCITED WHEN YOU SEE YOUR STUDENTS SWIMMING HAPPILY?
I UNDERSTAND HOW YOU FEEL...
...BUT YOU CAN'T ACT ON IT!
SORRY, LEAVE LANE FOUR OPEN!
MAYBE YOU'RE JUST NOT SUITED FOR THIS JOB, MAKI-CHAN.
I WANNA SWIM TOO.
PLEASE DO YOUR JOB, MAKI-SENSEI!!
HUP!
AS LONG AS YOU CAN ADMIT YOU HAVE A PROBLEM...
OH, BROTHER

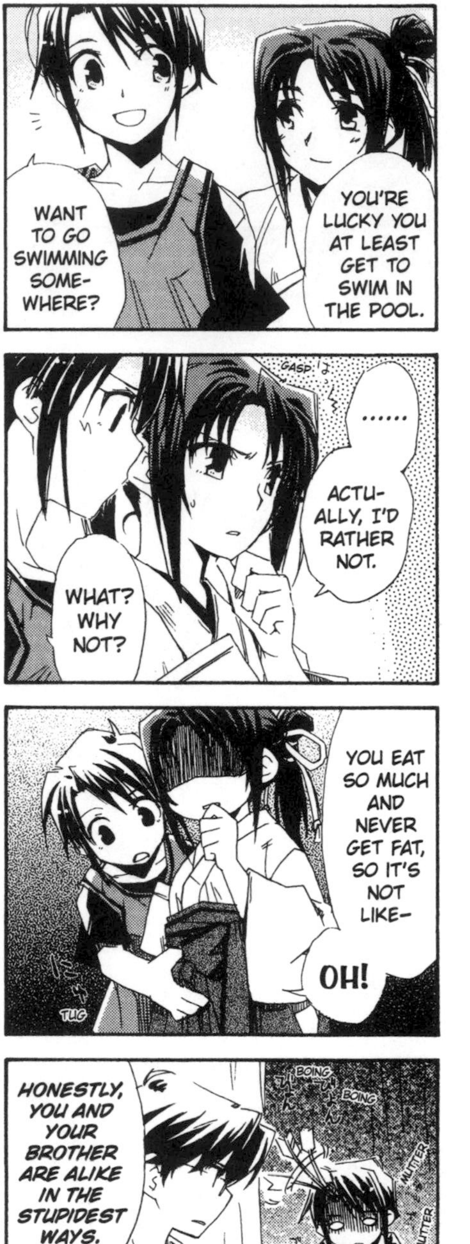
YOU'RE LUCKY YOU AT LEAST GET TO SWIM IN THE POOL.
WANT TO GO SWIMMING SOME-WHERE?
GASP
……
ACTU-ALLY, I'D RATHER NOT.
WHAT? WHY NOT?
YOU EAT SO MUCH AND NEVER GET FAT, SO IT'S NOT LIKE-
OH!
TUG
BOING
BOING
MUTTER
MUTTER
HONESTLY, YOU AND YOUR BROTHER ARE ALIKE IN THE STUPIDEST WAYS.
MUTTER
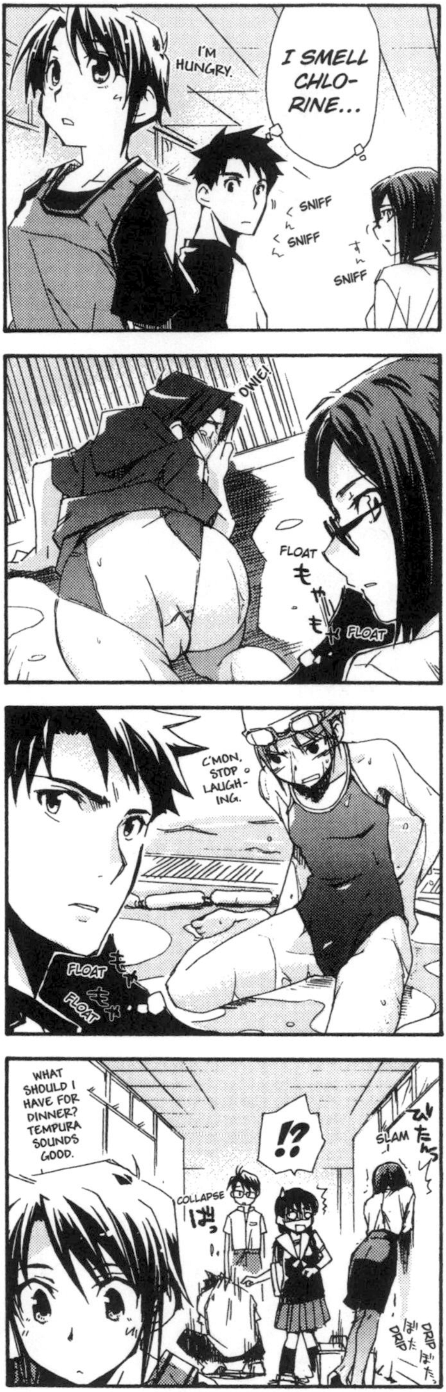
I SMELL CHLO-RINE...
I'M HUNGRY.
SNIFF
SNIFF
SNIFF
OWIE!
FLOAT
FLOAT
C'MON, STOP LAUGH-ING.
FLOAT
FLOAT
SLAM
!?
WHAT SHOULD I HAVE FOR DINNER? TEMPURA SOUNDS GOOD.
COLLAPSE
DRIP
DRIP

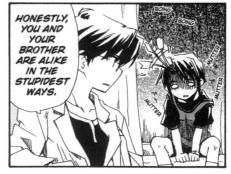

KANAME KARASUMA

CLASS: FOREIGN LANGUAGE TEACHER
GENDER: YURI
PERSONALITY: ROMANTIC
LEVEL: 9

E: SKIRT SUIT
E: DIGITAL CAMERA
E: BLOODY HANDKERCHIEF
E: GLASSES

(SKIN) HEALTH POINTS: SLIPPERY
MENTAL POINTS: BUTT OF THE JOKE
STRENGTH: WEAK ON THE FINISH
SPEED: NEVER MISSES A PHOTO OP
STAMINA: THERE'S NO BEATING AGE
INTELLIGENCE: TRILINGUAL
LUCK: HAPPINESS IN DEFEAT
GUTS: ANYTHING FOR HER

Y: IT'S ON ME!

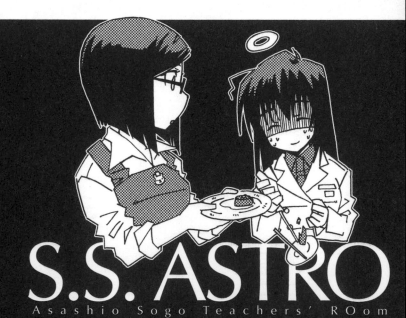

S.S. ASTRO
Asashio Sogo Teachers' ROom

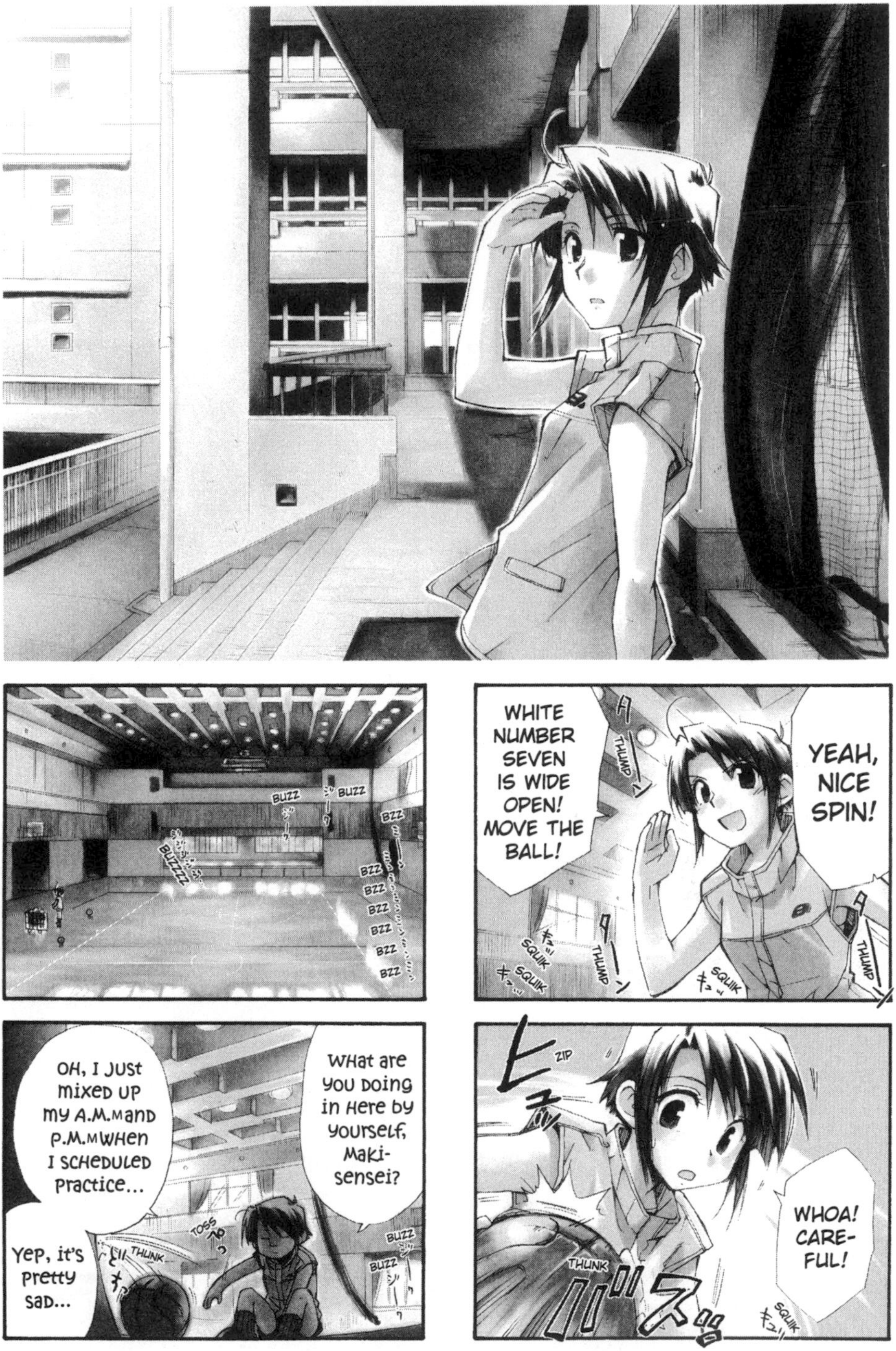
YEAH, NICE SPIN!
WHITE NUMBER SEVEN IS WIDE OPEN! MOVE THE BALL!
THUMP
THUMP
THUMP
SQUIK
SQUIK
SQUIK
BUZZ
BUZZ
BZZ
BUZZZZZ
BZZ
BZZ
BZZ
BZZ
BZZ
BZZ
ZIP
WHOA! CARE-FUL!
THUNK
SQUIK
What are you Doing in Here by yourself, Maki-sensei?
OH, I JUST mixed UP my A.M. and P.M. WHEN I SCHEDULED Practice...
Yep, it's pretty sad...
TOSS
THUNK
BUZZ
BUZZ

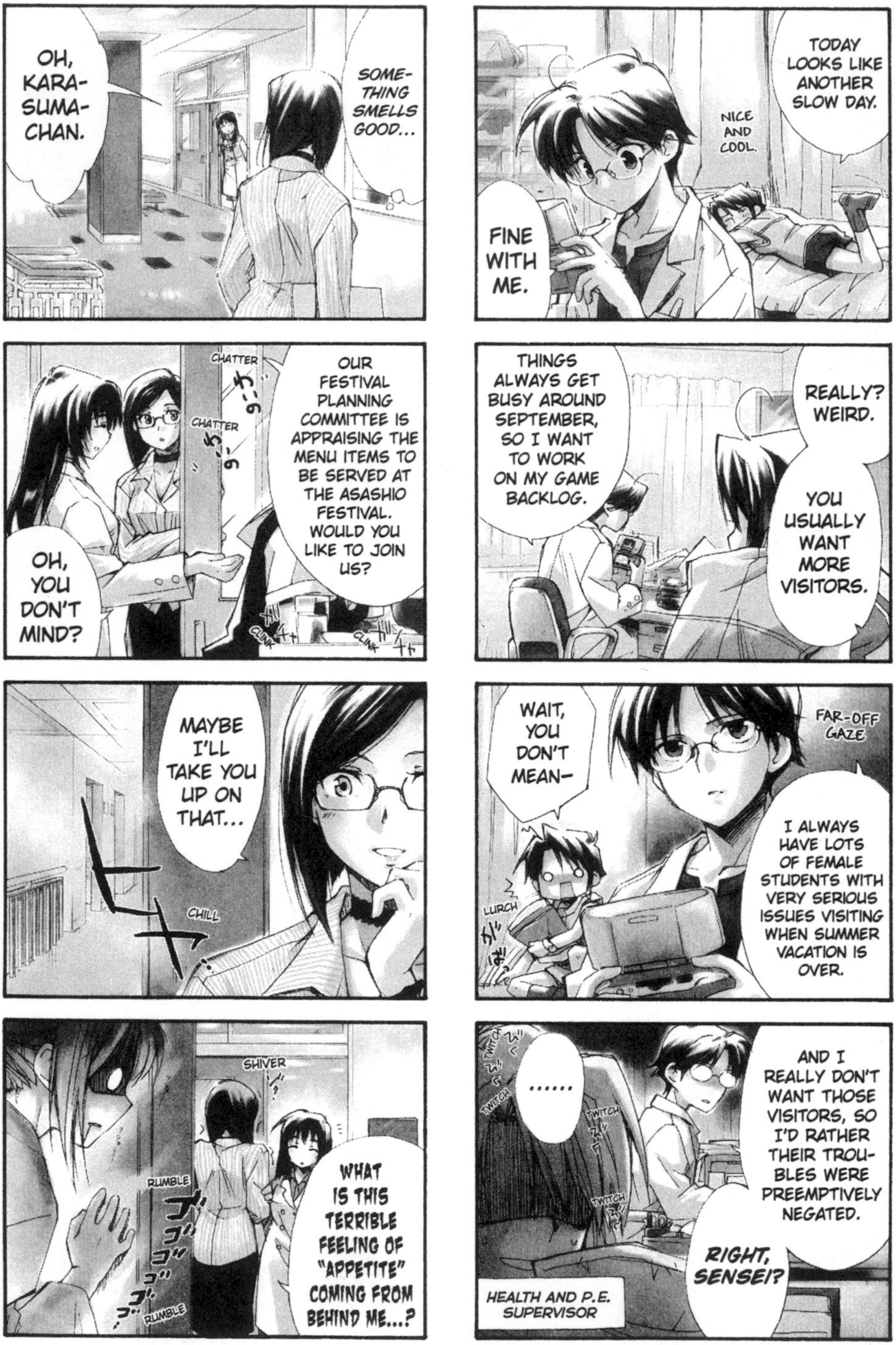
TODAY LOOKS LIKE ANOTHER SLOW DAY.
NICE AND COOL.
FINE WITH ME.
REALLY? WEIRD.
YOU USUALLY WANT MORE VISITORS.
THINGS ALWAYS GET BUSY AROUND SEPTEMBER, SO I WANT TO WORK ON MY GAME BACKLOG.
FAR-OFF GAZE
I ALWAYS HAVE LOTS OF FEMALE STUDENTS WITH VERY SERIOUS ISSUES VISITING WHEN SUMMER VACATION IS OVER.
WAIT, YOU DON'T MEAN—
LURCH
AND I REALLY DON'T WANT THOSE VISITORS, SO I'D RATHER THEIR TROU-BLES WERE PREEMPTIVELY NEGATED.
......
TWITCH
TWITCH
TWITCH
TWITCH
RIGHT, SENSEI?
HEALTH AND P.E. SUPERVISOR
SOME-THING SMELLS GOOD...
OH, KARA-SUMA-CHAN.
OUR FESTIVAL PLANNING COMMITTEE IS APPRAISING THE MENU ITEMS TO BE SERVED AT THE ASASHIO FESTIVAL. WOULD YOU LIKE TO JOIN US?
CHATTER
CHATTER
OH, YOU DON'T MIND?
CLINK
CLINK
MAYBE I'LL TAKE YOU UP ON THAT...
CHILL
SHIVER
WHAT IS THIS TERRIBLE FEELING OF "APPETITE" COMING FROM BEHIND ME...?
RUMBLE
RUMBLE

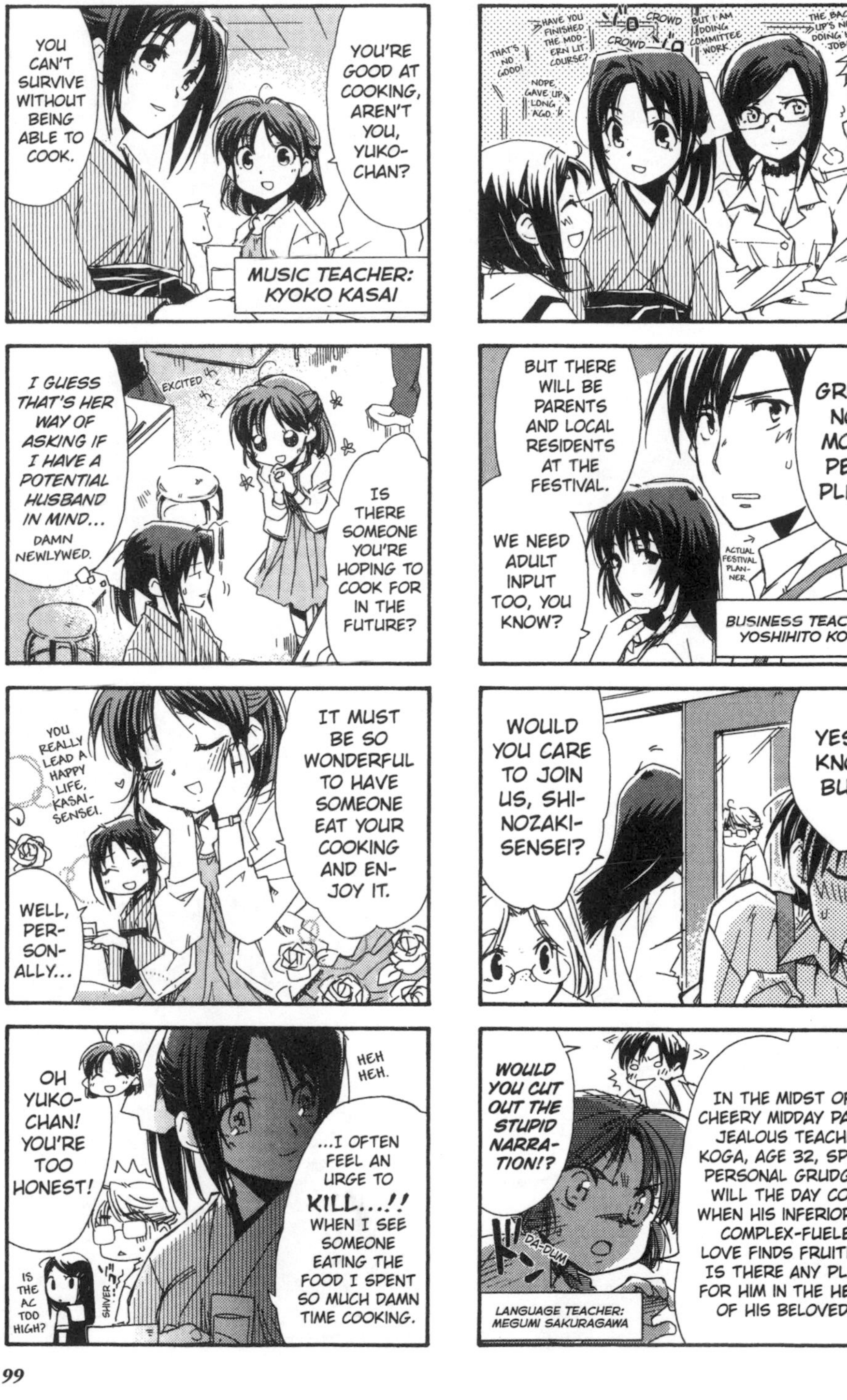
HEY!
THE BACK-UP'S NOT DOING HER JOB!
BUT I AM DOING COMMITTEE WORK
CROWD
CROWD
HAVE YOU FINISHED THE MODERN LIT. COURSE?
THAT'S NO GOOD!
NOPE, GAVE UP LONG AGO.
GREAT, NOT MORE PEOPLE...
BUT THERE WILL BE PARENTS AND LOCAL RESIDENTS AT THE FESTIVAL.
WE NEED ADULT INPUT TOO, YOU KNOW?
ACTUAL FESTIVAL PLANNER
BUSINESS TEACHER: YOSHIHITO KOGA
YES, I KNOW, BUT–
WOULD YOU CARE TO JOIN US, SHINOZAKI-SENSEI?
IN THE MIDST OF A CHEERY MIDDAY PARTY, JEALOUS TEACHER KOGA, AGE 32, SPEWS PERSONAL GRUDGES. WILL THE DAY COME WHEN HIS INFERIORITY-COMPLEX-FUELED LOVE FINDS FRUITION? IS THERE ANY PLACE FOR HIM IN THE HEART OF HIS BELOVED!?
WOULD YOU CUT OUT THE STUPID NARRATION!?
DA-DUM
LANGUAGE TEACHER: MEGUMI SAKURAGAWA
YOU'RE GOOD AT COOKING, AREN'T YOU, YUKO-CHAN?
YOU CAN'T SURVIVE WITHOUT BEING ABLE TO COOK.
MUSIC TEACHER: KYOKO KASAI
IS THERE SOMEONE YOU'RE HOPING TO COOK FOR IN THE FUTURE?
EXCITED
I GUESS THAT'S HER WAY OF ASKING IF I HAVE A POTENTIAL HUSBAND IN MIND...
DAMN NEWLYWED.
IT MUST BE SO WONDERFUL TO HAVE SOMEONE EAT YOUR COOKING AND ENJOY IT.
YOU REALLY LEAD A HAPPY LIFE, KASAI-SENSEI.
WELL, PERSONALLY...
HEH HEH.
...I OFTEN FEEL AN URGE TO KILL...!! WHEN I SEE SOMEONE EATING THE FOOD I SPENT SO MUCH DAMN TIME COOKING.
OH YUKO-CHAN! YOU'RE TOO HONEST!
SHIVER
IS THE AC TOO HIGH?

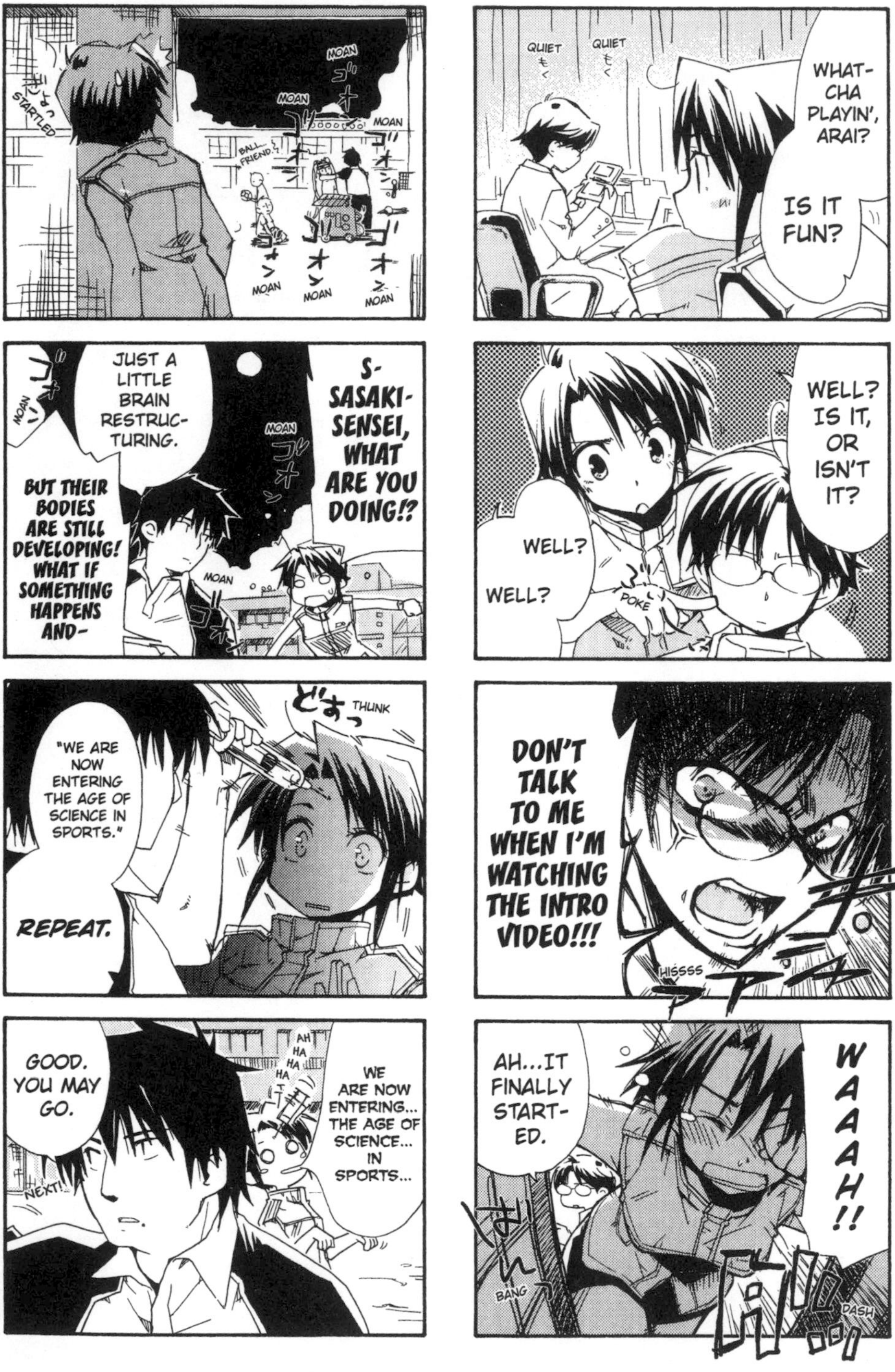
QUIET
QUIET
WHAT-CHA PLAYIN', ARAI?
IS IT FUN?
WELL? IS IT, OR ISN'T IT?
WELL?
WELL?
POKE
DON'T TALK TO ME WHEN I'M WATCHING THE INTRO VIDEO!!!
HISSSS
WAAAAH!!
AH...IT FINALLY START-ED.
BANG
DASH
MOAN
MOAN
MOAN
STARTLED
BALL... FRIEND.
MOAN
MOAN
MOAN
S-SASAKI-SENSEI, WHAT ARE YOU DOING!?
JUST A LITTLE BRAIN RESTRUC-TURING.
BUT THEIR BODIES ARE STILL DEVELOPING! WHAT IF SOMETHING HAPPENS AND-
MOAN
MOAN
MOAN
THUNK
"WE ARE NOW ENTERING THE AGE OF SCIENCE IN SPORTS."
REPEAT.
WE ARE NOW ENTERING... THE AGE OF SCIENCE... IN SPORTS...
AH HA HA HA
GOOD. YOU MAY GO.
NEXT!

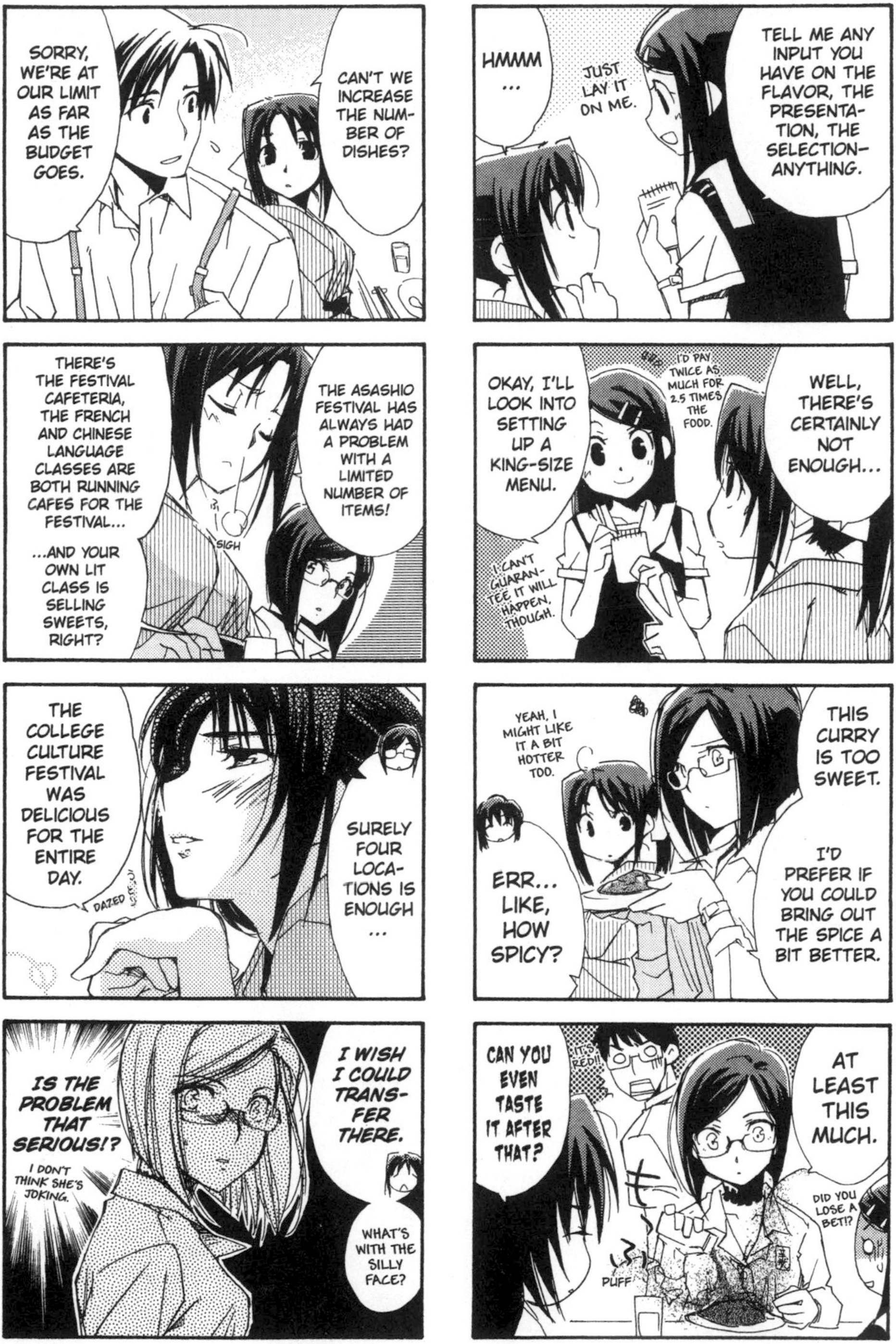
TELL ME ANY INPUT YOU HAVE ON THE FLAVOR, THE PRESENTATION, THE SELECTION—ANYTHING.
JUST LAY IT ON ME.
HMMM ...
WELL, THERE'S CERTAINLY NOT ENOUGH...
I'D PAY TWICE AS MUCH FOR 2.5 TIMES THE FOOD.
OKAY, I'LL LOOK INTO SETTING UP A KING-SIZE MENU.
I CAN'T GUARANTEE IT WILL HAPPEN, THOUGH.
THIS CURRY IS TOO SWEET.
I'D PREFER IF YOU COULD BRING OUT THE SPICE A BIT BETTER.
YEAH, I MIGHT LIKE IT A BIT HOTTER TOO.
ERR... LIKE, HOW SPICY?
AT LEAST THIS MUCH.
DID YOU LOSE A BET!?
IT'S RED!!
CAN YOU EVEN TASTE IT AFTER THAT?
PUFF
CAN'T WE INCREASE THE NUMBER OF DISHES?
SORRY, WE'RE AT OUR LIMIT AS FAR AS THE BUDGET GOES.
THE ASASHIO FESTIVAL HAS ALWAYS HAD A PROBLEM WITH A LIMITED NUMBER OF ITEMS!
SIGH
THERE'S THE FESTIVAL CAFETERIA, THE FRENCH AND CHINESE LANGUAGE CLASSES ARE BOTH RUNNING CAFES FOR THE FESTIVAL...
...AND YOUR OWN LIT CLASS IS SELLING SWEETS, RIGHT?
SURELY FOUR LOCATIONS IS ENOUGH ...
THE COLLEGE CULTURE FESTIVAL WAS DELICIOUS FOR THE ENTIRE DAY.
DAZED
I WISH I COULD TRANSFER THERE.
WHAT'S WITH THE SILLY FACE?
IS THE PROBLEM THAT SERIOUS!?
I DON'T THINK SHE'S JOKING.

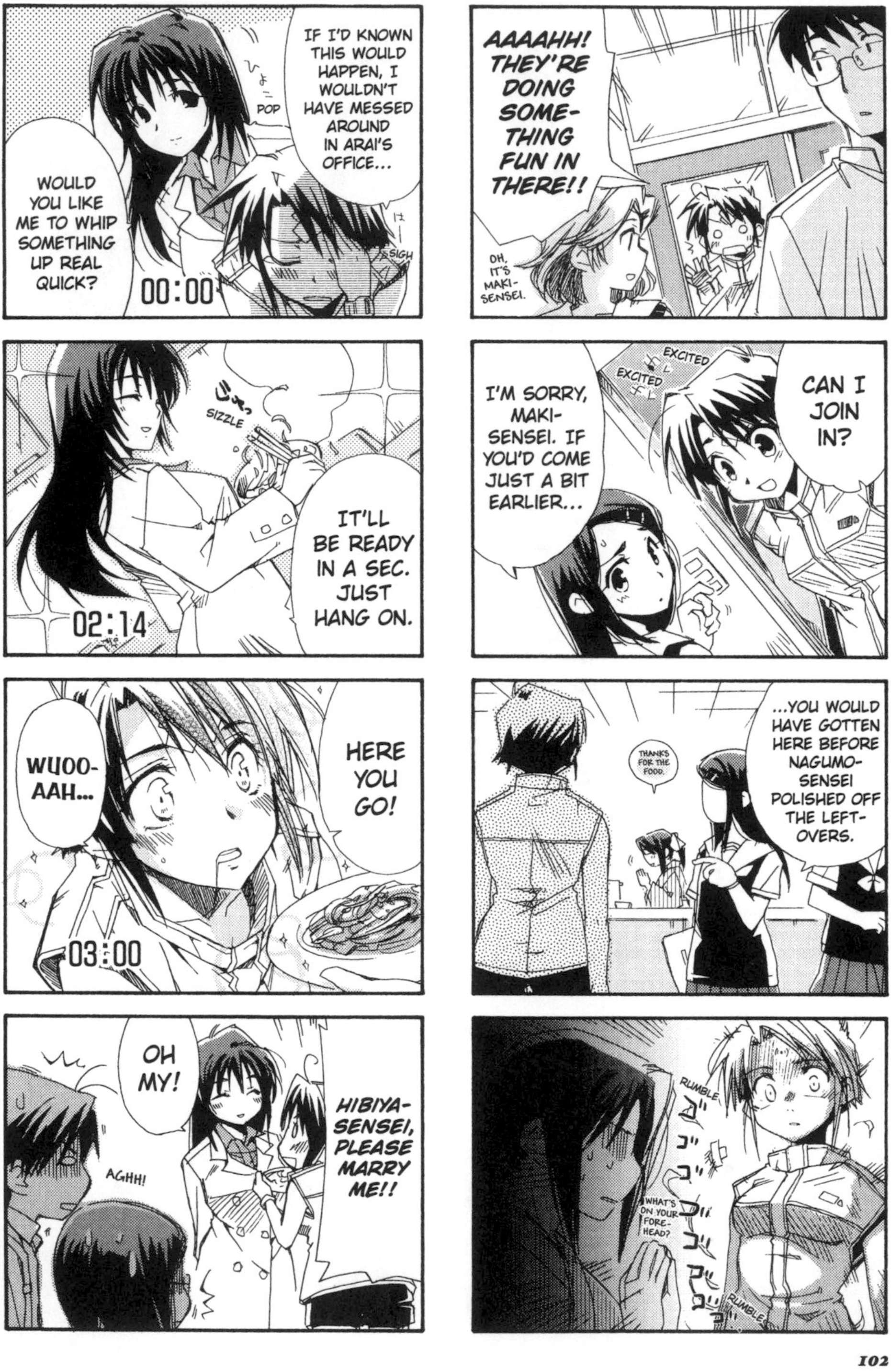
AAAAHH! THEY'RE DOING SOME-THING FUN IN THERE!!
OH, IT'S MAKI-SENSEI.
IF I'D KNOWN THIS WOULD HAPPEN, I WOULDN'T HAVE MESSED AROUND IN ARAI'S OFFICE...
POP
SIGH
WOULD YOU LIKE ME TO WHIP SOMETHING UP REAL QUICK?
00:00
CAN I JOIN IN?
EXCITED
EXCITED
I'M SORRY, MAKI-SENSEI. IF YOU'D COME JUST A BIT EARLIER...
SIZZLE
IT'LL BE READY IN A SEC. JUST HANG ON.
02:14
...YOU WOULD HAVE GOTTEN HERE BEFORE NAGUMO-SENSEI POLISHED OFF THE LEFT-OVERS.
THANKS FOR THE FOOD.
HERE YOU GO!
WUOO-AAH...
03:00
RUMBLE
WHAT'S ON YOUR FORE-HEAD?
RUMBLE
HIBIYA-SENSEI, PLEASE MARRY ME!!
OH MY!
AGHH!

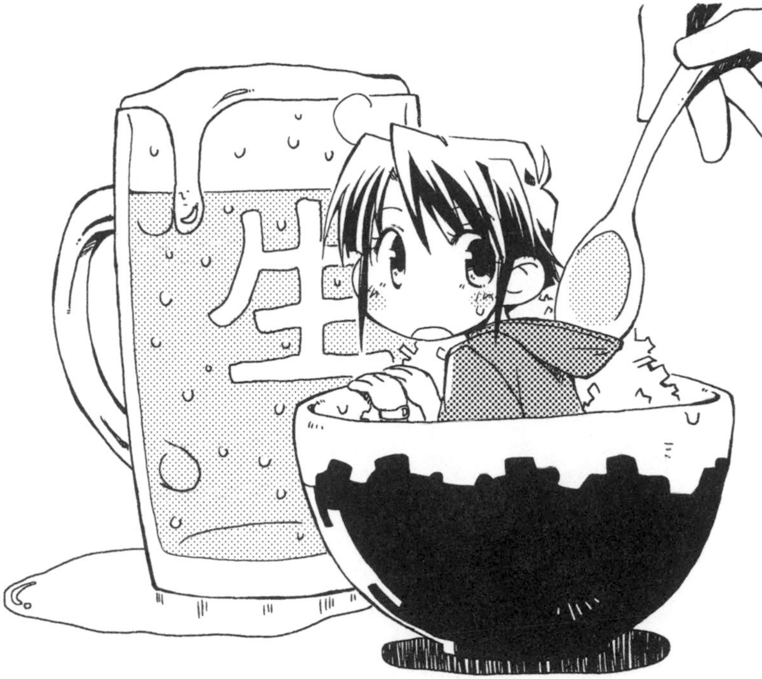
生

MUG: DRAFT

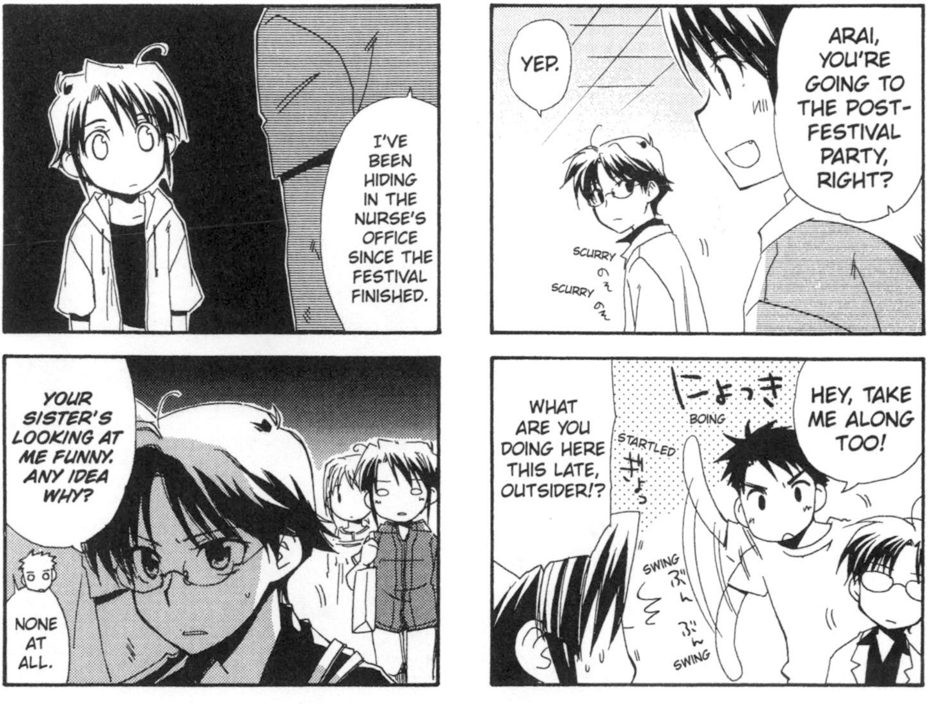
ARAI, YOU'RE GOING TO THE POST-FESTIVAL PARTY, RIGHT?
YEP.
SCURRY のそ
SCURRY のそ
I'VE BEEN HIDING IN THE NURSE'S OFFICE SINCE THE FESTIVAL FINISHED.
HEY, TAKE ME ALONG TOO!
にょっき BOING
WHAT ARE YOU DOING HERE THIS LATE, OUTSIDER!?
STARTLED ぎょっ
SWING ぶん
ぶん SWING
YOUR SISTER'S LOOKING AT ME FUNNY. ANY IDEA WHY?
NONE AT ALL.

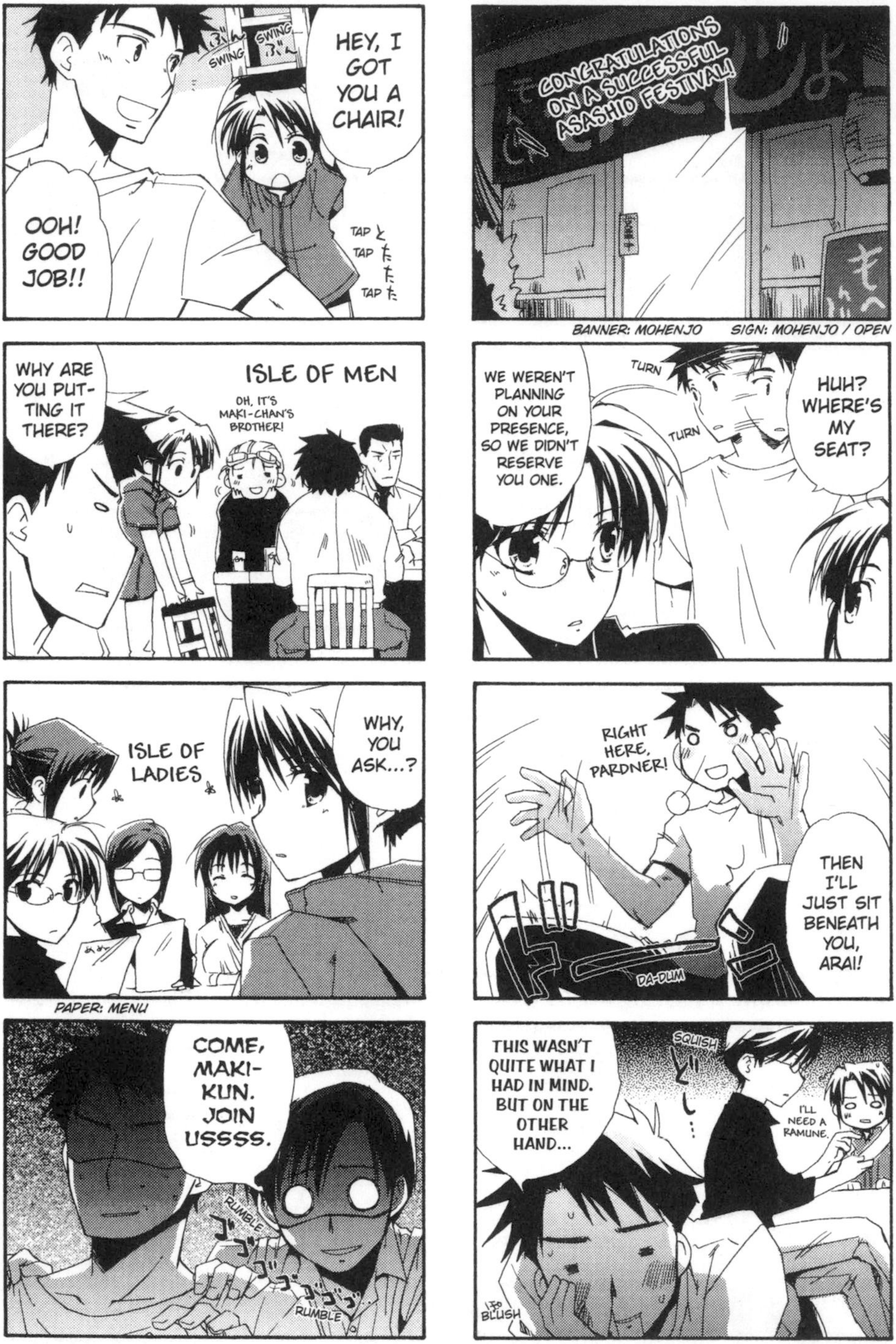
CONGRATULATIONS ON A SUCCESSFUL ASASHIO FESTIVAL!
BANNER: MOHENJO
SIGN: MOHENJO / OPEN
HUH? WHERE'S MY SEAT?
TURN
TURN
WE WEREN'T PLANNING ON YOUR PRESENCE, SO WE DIDN'T RESERVE YOU ONE.
RIGHT HERE, PARDNER!
THEN I'LL JUST SIT BENEATH YOU, ARAI!
DA-DUM
SQUISH
THIS WASN'T QUITE WHAT I HAD IN MIND. BUT ON THE OTHER HAND...
I'LL NEED A RAMUNE.
BLUSH
HEY, I GOT YOU A CHAIR!
SWING
SWING
OOH! GOOD JOB!!
TAP
TAP
TAP
ISLE OF MEN
WHY ARE YOU PUTTING IT THERE?
OH, IT'S MAKI-CHAN'S BROTHER!
WHY, YOU ASK...?
ISLE OF LADIES
PAPER: MENU
COME, MAKI-KUN. JOIN USSSS.
RUMBLE
RUMBLE

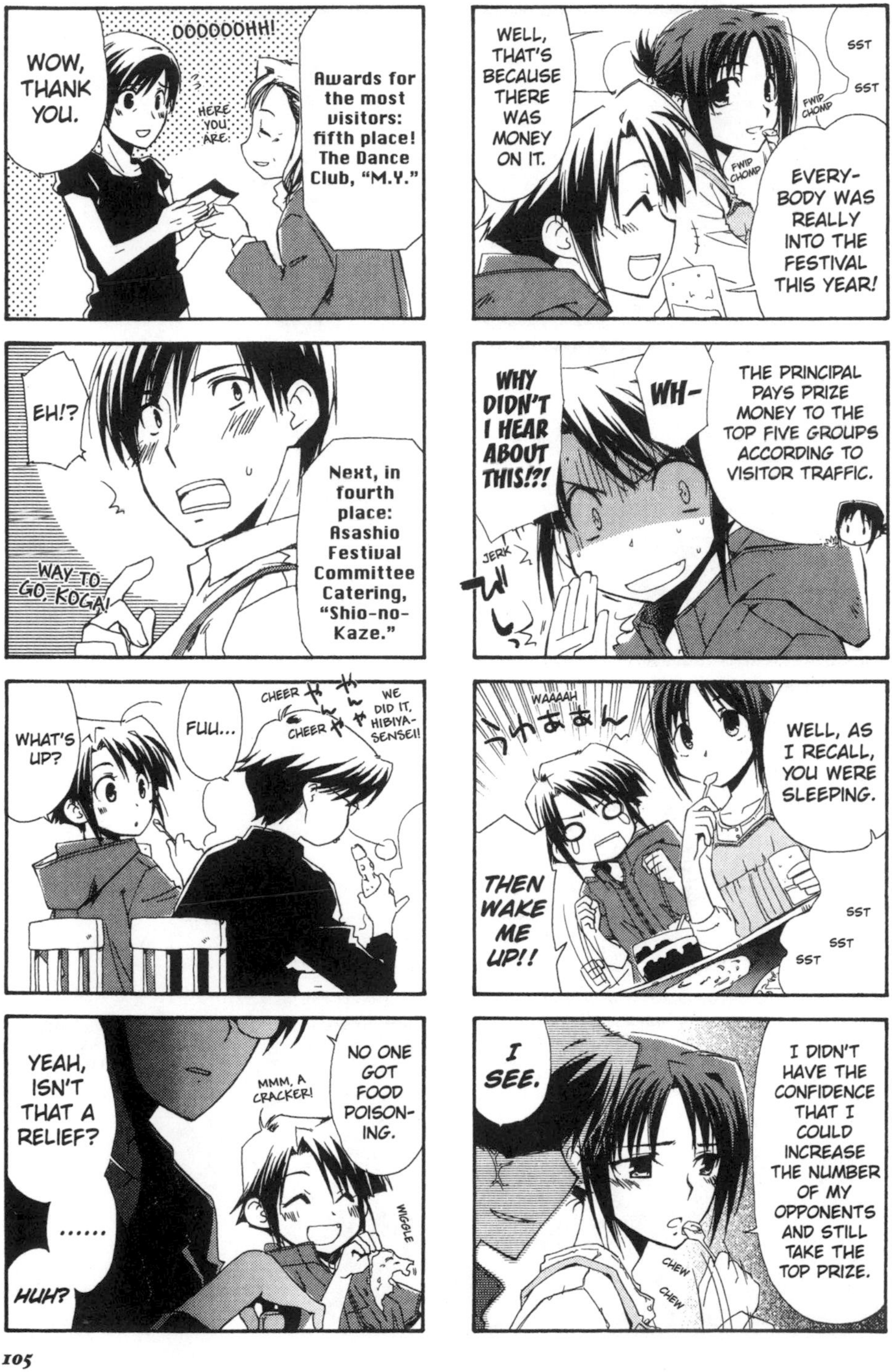
SST
SST
FWIP CHOMP
FWIP CHOMP
EVERY-BODY WAS REALLY INTO THE FESTIVAL THIS YEAR!
WELL, THAT'S BECAUSE THERE WAS MONEY ON IT.
Awards for the most visitors: fifth place! The Dance Club, "M.Y."
OOOOOOHH!
HERE YOU ARE.
WOW, THANK YOU.
THE PRINCIPAL PAYS PRIZE MONEY TO THE TOP FIVE GROUPS ACCORDING TO VISITOR TRAFFIC.
WH-
WHY DIDN'T I HEAR ABOUT THIS!?!
JERK
Next, in fourth place: Asashio Festival Committee Catering, "Shio-no-Kaze."
EH!?
WAY TO GO, KOGA!
WELL, AS I RECALL, YOU WERE SLEEPING.
WAAAAH
うわああん
THEN WAKE ME UP!!
SST
SST
SST
WE DID IT, HIBIYA-SENSEI!
CHEER
CHEER
FUU...
WHAT'S UP?
I DIDN'T HAVE THE CONFIDENCE THAT I COULD INCREASE THE NUMBER OF MY OPPONENTS AND STILL TAKE THE TOP PRIZE.
I SEE.
CHEW
CHEW
NO ONE GOT FOOD POISONING.
MMM, A CRACKER!
YEAH, ISN'T THAT A RELIEF?
WIGGLE
......
HUH?

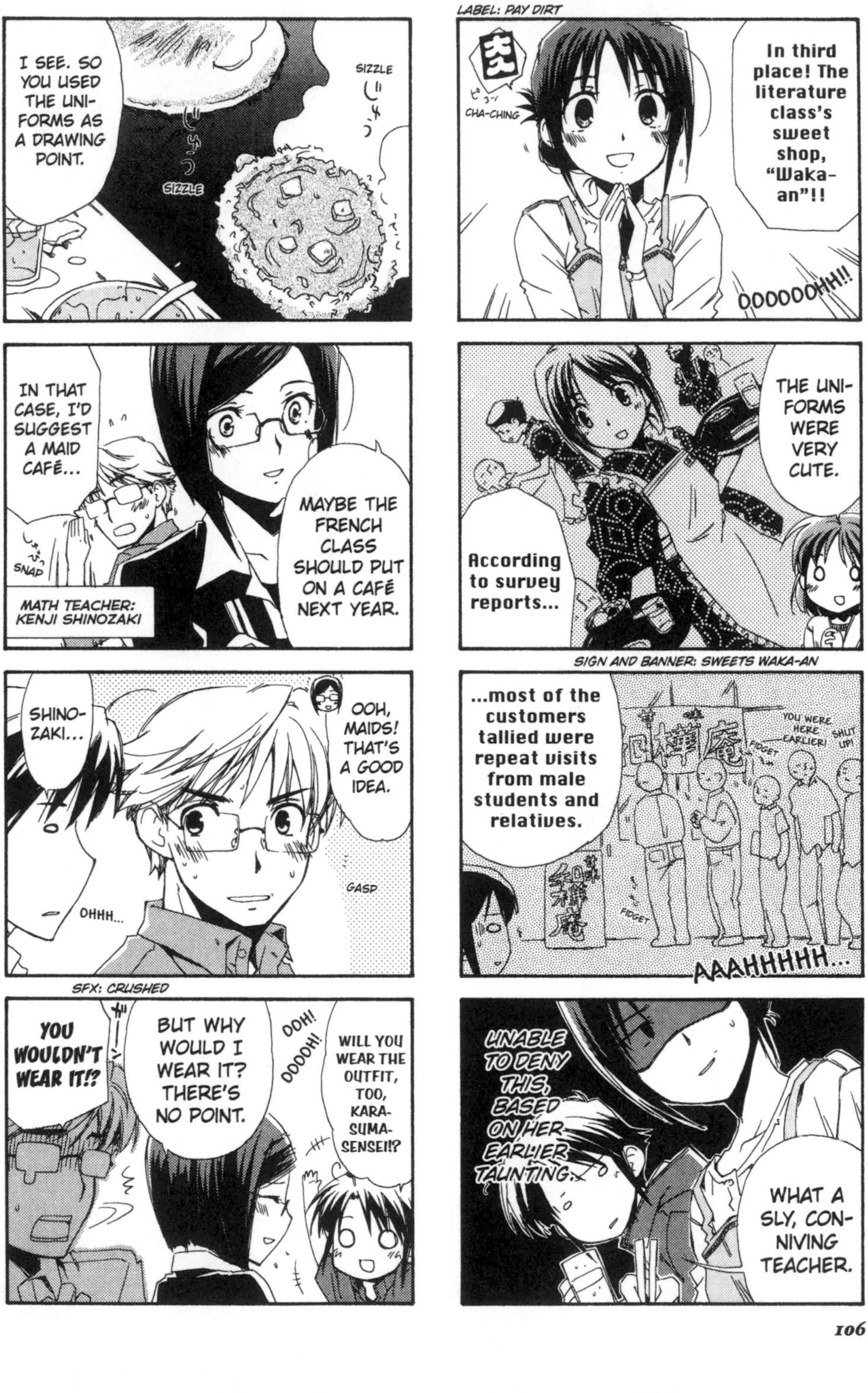
LABEL: PAY DIRT
CHA-CHING
In third place! The literature class's sweet shop, "Waka-an"!!
OOOOOOHH!!
THE UNIFORMS WERE VERY CUTE.
According to survey reports...
SIGN AND BANNER: SWEETS WAKA-AN
...most of the customers tallied were repeat visits from male students and relatives.
YOU WERE HERE EARLIER!
SHUT UP!
FIDGET
FIDGET
AAAHHHHH...
UNABLE TO DENY THIS, BASED ON HER EARLIER TAUNTING.
WHAT A SLY, CONNIVING TEACHER.
I SEE. SO YOU USED THE UNIFORMS AS A DRAWING POINT.
SIZZLE
SIZZLE
IN THAT CASE, I'D SUGGEST A MAID CAFÉ...
MAYBE THE FRENCH CLASS SHOULD PUT ON A CAFÉ NEXT YEAR.
SNAP
MATH TEACHER: KENJI SHINOZAKI
SHINOZAKI...
OOH, MAIDS! THAT'S A GOOD IDEA.
GASP
OHHH...
SFX: CRUSHED
YOU WOULDN'T WEAR IT!?
BUT WHY WOULD I WEAR IT? THERE'S NO POINT.
OOH! OOOOH!
WILL YOU WEAR THE OUTFIT, TOO, KARASUMA-SENSEI!?

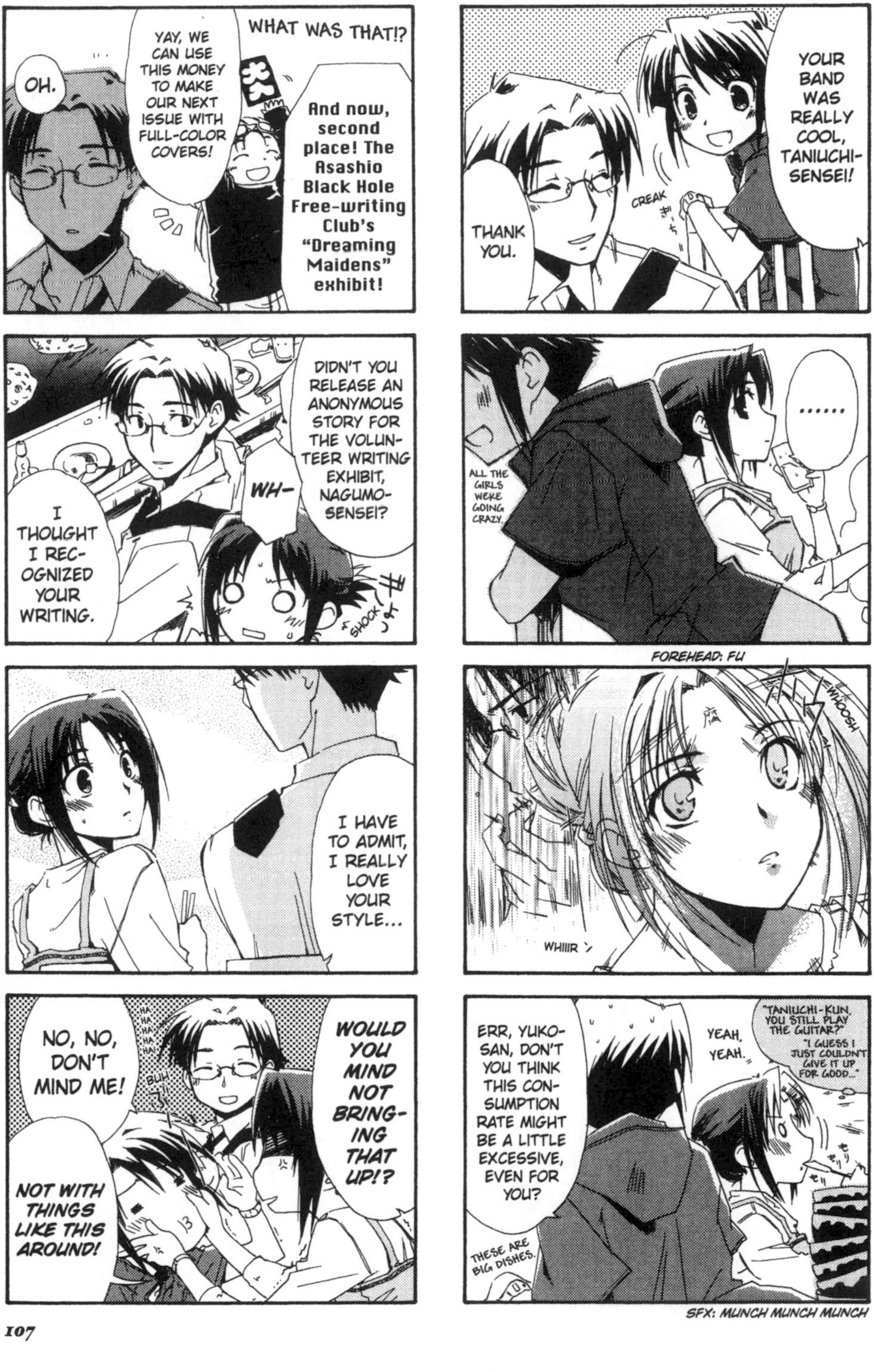
YOUR BAND WAS REALLY COOL, TANIUCHI-SENSEI!
CREAK
THANK YOU.
WHAT WAS THAT!?
And now, second place! The Asashio Black Hole Free-writing Club's "Dreaming Maidens" exhibit!
YAY, WE CAN USE THIS MONEY TO MAKE OUR NEXT ISSUE WITH FULL-COLOR COVERS!
OH.
......
ALL THE GIRLS WERE GOING CRAZY.
DIDN'T YOU RELEASE AN ANONYMOUS STORY FOR THE VOLUNTEER WRITING EXHIBIT, NAGUMO-SENSEI?
WH-
I THOUGHT I RECOGNIZED YOUR WRITING.
SHOCK
FOREHEAD: FU
WHOOSH
WHIIIR
I HAVE TO ADMIT, I REALLY LOVE YOUR STYLE...
"TANIUCHI-KUN, YOU STILL PLAY THE GUITAR?"
"I GUESS I JUST COULDN'T GIVE IT UP FOR GOOD..."
YEAH, YEAH.
ERR, YUKO-SAN, DON'T YOU THINK THIS CONSUMPTION RATE MIGHT BE A LITTLE EXCESSIVE, EVEN FOR YOU?
THESE ARE BIG DISHES.
WOULD YOU MIND NOT BRINGING THAT UP!?
HA HA HA HA HA!
NO, NO, DON'T MIND ME!
BLUH
NOT WITH THINGS LIKE THIS AROUND!
SFX: MUNCH MUNCH MUNCH

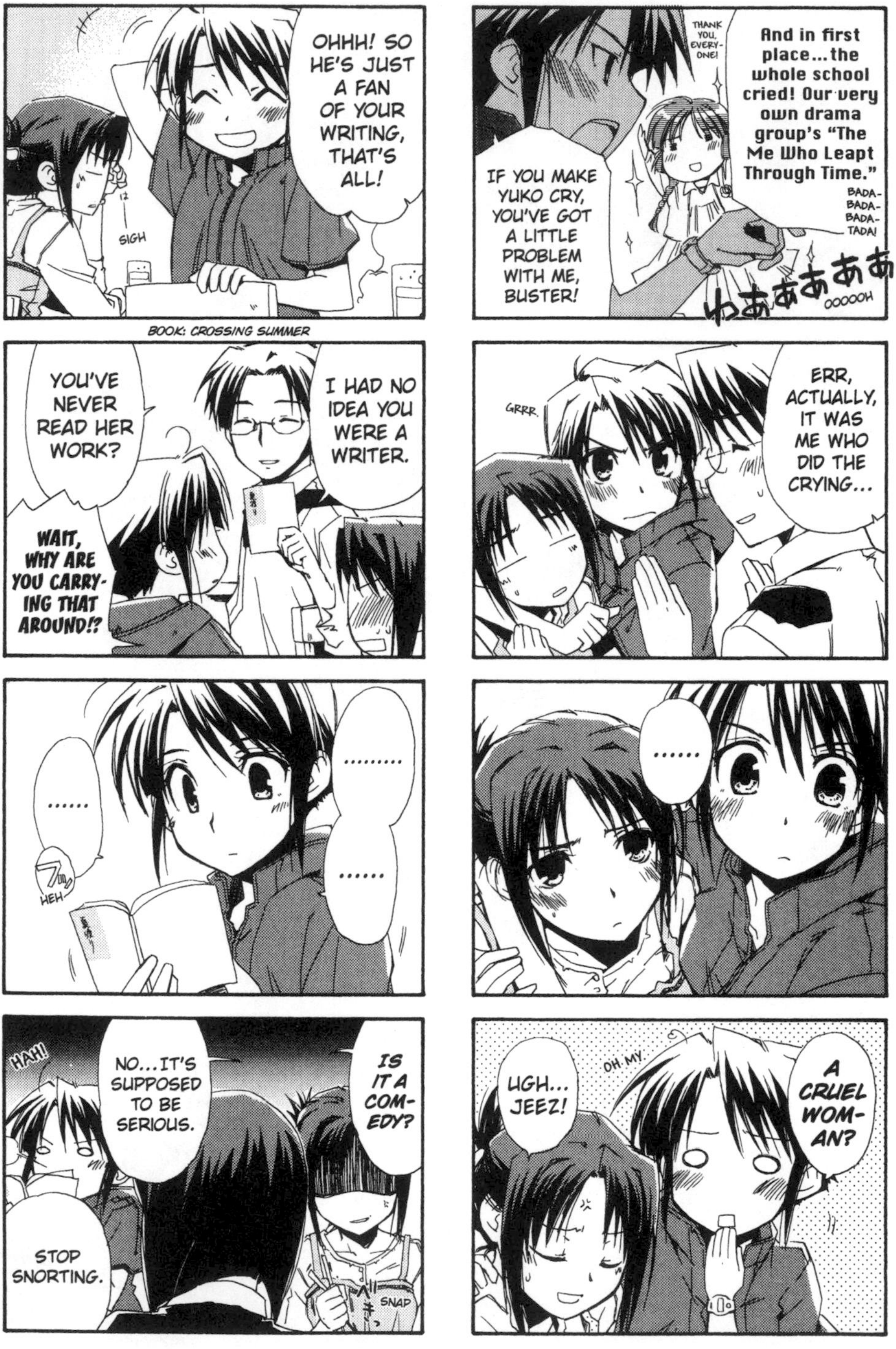
And in first place... the whole school cried! Our very own drama group's "The Me Who Leapt Through Time."
THANK YOU, EVERY-ONE!
BADA-BADA-BADA-TADA!
IF YOU MAKE YUKO CRY, YOU'VE GOT A LITTLE PROBLEM WITH ME, BUSTER!
わあああああ
OOOOOH
ERR, ACTUALLY, IT WAS ME WHO DID THE CRYING...
GRRR.
......
A CRUEL WOMAN?
OH MY
UGH... JEEZ!
OHHH! SO HE'S JUST A FAN OF YOUR WRITING, THAT'S ALL!
SIGH
BOOK: CROSSING SUMMER
I HAD NO IDEA YOU WERE A WRITER.
YOU'VE NEVER READ HER WORK?
WAIT, WHY ARE YOU CARRYING THAT AROUND!?
....
......
......
HEH
IS IT A COMEDY?
NO... IT'S SUPPOSED TO BE SERIOUS.
HAH!
SNAP
STOP SNORTING.

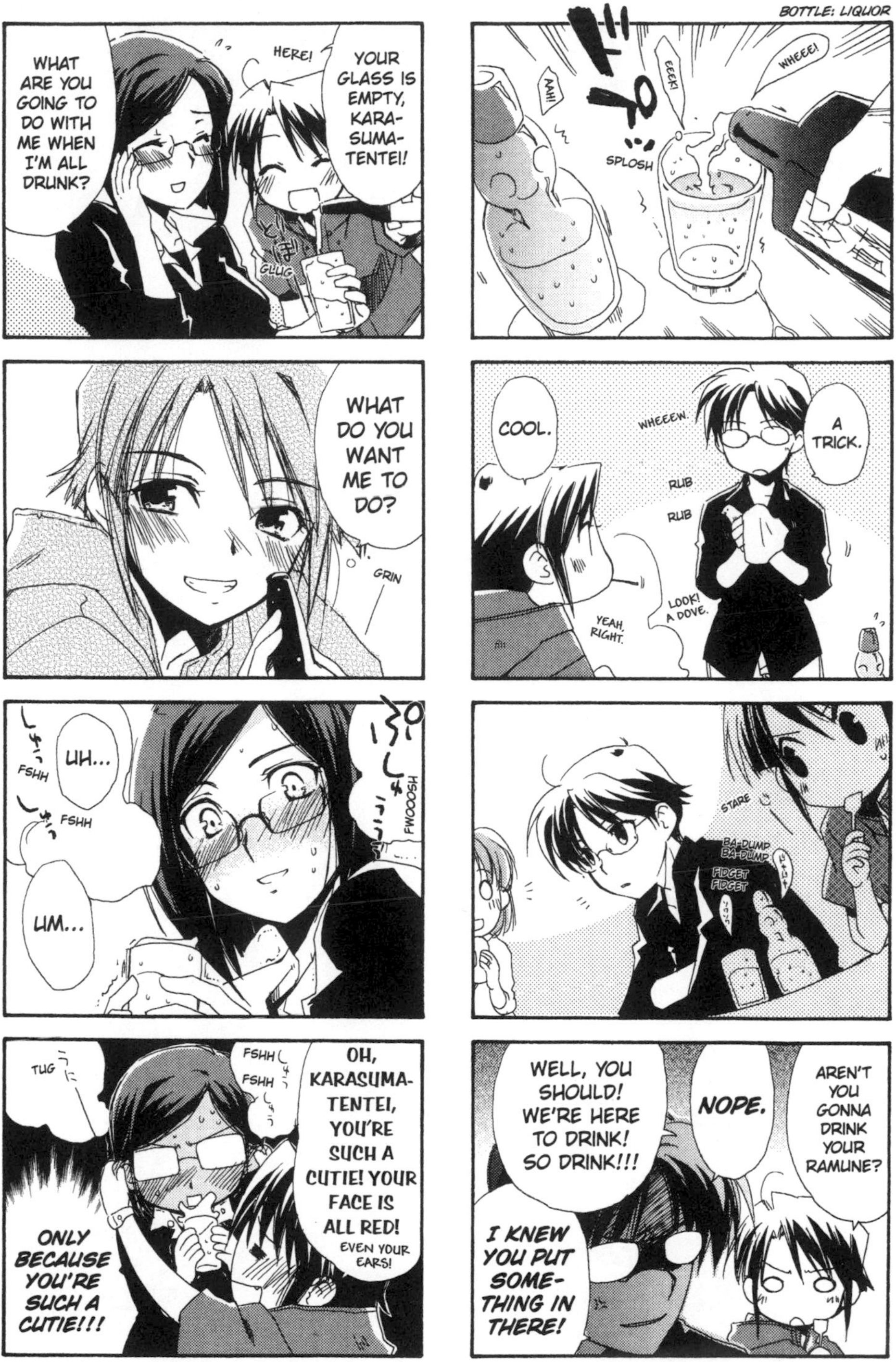
BOTTLE: LIQUOR
WHEEE!
EEEK!
AAH!
SPLOSH
A TRICK.
WHEEEW.
COOL.
RUB
RUB
LOOK! A DOVE.
YEAH, RIGHT.
STARE
BA-DUMP BA-DUMP
FIDGET FIDGET
AREN'T YOU GONNA DRINK YOUR RAMUNE?
NOPE.
WELL, YOU SHOULD! WE'RE HERE TO DRINK! SO DRINK!!!
I KNEW YOU PUT SOMETHING IN THERE!
YOUR GLASS IS EMPTY, KARASUMA-TENTEI!
HERE!
WHAT ARE YOU GOING TO DO WITH ME WHEN I'M ALL DRUNK?
GLUG
WHAT DO YOU WANT ME TO DO?
GRIN
FWOOOSH
UH...
FSHH
FSHH
UM...
OH, KARASUMA-TENTEI, YOU'RE SUCH A CUTIE! YOUR FACE IS ALL RED!
EVEN YOUR EARS!
FSHH
FSHH
TUG
ONLY BECAUSE YOU'RE SUCH A CUTIE!!!

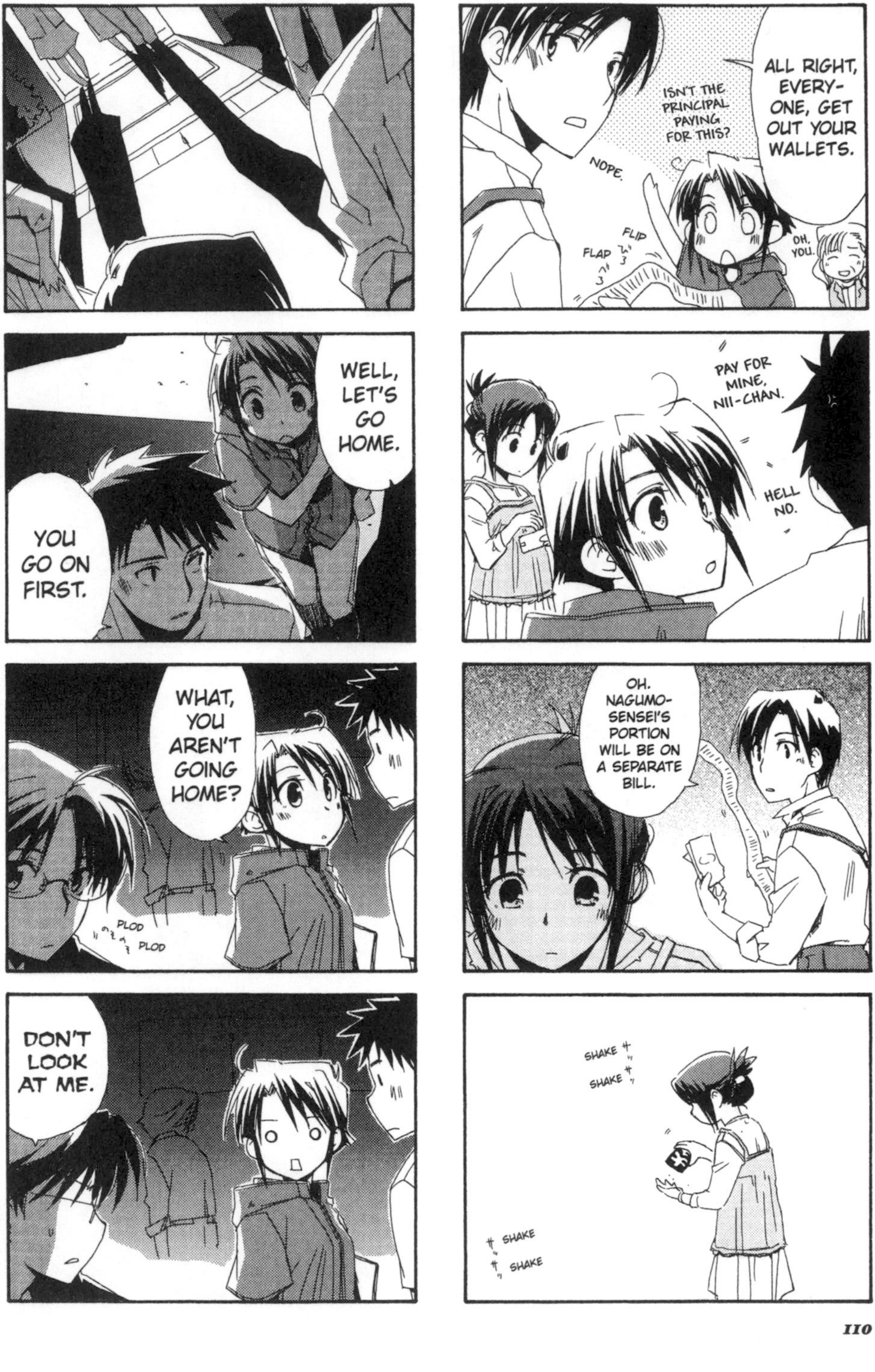
ALL RIGHT, EVERY-ONE, GET OUT YOUR WALLETS.
ISN'T THE PRINCIPAL PAYING FOR THIS?
NOPE.
OH, YOU.
FLIP
FLAP
PAY FOR MINE, NII-CHAN.
HELL NO.
OH. NAGUMO-SENSEI'S PORTION WILL BE ON A SEPARATE BILL.
SHAKE
SHAKE
SHAKE
SHAKE
WELL, LET'S GO HOME.
YOU GO ON FIRST.
WHAT, YOU AREN'T GOING HOME?
PLOD
PLOD
DON'T LOOK AT ME.

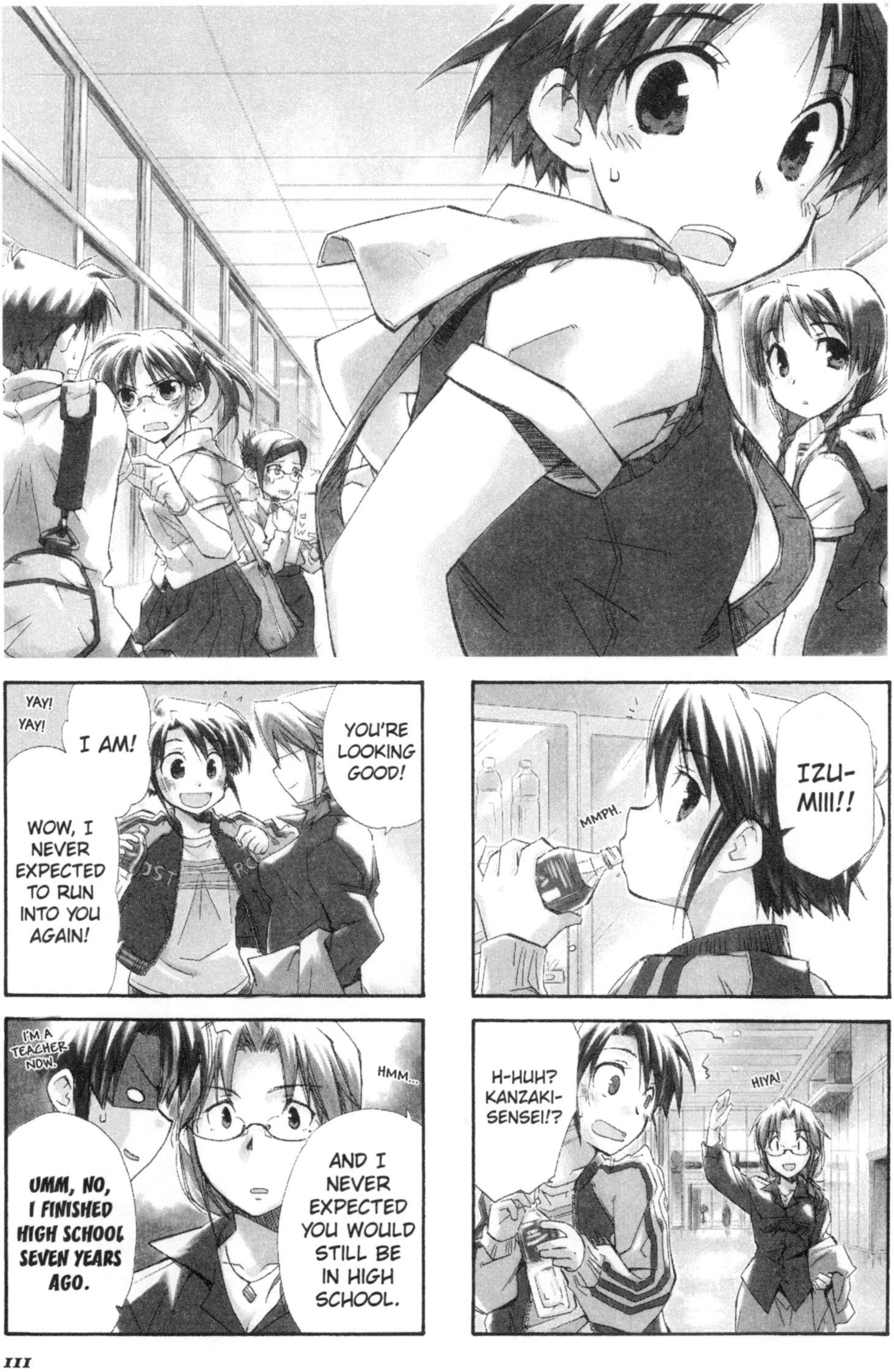
IZU-MIII!!
MMPH.
YOU'RE LOOKING GOOD!
I AM!
YAY! YAY!
WOW, I NEVER EXPECTED TO RUN INTO YOU AGAIN!
HIYA!
H-HUH? KANZAKI-SENSEI!?
HMM...
AND I NEVER EXPECTED YOU WOULD STILL BE IN HIGH SCHOOL.
I'M A TEACHER NOW.
UMM, NO, I FINISHED HIGH SCHOOL SEVEN YEARS AGO.

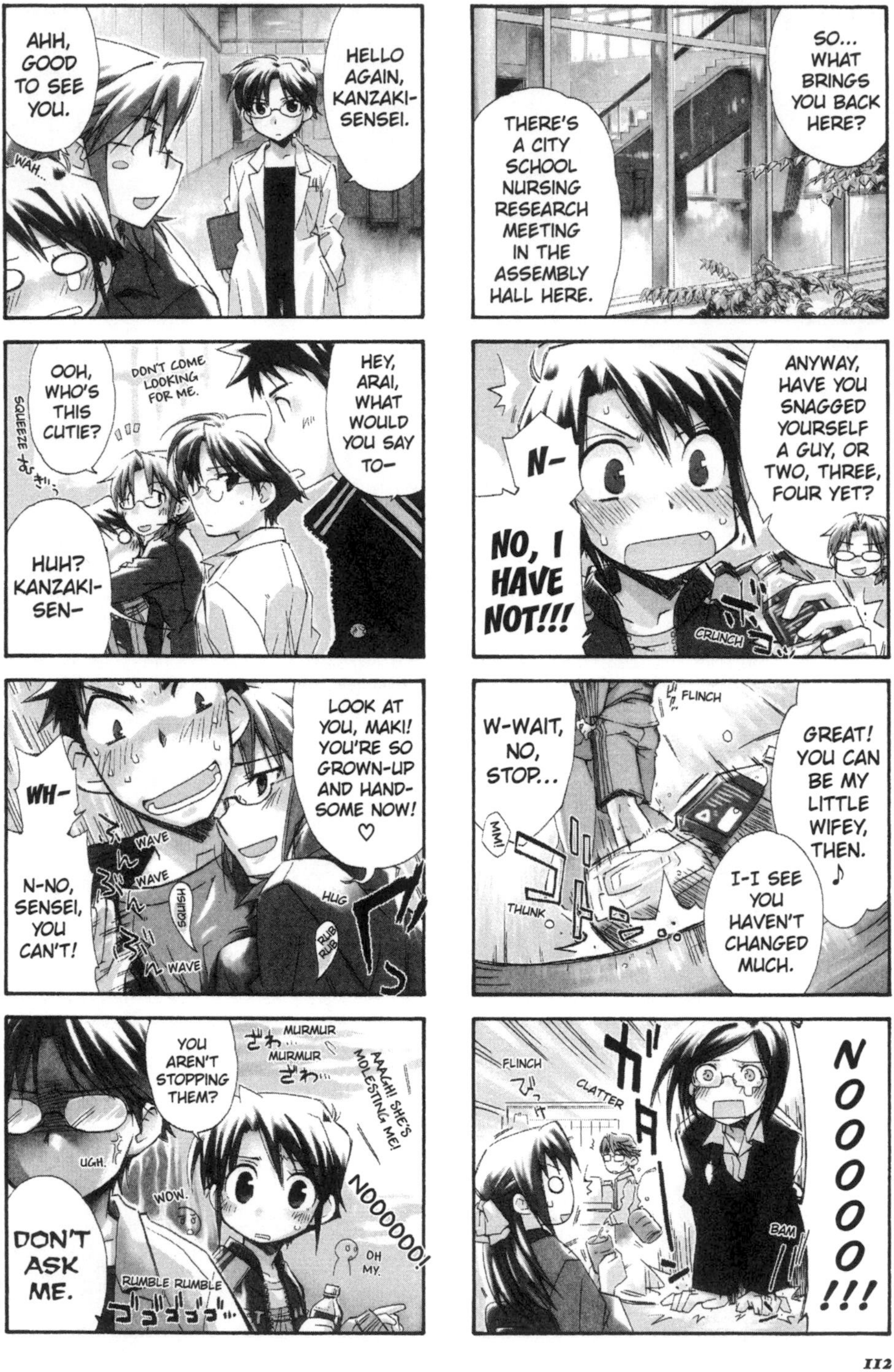
SO... WHAT BRINGS YOU BACK HERE?
THERE'S A CITY SCHOOL NURSING RESEARCH MEETING IN THE ASSEMBLY HALL HERE.
HELLO AGAIN, KANZAKI-SENSEI.
AHH, GOOD TO SEE YOU.
WAH...
ANYWAY, HAVE YOU SNAGGED YOURSELF A GUY, OR TWO, THREE, FOUR YET?
N-
NO, I HAVE NOT!!!
CRUNCH
HEY, ARAI, WHAT WOULD YOU SAY TO-
DON'T COME LOOKING FOR ME.
OOH, WHO'S THIS CUTIE?
SQUEEZE
HUH? KANZAKI-SEN-
FLINCH
GREAT! YOU CAN BE MY LITTLE WIFEY, THEN. ♪
W-WAIT, NO, STOP...
MM!
I-I SEE YOU HAVEN'T CHANGED MUCH.
THUNK
LOOK AT YOU, MAKI! YOU'RE SO GROWN-UP AND HAND-SOME NOW! ♡
WH-
WAVE
WAVE
HUG
SQUISH
RUB RUB
N-NO, SENSEI, YOU CAN'T!
WAVE
NOOOOOO!!!
CLATTER
FLINCH
BAM
AAAGH! SHE'S MOLESTING ME!
MURMUR
MURMUR
YOU AREN'T STOPPING THEM?
NOOOOOO!
UGH.
WOW.
OH MY.
DON'T ASK ME.
RUMBLE RUMBLE

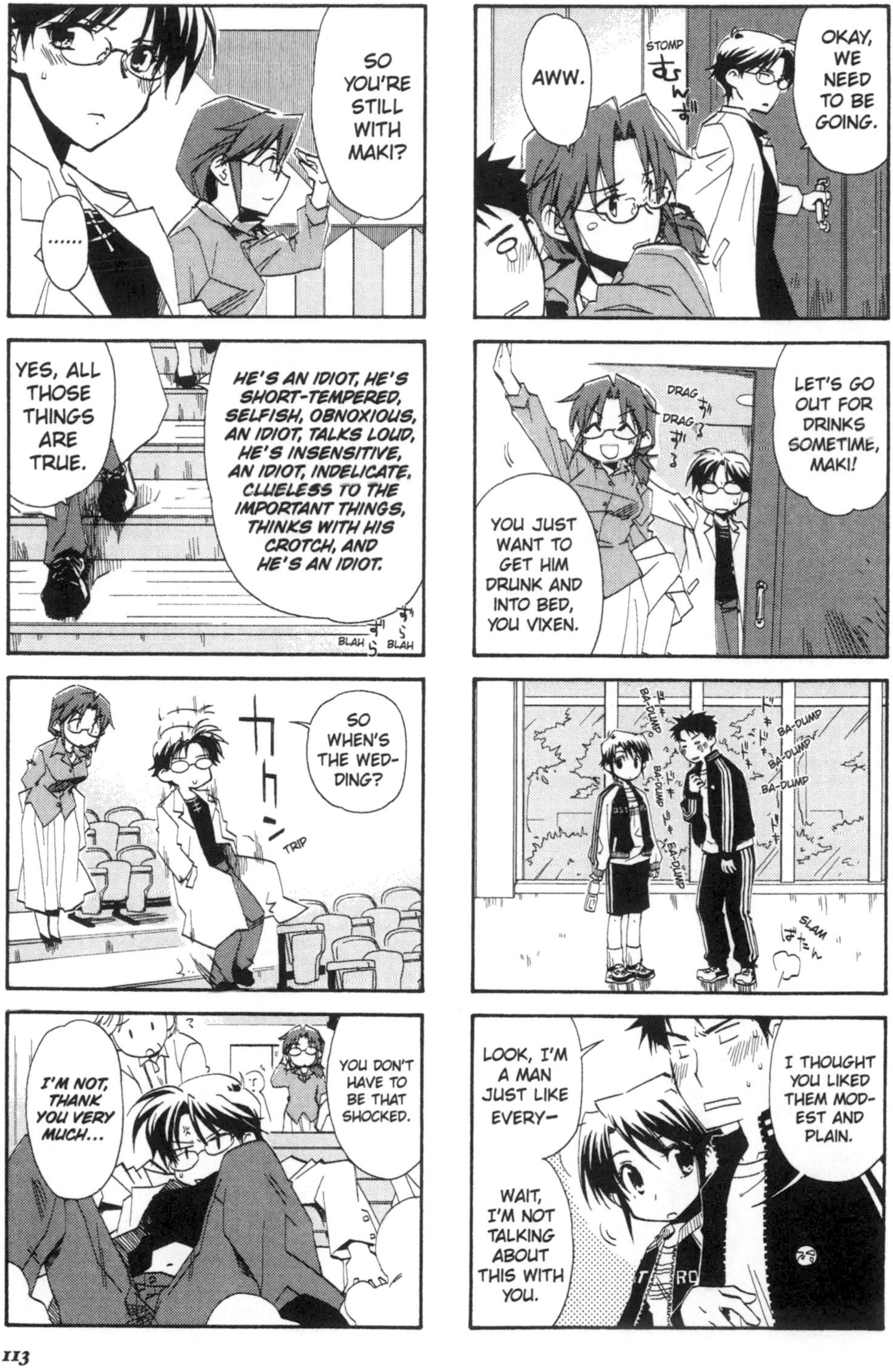
OKAY, WE NEED TO BE GOING.
STOMP
AWW.
LET'S GO OUT FOR DRINKS SOMETIME, MAKI!
DRAG
DRAG
YOU JUST WANT TO GET HIM DRUNK AND INTO BED, YOU VIXEN.
BA-DUMP
BA-DUMP
BA-DUMP
BA-DUMP
BA-DUMP
BA-DUMP
SLAM
I THOUGHT YOU LIKED THEM MOD-EST AND PLAIN.
LOOK, I'M A MAN JUST LIKE EVERY—
WAIT, I'M NOT TALKING ABOUT THIS WITH YOU.
SO YOU'RE STILL WITH MAKI?
......
HE'S AN IDIOT, HE'S SHORT-TEMPERED, SELFISH, OBNOXIOUS, AN IDIOT, TALKS LOUD, HE'S INSENSITIVE, AN IDIOT, INDELICATE, CLUELESS TO THE IMPORTANT THINGS, THINKS WITH HIS CROTCH, AND HE'S AN IDIOT.
YES, ALL THOSE THINGS ARE TRUE.
BLAH BLAH
SO WHEN'S THE WED-DING?
TRIP
YOU DON'T HAVE TO BE THAT SHOCKED.
I'M NOT, THANK YOU VERY MUCH...

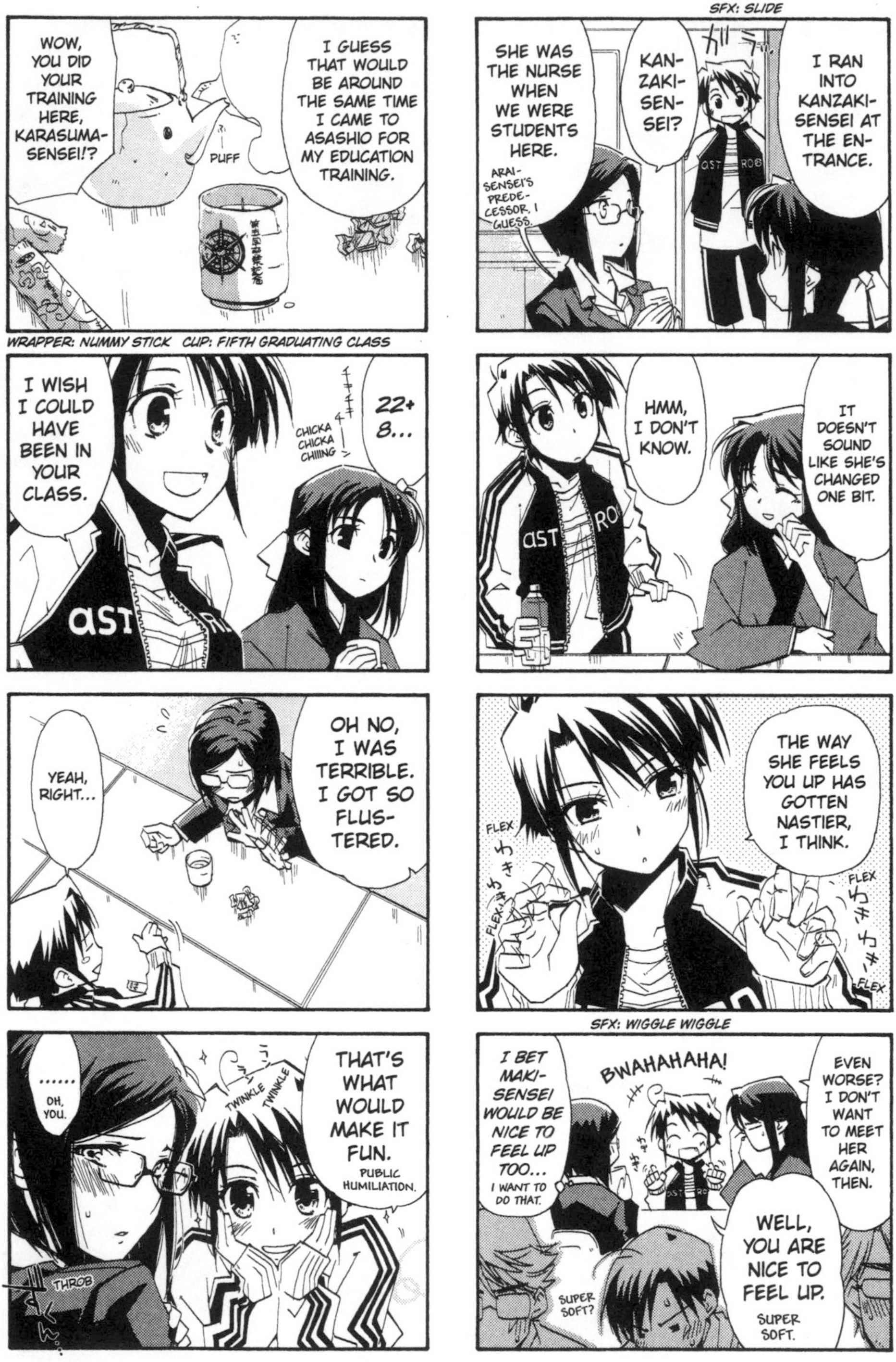
SFX: SLIDE
I RAN INTO KANZAKI-SENSEI AT THE ENTRANCE.
KANZAKI-SENSEI?
SHE WAS THE NURSE WHEN WE WERE STUDENTS HERE.
ARAI-SENSEI'S PREDECESSOR, I GUESS.
I GUESS THAT WOULD BE AROUND THE SAME TIME I CAME TO ASASHIO FOR MY EDUCATION TRAINING.
PUFF
WOW, YOU DID YOUR TRAINING HERE, KARASUMA-SENSEI!?
WRAPPER: NUMMY STICK CUP: FIFTH GRADUATING CLASS
IT DOESN'T SOUND LIKE SHE'S CHANGED ONE BIT.
HMM, I DON'T KNOW.
22+8...
CHICKA CHICKA CHIIING
I WISH I COULD HAVE BEEN IN YOUR CLASS.
THE WAY SHE FEELS YOU UP HAS GOTTEN NASTIER, I THINK.
FLEX
FLEX
FLEX
FLEX
SFX: WIGGLE WIGGLE
OH NO, I WAS TERRIBLE. I GOT SO FLUSTERED.
YEAH, RIGHT...
EVEN WORSE? I DON'T WANT TO MEET HER AGAIN, THEN.
BWAHAHAHA!
I BET MAKI-SENSEI WOULD BE NICE TO FEEL UP TOO...
I WANT TO DO THAT.
WELL, YOU ARE NICE TO FEEL UP.
SUPER SOFT.
SUPER SOFT?
THAT'S WHAT WOULD MAKE IT FUN.
PUBLIC HUMILIATION.
TWINKLE
TWINKLE
......
OH, YOU.
THROB

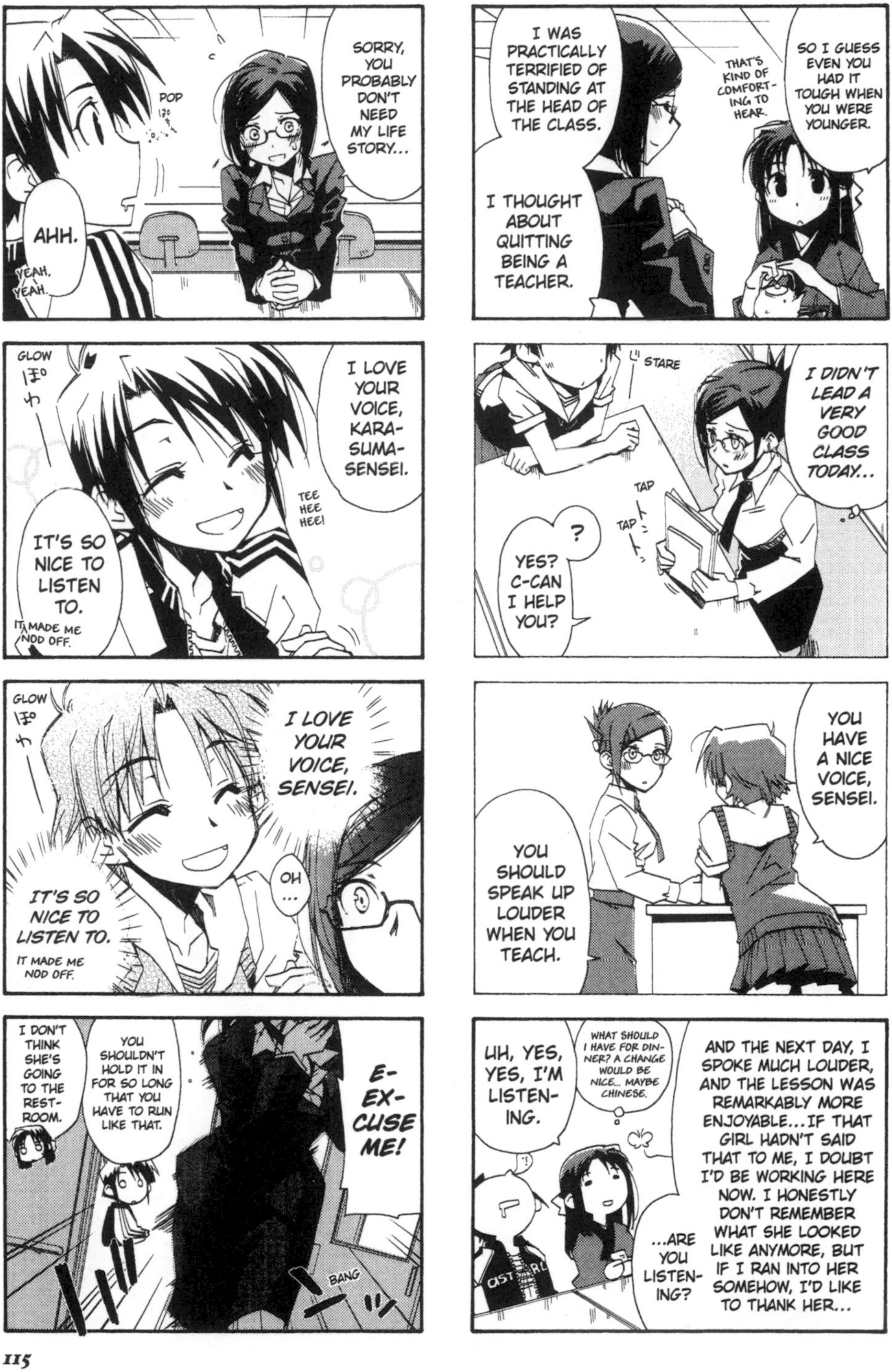
SO I GUESS EVEN YOU HAD IT TOUGH WHEN YOU WERE YOUNGER.
THAT'S KIND OF COMFORTING TO HEAR.
I WAS PRACTICALLY TERRIFIED OF STANDING AT THE HEAD OF THE CLASS.
I THOUGHT ABOUT QUITTING BEING A TEACHER.
STARE
I DIDN'T LEAD A VERY GOOD CLASS TODAY...
TAP
TAP
?
YES? C-CAN I HELP YOU?
YOU HAVE A NICE VOICE, SENSEI.
YOU SHOULD SPEAK UP LOUDER WHEN YOU TEACH.
AND THE NEXT DAY, I SPOKE MUCH LOUDER, AND THE LESSON WAS REMARKABLY MORE ENJOYABLE...IF THAT GIRL HADN'T SAID THAT TO ME, I DOUBT I'D BE WORKING HERE NOW. I HONESTLY DON'T REMEMBER WHAT SHE LOOKED LIKE ANYMORE, BUT IF I RAN INTO HER SOMEHOW, I'D LIKE TO THANK HER...
WHAT SHOULD I HAVE FOR DINNER? A CHANGE WOULD BE NICE... MAYBE CHINESE.
UH, YES, YES, I'M LISTENING.
...ARE YOU LISTENING?
SORRY, YOU PROBABLY DON'T NEED MY LIFE STORY...
POP
AHH.
YEAH, YEAH.
I LOVE YOUR VOICE, KARASUMA-SENSEI.
GLOW
TEE HEE HEE!
IT'S SO NICE TO LISTEN TO.
IT MADE ME NOD OFF.
I LOVE YOUR VOICE, SENSEI.
GLOW
OH ...
IT'S SO NICE TO LISTEN TO.
IT MADE ME NOD OFF.
E-EXCUSE ME!
YOU SHOULDN'T HOLD IT IN FOR SO LONG THAT YOU HAVE TO RUN LIKE THAT.
I DON'T THINK SHE'S GOING TO THE RESTROOM.
BANG

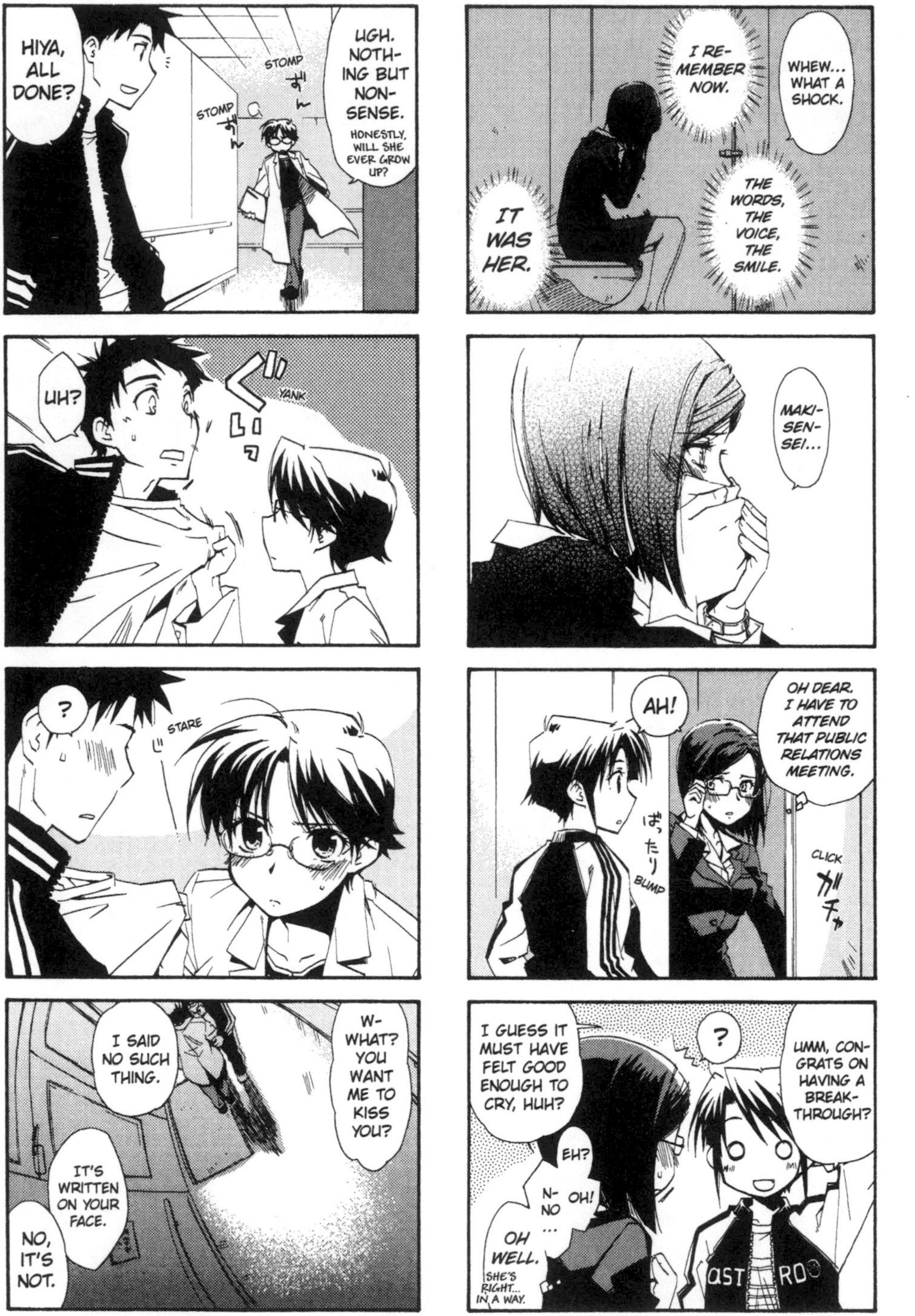
WHEW... WHAT A SHOCK.
I RE-MEMBER NOW.
THE WORDS, THE VOICE, THE SMILE.
IT WAS HER.
MAKI-SENSEI...
OH DEAR. I HAVE TO ATTEND THAT PUBLIC RELATIONS MEETING.
CLICK
ガチャ
AH!
ばったり
BUMP
UMM, CON-GRATS ON HAVING A BREAK-THROUGH?
?
I GUESS IT MUST HAVE FELT GOOD ENOUGH TO CRY, HUH?
EH?
OH!
N-NO ...
OH WELL.
SHE'S RIGHT... IN A WAY.
UGH. NOTH-ING BUT NON-SENSE.
HONESTLY, WILL SHE EVER GROW UP?
STOMP
ずん
STOMP
ずん
HIYA, ALL DONE?
YANK
ぐいっ
UH?
STARE
じ
?
W-WHAT? YOU WANT ME TO KISS YOU?
I SAID NO SUCH THING.
IT'S WRITTEN ON YOUR FACE.
NO, IT'S NOT.

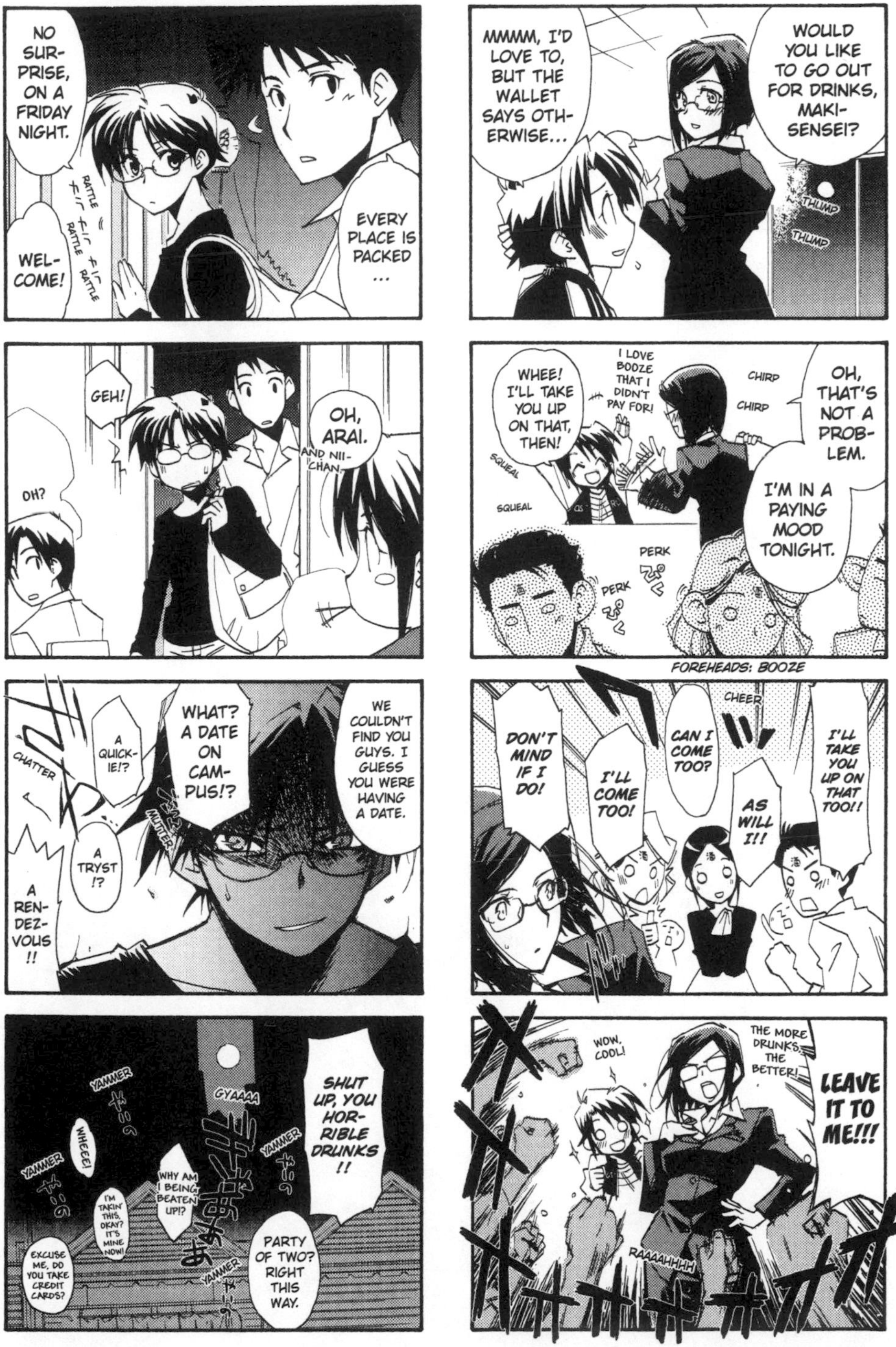
WOULD YOU LIKE TO GO OUT FOR DRINKS, MAKI-SENSEI?
MMMM, I'D LOVE TO, BUT THE WALLET SAYS OTH-ERWISE...
THUMP
THUMP
OH, THAT'S NOT A PROB-LEM.
I'M IN A PAYING MOOD TONIGHT.
CHIRP
CHIRP
I LOVE BOOZE THAT I DIDN'T PAY FOR!
WHEE! I'LL TAKE YOU UP ON THAT, THEN!
SQUEAL
SQUEAL
PERK
PERK
FOREHEADS: BOOZE
CHEER
I'LL TAKE YOU UP ON THAT TOO!!
AS WILL I!!
CAN I COME TOO?
I'LL COME TOO!
DON'T MIND IF I DO!
LEAVE IT TO ME!!!
THE MORE DRUNKS, THE BETTER!
WOW, COOL!
RAAAAHHHH
NO SUR-PRISE, ON A FRIDAY NIGHT.
EVERY PLACE IS PACKED ...
RATTLE RATTLE RATTLE
WEL-COME!
OH, ARAI.
AND NII-CHAN.
GEH!
OH?
WE COULDN'T FIND YOU GUYS. I GUESS YOU WERE HAVING A DATE.
WHAT? A DATE ON CAM-PUS!?
MUTTER
A QUICK-IE!?
CHATTER
A TRYST !?
A REN-DEZ-VOUS !!
SHUT UP, YOU HOR-RIBLE DRUNKS !!
GYAAAA
YAMMER
PARTY OF TWO? RIGHT THIS WAY.
YAMMER
WHY AM I BEING BEATEN UP!?
I'M TAKIN' THIS, OKAY? IT'S MINE NOW!
YAMMER
WHEEE!
YAMMER
EXCUSE ME, DO YOU TAKE CREDIT CARDS?

ARAI-TENTEI EXPLAINS IT ALL!

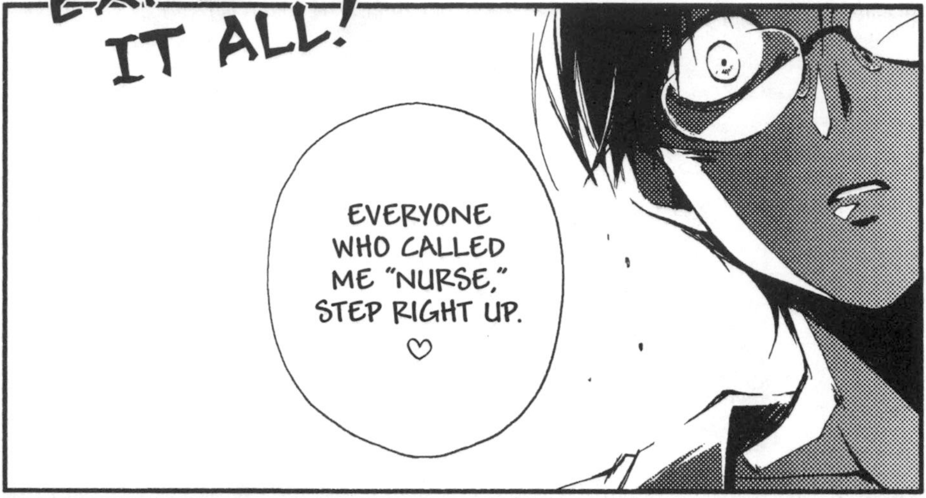
EVERYONE WHO CALLED ME "NURSE," STEP RIGHT UP. ♡

EXPLANATION ❀ THE TEACHER WHO WORKS IN THE SCHOOL INFIRMARY IS KNOWN AS A "NURSING TEACHER." THE TITLES OF "NURSE" OR "DOCTOR" THAT APPEAR IN THIS MANGA ARE TECHNICALLY INCORRECT. THERE IS NO ACTUAL NURSE POSITION IN SCHOOL, AND AN ACTUAL NURSE'S WORK IS COMPLETELY DIFFERENT. ALSO, THE NURSING TEACHER IS NOT ACTUALLY AN INSTRUCTOR, BUT A MEDICAL PROFESSIONAL, AND THUS TECHNICALLY A PART-TIME EMPLOYEE.

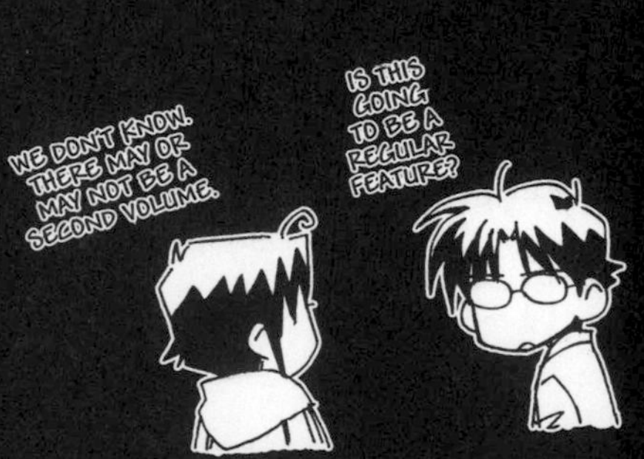
IS THIS GOING TO BE A REGULAR FEATURE?
WE DON'T KNOW. THERE MAY OR MAY NOT BE A SECOND VOLUME.

The Asashio Integrated High School Symbol

This school badge is a representation of a telescope and compass. The far end of the horizon, as seen through the telescope finder in the middle, represents the unlimited future of the school's students, and the compass represents the guidance of the school's faculty, to keep the students from being lost upon entering the wide world of society. The six compass pointers symbolize the sixfold system of "information systems," "international business," "linguistic communication," "the fine arts," "society and business," and "natural science."

S.S. ASTRO 1
Asashio Sogo Teachers' ROom

Special Thanks.   Tokyo metro HS senior high school , OGs , OBs , Teachers
                  Y. Ito   K. Noguchi   GLAY GLASSES
                  my Family   H. Kobayashi

2007. Feb.   Negi Banno   Thank you for reading!

THIS BOOK CONTAINS MATERIAL FIRST PUBLISHED IN:
MANGA TIME KIRARA CARAT, JUNE, JULY, AND NOVEMBER 2005 THROUGH NOVEMBER 2006
AND MATERIAL DRAWN SPECIFICALLY FOR THIS BOOK EDITION.

Translation Notes

Throughout the series Izumi addresses herself with *ore*, the masculine form of "I," rather than the unisex/formal *watashi or* the casual, feminine *atashi*. It's indicative of how much of a tomboy she is.

While the yen-to-dollar value is constantly fluctuating, a quick conversion is ¥100 = $1.

page 2
The red stamps in the upper right corner of these profiles are personalized signature stamps called ***hanko***. Every Japanese adult has their own hanko, marked with the kanji of their name, which is used to authorize official documents instead of a written signature.

page 6-7
Soba is a type of traditional noodle made from buckwheat, which makes it darker and more grainy than ramen. It is often served in a square dish with a small cup of broth to dip the noodles into.

Monjayaki is a regional cousin of the famous *okonomiyaki*. These dishes are made by pouring batter onto a grill, much like pancakes, but with savory ingredients and meat or seafood. Okonomiyaki comes from western Japan around Osaka and Kyoto, while monjayaki is a specialty of eastern Japan near Tokyo. Based on the frequency that this appears in the manga, we can guess that the author is a big fan.

page 9
Homeroom teacher: The Japanese version of "homeroom" is similar to the American, but not quite the same. Unlike Western schools, in which students attend homeroom for roll call and announcements and then walk to their different teachers' classrooms according to personal schedule, Japanese homerooms are where students spend most of the day, while it is the teachers who travel from class to class to teach their subjects. In addition, students are given more duties through homeroom, including school clean-up and planning for activities such as school fairs.

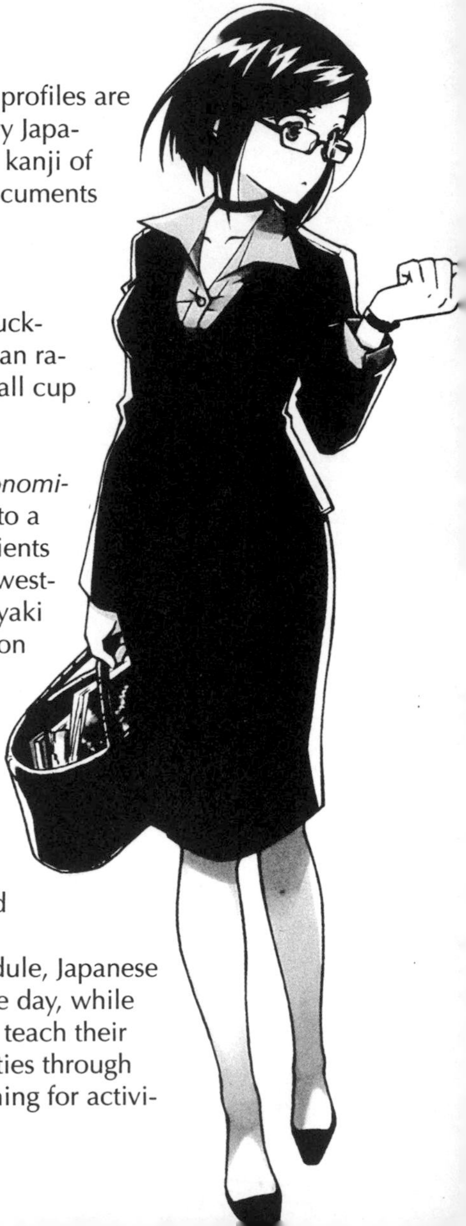

page 13
Along with the ultra-formal tone of voice and dress, Yuko-sensei's bowing while kneeling on top of the desk is quite out of place at school. In fact, it's unlikely that most Japanese would ever encounter this type of bowing in their lives outside of a tea ceremony, and those are rare enough in contemporary Japan.

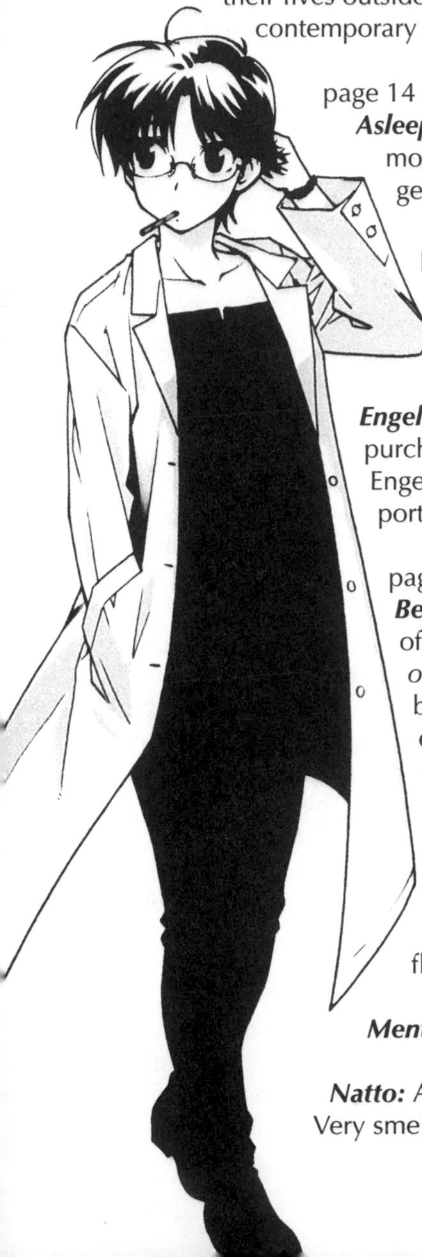

page 14
Asleep fist: This is a parody of the Hong Kong kung-fu movie staple, the "drunken fist," in which the character gets drunk to use a special kind of kung-fu.

page 19
Tentei: This is not an actual Japanese suffix, it's just a babyish mispronunciation of *sensei*.

page 20
Engel's coefficient: The proportion of a household's total purchases which go toward buying food. Introduced in Engel's law, which states that as income rises, the proportion of money spent on food decreases.

page 23
Bento: A traditional Japanese boxed lunch consisting of white rice and several different toppings (known as *okazu*) in separate compartments. The multi-layered bento that Yuko-sensei is seen eating from is the equivalent of a multi-course meal and would be overkill for a packed lunch, not to mention impractical to lug around.

Nummy Stick: A parody ("Umaa Bo") of the real-life snack *Umai Bo*, or "Yummy Stick," which is a puffed corn snack that comes in many different flavors, including mentaiko and natto.

Mentaiko: Marinated pollock (a type of fish) eggs.

Natto: A traditional dish made with fermented soybeans. Very smelly and sticky.

page 25
This is a parody of RPG video game status screens, particularly *Dragon Quest*. The "closet pervert" personality is a feature from *Dragon Quest III*, and the "E" refers to items which the character is currently equipping.

page 54
Bishoujo games: A genre of computer games wherein the player must romance *bishoujo* ("pretty girls") in ways that can be either suitable for minors or not. What Setsuna is insinuating — and Yuko is trying to cover up — is the fact that Yuko enjoys playing yaoi games featuring gay men.

page 56
Many schools in Japan have a once-a-year field trip for the entire school. While Kyoto is a common destination for Tokyo area schools due to its many historic sights, the southern island of Okinawa, which is warm year-round and resembles Hawaii, is perhaps the most popular.

page 64
Hanami, or "flower viewing," is a traditional activity undertaken during the short period of the spring months when *sakura* (cherry blossom) trees are in flower. A typical practice is to set down blankets underneath the flowering trees and hold a party with food and sake.

Yuko's sneeze while the other teachers are talking about her is based on the Japanese belief that a sudden sneeze means someone is talking about you.

page 69
The Fu symbol: The "mental points" section of these character bios has a hidden meaning; it actually refers to their predilection for girly "otaku" fetishes, most specifically the *yaoi* or BL (boy's love) subculture. Imagining situations in which fictional male characters might be gay and attracted to each other is a common activity for what the Japanese call *fujoshi*, a pun on the word for "lady" that, when spelled with a different kanji, means "dirty woman." This self-mocking term, used by fans of yaoi/BL to describe themselves, refers to the "shameful" or "dirty" fantasies that they hold. The fu symbol is the kanji for "dirty," and is shown on Yuko's forehead in this story when she is imagining such connections between her male coworkers.

page 72
108 characters: This is a reference to the *Suikoden* videogame series. The *Suikoden* RPG games are based on a classic Chinese novel that features 108 characters known at the 108 Stars. One of the features of the *Suikoden* series is that the player can recruit and use all 108 of these characters in each game.

page 76
Seme: In yaoi material, there is a very common dynamic called *seme/uke*. Seme refers to the dominant member of a partnership, while uke refers to the submissive member.

Doujinshi circle: A *doujinshi* is a fan-published magazine of drawn and/or written material, the bread and butter of otaku and fujoshi subculture. They are often made by groups of people, known as "circles," which might be gathered together as students of the same college, fans of a particular manga/anime series or even a specific character pairing. A circle will typically put together a dojinshi for sale at events organized a few times a year, such as Comic Market.

page 87
Initial R: A joke combining the first letter of "roach" with the popular street racing manga/anime, *Initial D*.

page 95
Yuri: As yaoi refers to depictions of gay men, yuri is its counterpart featuring lesbian women.

page 104
Ramune: A well-known brand of lemon-lime flavored Japanese soft drink. The glass bottle version comes with a special dimple in the neck that holds a glass marble once the top has been popped. It is drunk most often in the summer months.

GJ: Online gaming or IM shorthand for "good job."

page 108
The Me Who Leapt Through Time: A play on a famous Japanese 1960s sci-fi short story, *The Girl Who Leapt Through Time*. The story has been adapted to television and film multiple times, most recently in the 2006 animated film of the same name.

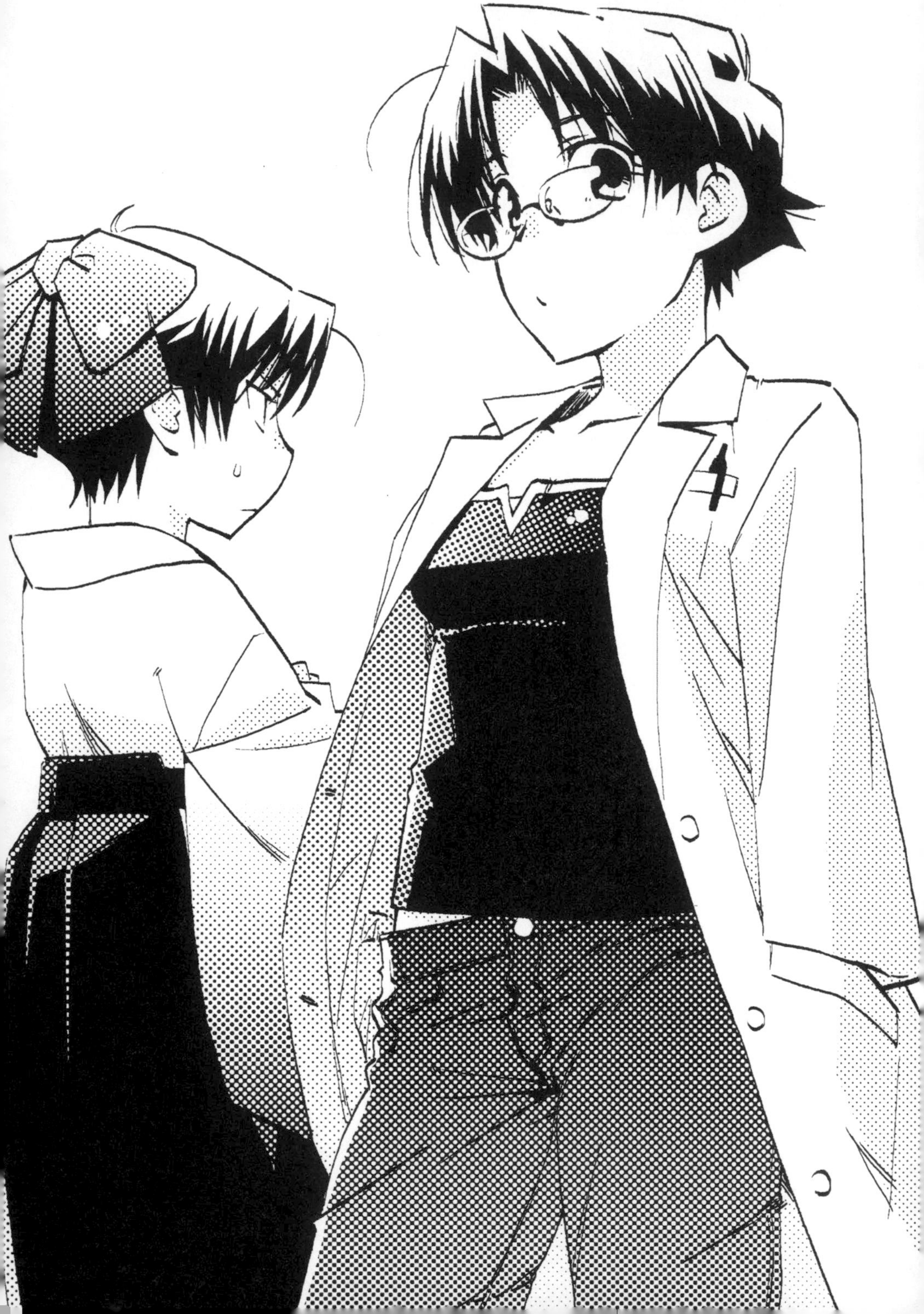

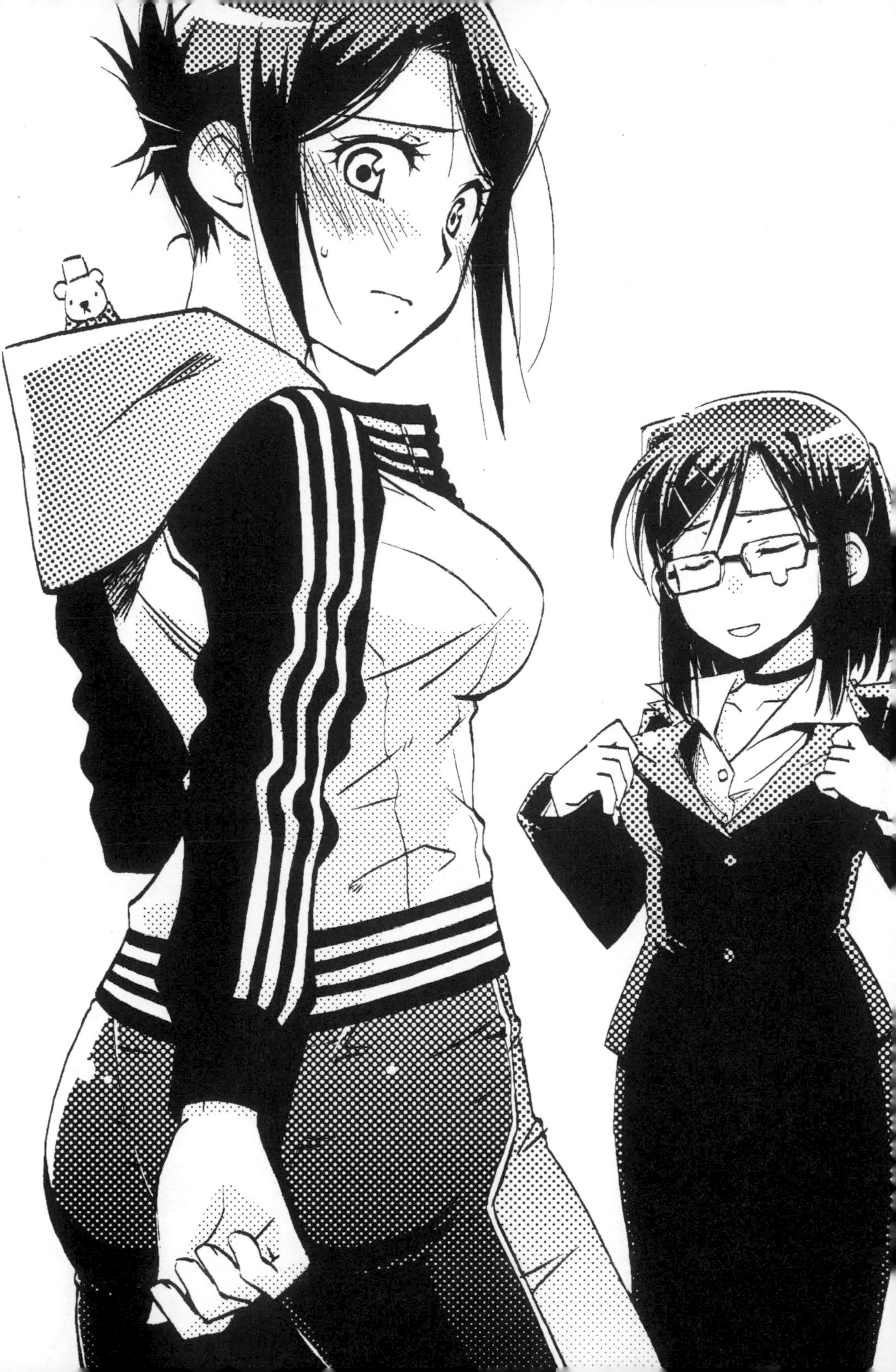

Suzunari!

VOLUME 1
PREVIEW

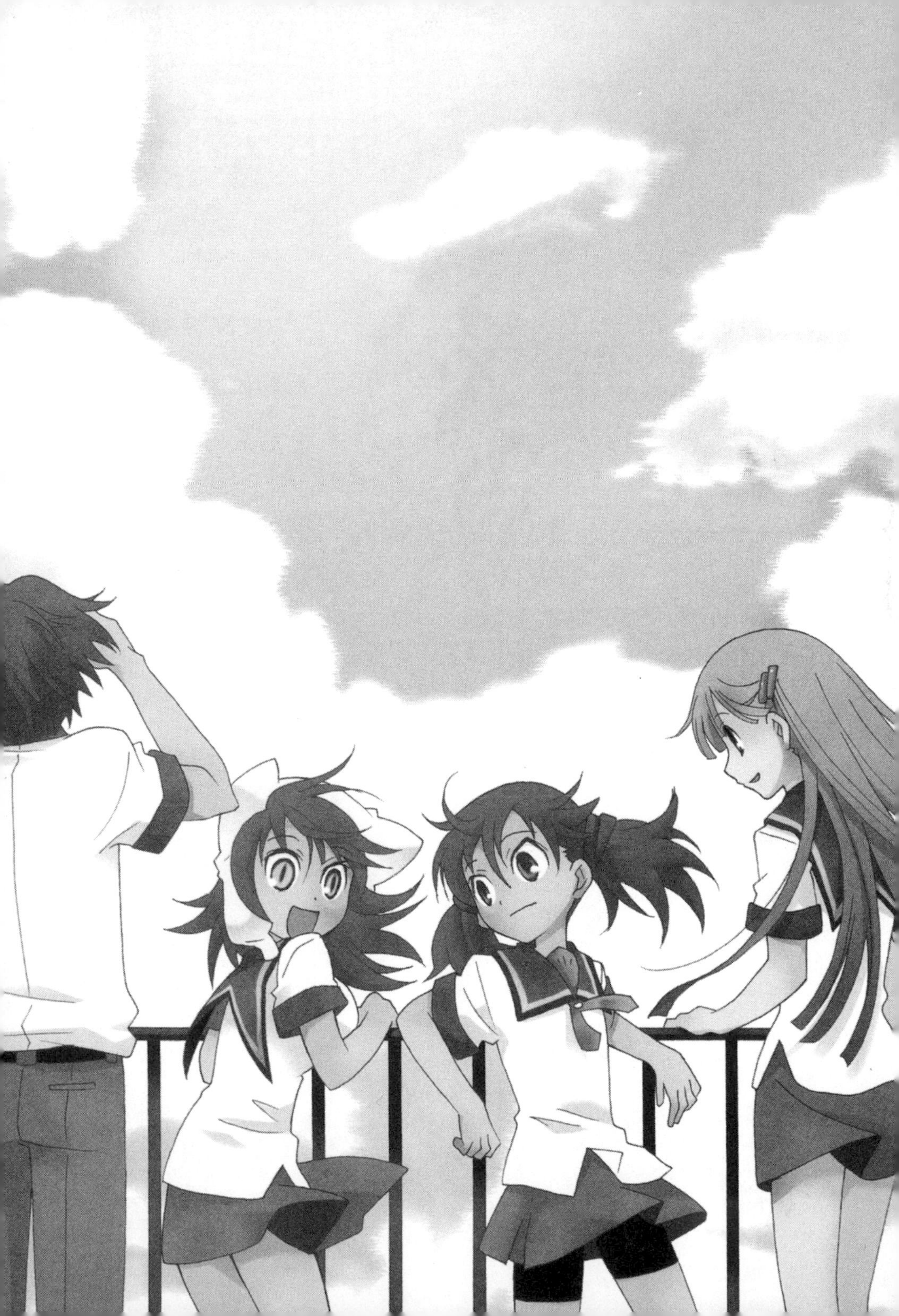

CHARACTERS

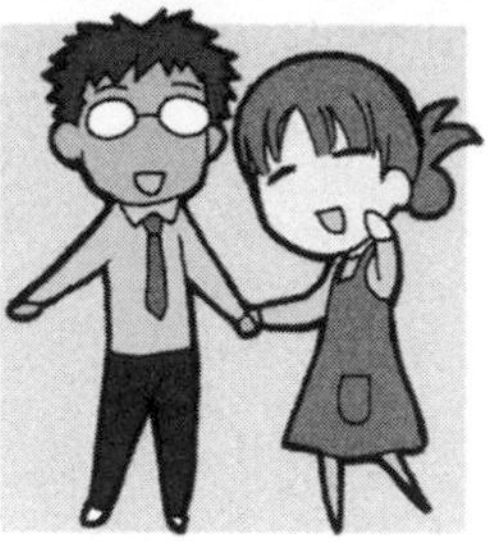

YORIHARU & MINATO TAKAMURA

KAEDE'S PARENTS. HER FATHER WORKS AT CITY HALL, AND HER MOTHER IS A HOUSEWIFE. EVEN AFTER MANY YEARS OF MARRIAGE, THE COUPLE IS STILL MADLY IN LOVE WITH EACH OTHER.

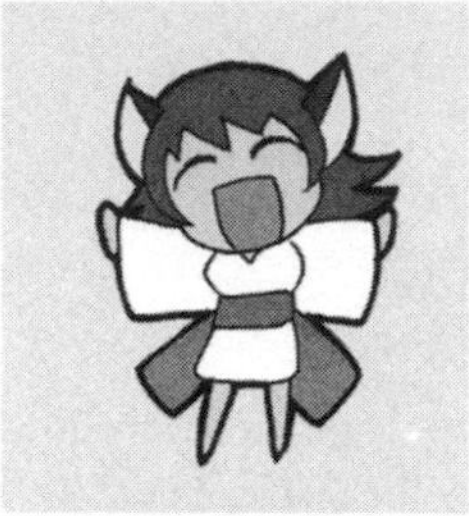

SUZU TAKAMURA

A MYSTERIOUS CATGIRL AND KAEDE'S LOOK-ALIKE WHO MADE A SUDDEN APPEARANCE. SHE IS COMPLETELY ENAMORED WITH KAEDE.

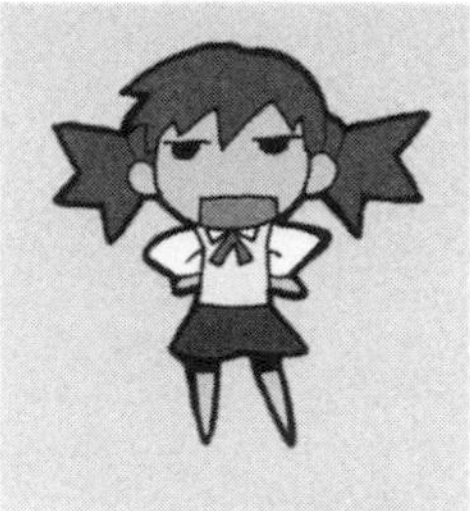

KAEDE TAKAMURA

A SMALL, ENERGETIC GIRL. BEING BROUGHT UP BY NONCHALANT PARENTS HAS POSSIBLY MADE HER A RELIABLE PERSON.

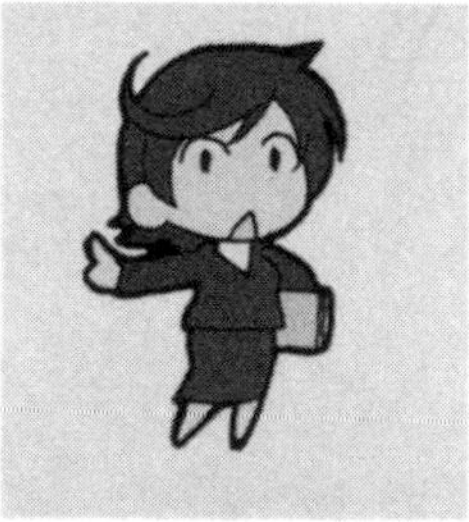

ETOH-SENSEI

KAEDE AND SUZU'S TEACHER. SHE IS A PATHETIC, GAMBLING-LOVING TEACHER WHO STAKES HER FORTUNE ON BETTING.

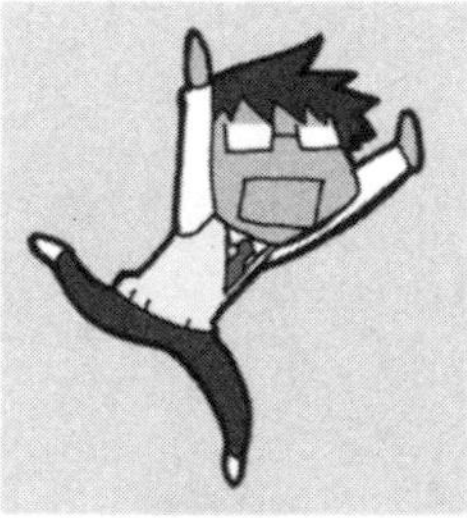

IINCHOU

KAEDE AND SUZU'S CLASS PRESIDENT. HE IS AN ENTHUSIASTIC MAN DEVOTED TO THE GOD OF MOE. HIS REAL NAME IS A MYSTERY.

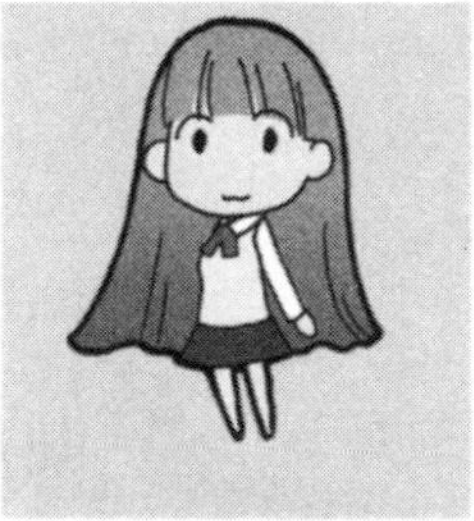

NATSUMI

KAEDE AND SUZU'S CLASSMATE. THIS GIRL LOVES THE OCCULT AND SPECIALIZES IN FORTUNE-TELLING, THOUGH THERE IS NO GUARANTEE THAT WHAT SHE FORETELLS WILL COME TRUE.

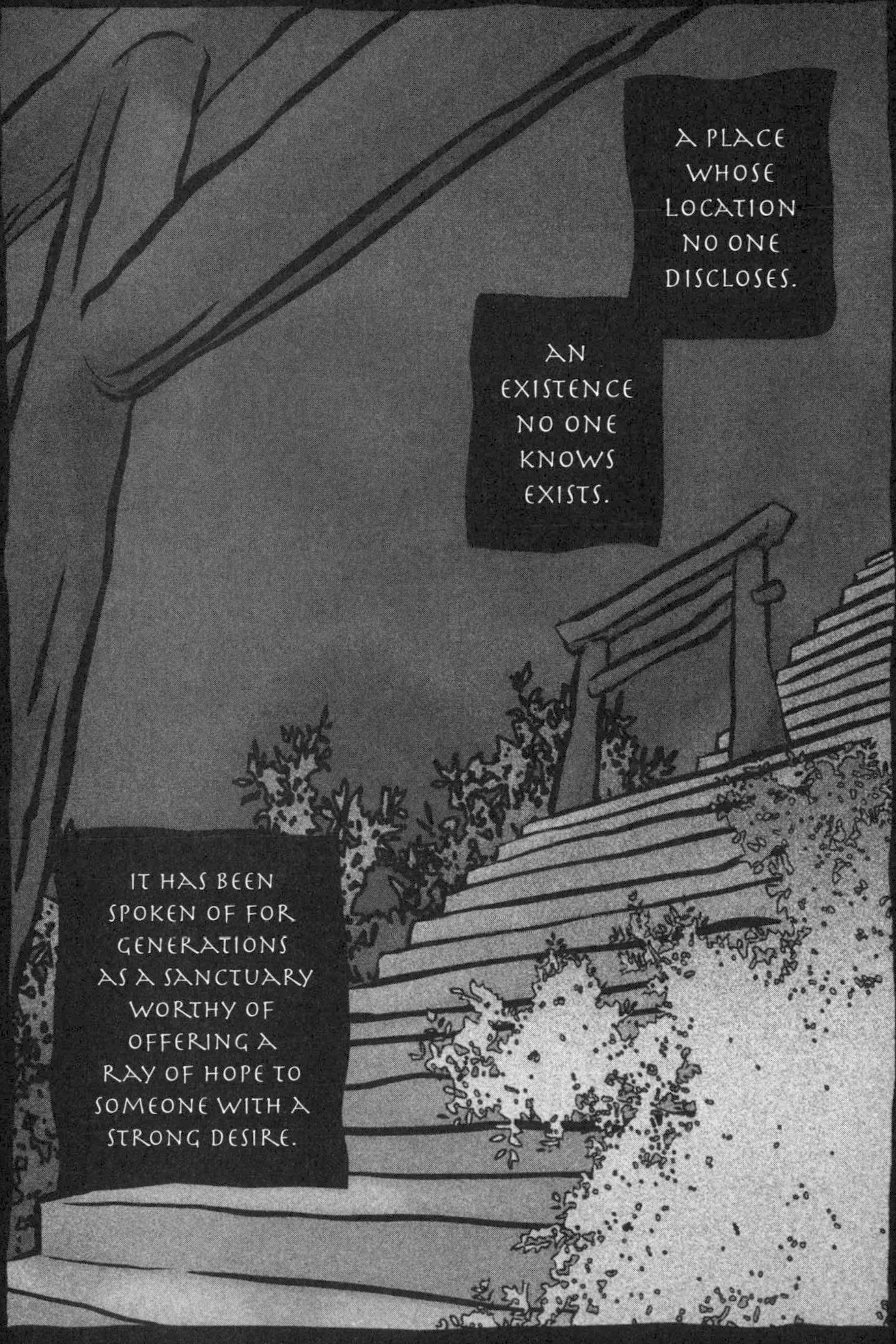
A PLACE WHOSE LOCATION NO ONE DISCLOSES.
AN EXISTENCE NO ONE KNOWS EXISTS.
IT HAS BEEN SPOKEN OF FOR GENERATIONS AS A SANCTUARY WORTHY OF OFFERING A RAY OF HOPE TO SOMEONE WITH A STRONG DESIRE.

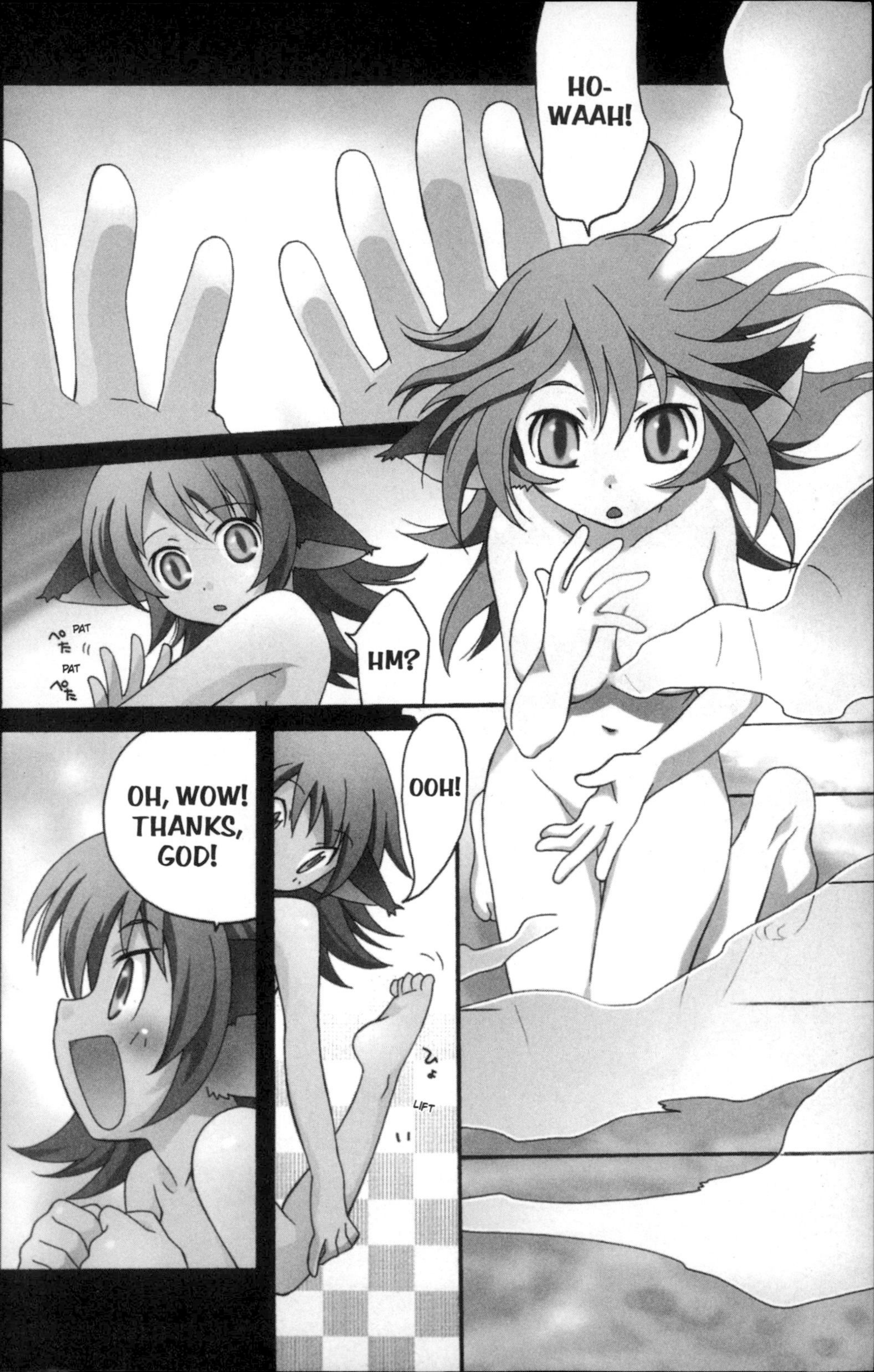
HO-WAAH!
HM?
PAT
PAT
OOH!
LIFT
OH, WOW! THANKS, GOD!

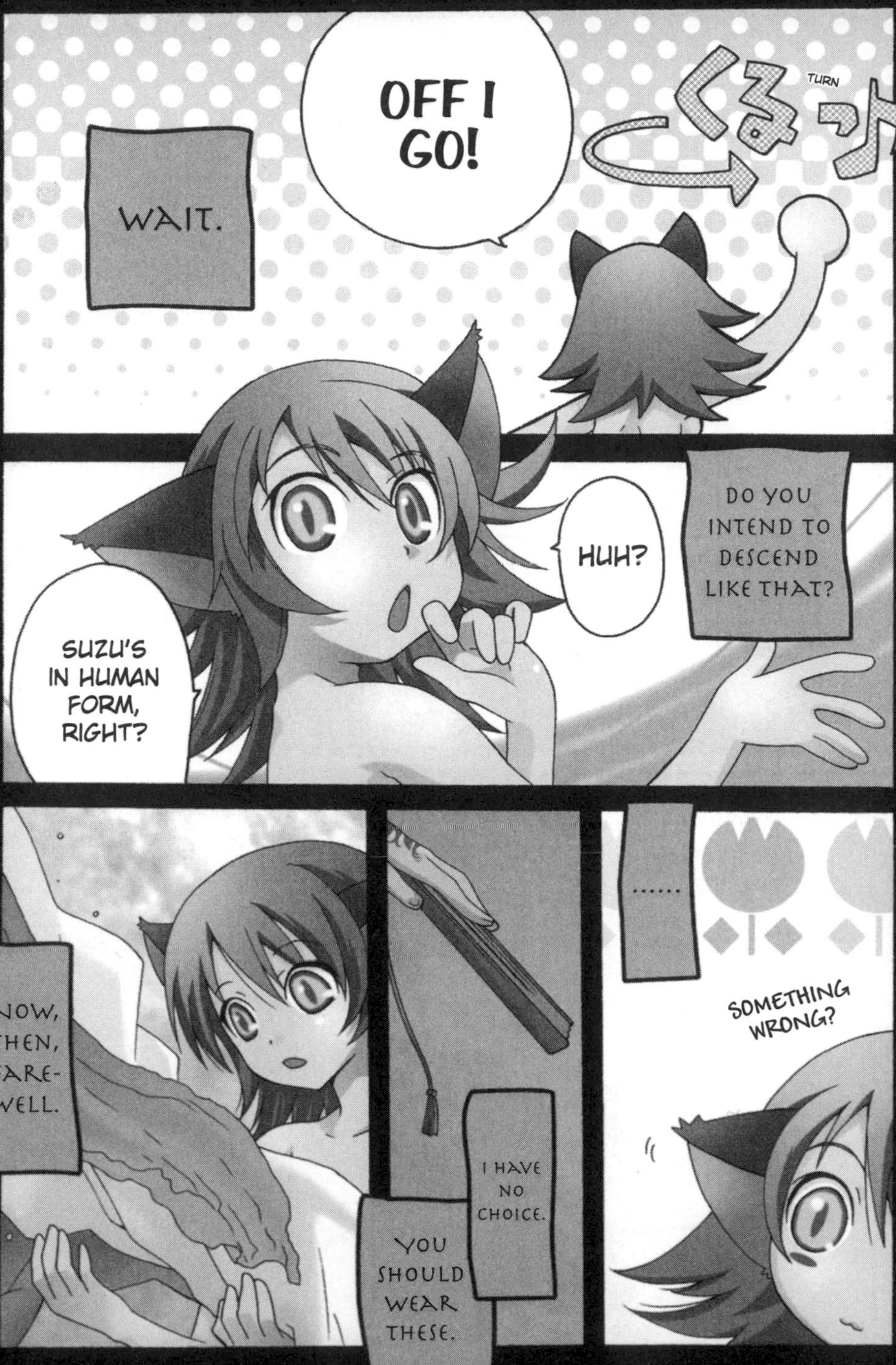
くるっ
TURN
OFF I GO!
WAIT.
DO YOU INTEND TO DESCEND LIKE THAT?
HUH?
SUZU'S IN HUMAN FORM, RIGHT?
......
SOMETHING WRONG?
I HAVE NO CHOICE.
YOU SHOULD WEAR THESE.
NOW, THEN, FAREWELL.

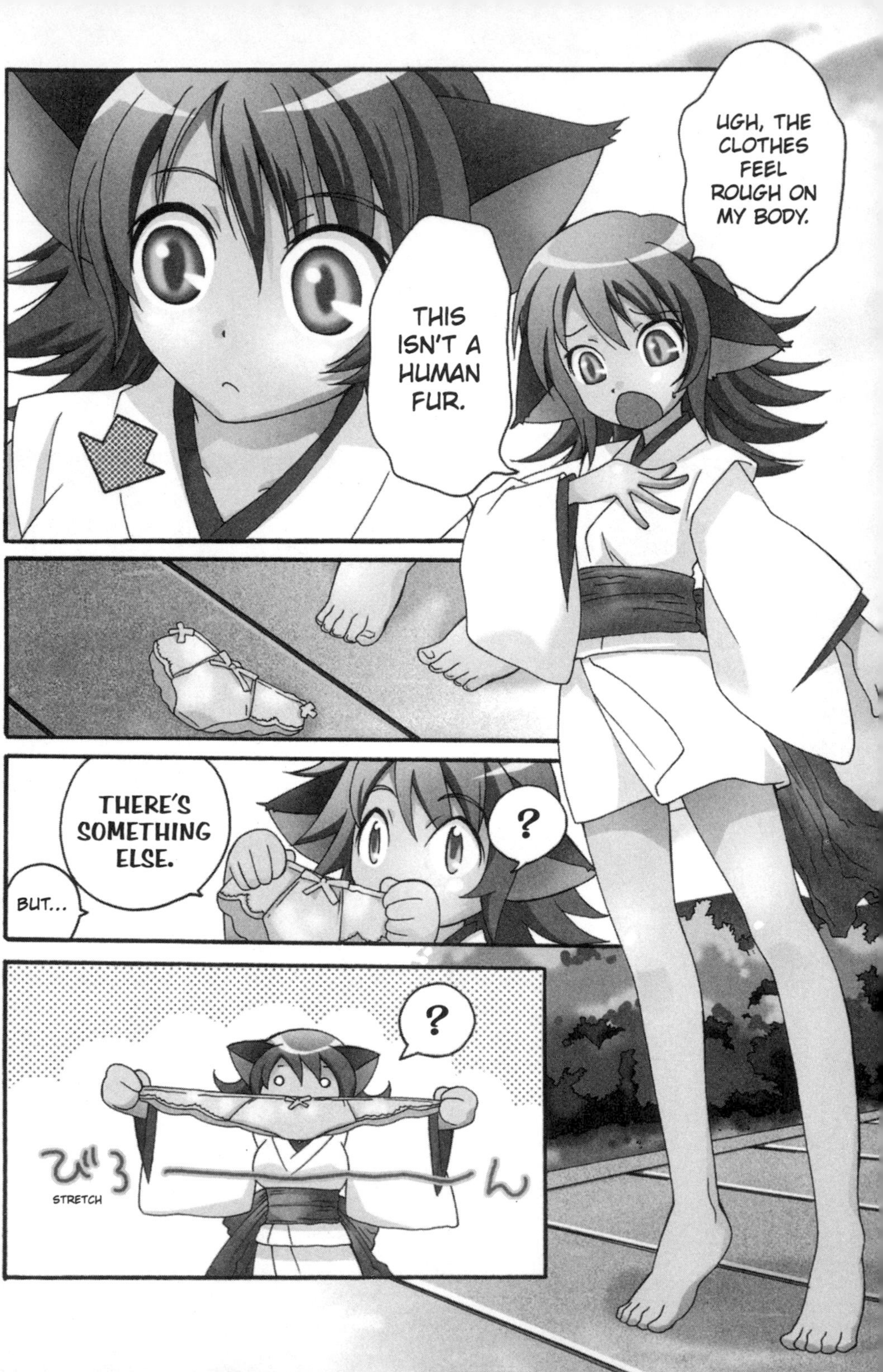
UGH, THE CLOTHES FEEL ROUGH ON MY BODY.
THIS ISN'T A HUMAN FUR.
?
THERE'S SOMETHING ELSE.
BUT…
?
びろーーーーん
STRETCH

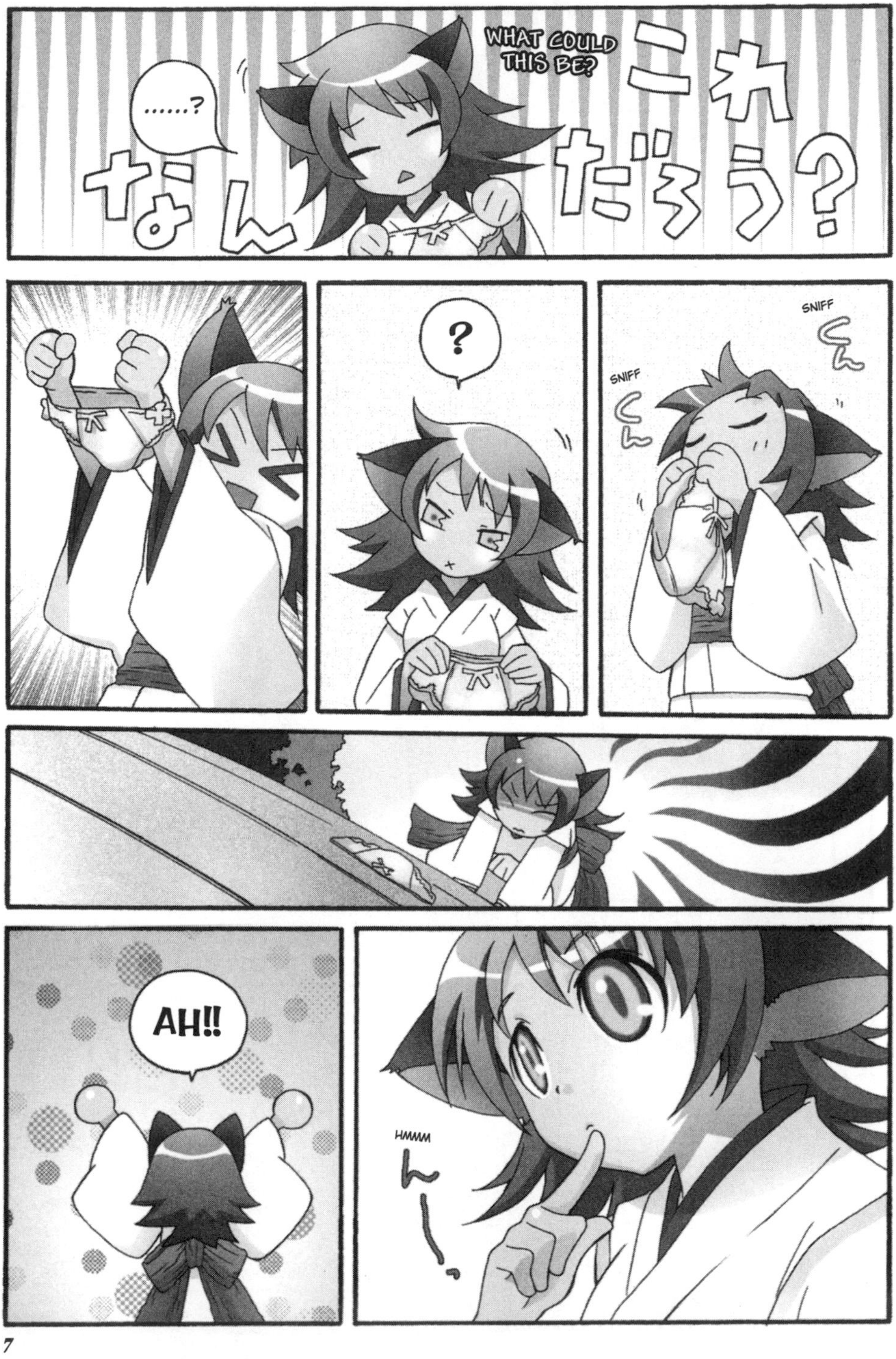
WHAT COULD THIS BE?
これなんだろう？
......?
SNIFF
くん
SNIFF
くん
?
HMMM
んー
AH!!

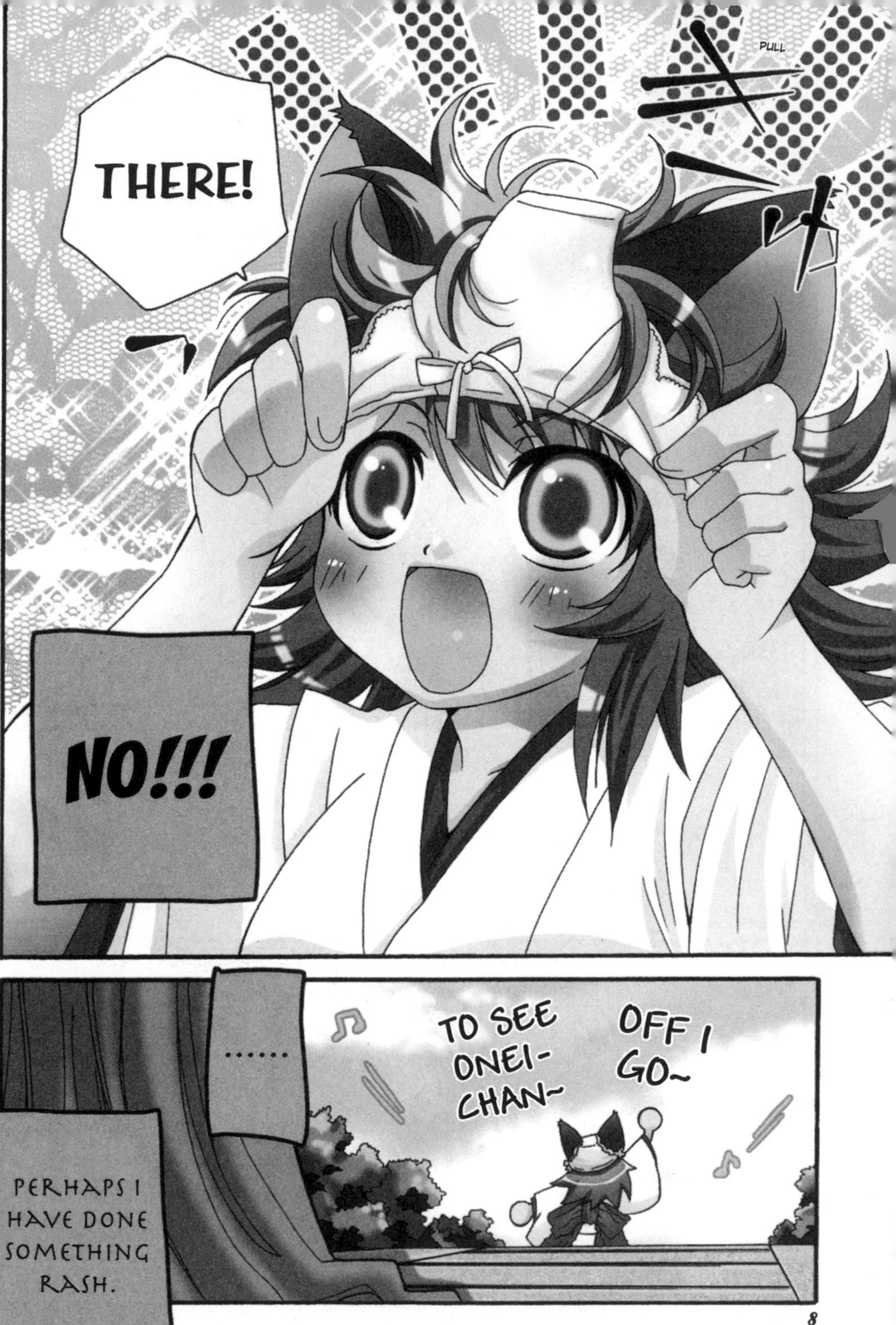
PULL
THERE!
NO!!!
OFF I GO~
TO SEE ONEI-CHAN~
......
PERHAPS I HAVE DONE SOMETHING RASH.

TO BE CONTINUED IN...

AVAILABLE NOW
FROM YEN PRESS!

S.S. ASTRO ①

NEGI BANNO

Translation: Stephen Paul

Lettering: Alexis Eckerman

KYOKAN ASTRO Vol. 1 © 2007 Negi Banno. All rights reserved. First published in Japan in 2007 by HOUBUNSHA CO., LTD. English translation rights in the United States, Canada, and United Kingdom arranged with HOUBUNSHA CO., LTD. through Tuttle-Mori Agency, Inc., Tokyo.

English translation copyright © 2008 by Hachette Book Group USA, Inc.

Yen Press
Hachette Book Group USA
237 Park Avenue, New York, NY 10017

Visit our Web sites at www.HachetteBookGroupUSA.com and www.YenPress.com.

Yen Press is an imprint of Hachette Book Group USA, Inc. The Yen Press name and logo are trademarks of Hachette Book Group USA, Inc.

First Edition: August 2008

ISBN-10: 0-7595-2898-5
ISBN-13: 978-0-7595-2898-7

10 9 8 7 6 5 4 3 2 1

BVG

Printed in the United States of America